Making Collector's Dolls

Making Collector's Dolls

Venus A. Dodge

with drawings by Martin Dodge

Sterling Publishing Co., Inc.   New York

Library of Congress Cataloging in Publication Data

Dodge, Venus.
    Making collector's dolls.

    Bibliography: P.
    Includes index
    1. Dollmaking   I. Title.
TT175.D56   1984   745.592'21   83-17163
ISBN 0-8069-5506-6
ISBN 0-8069-7800-7 (pbk.)

Published in 1983 by Sterling Publishing Co., Inc.
Two Park Avenue, New York, N.Y. 10016
First published in Great Britain under the title
"Making Collector's Dolls"
by David & Charles (Publishers) Limited, Newton Abbot

Copyright © Venus Dodge 1983

ISBN 0-8069-5506-6 (trade)
ISBN 0-8069-7800-7 (pbk)

Distributed in Canada by Oak Tree Press Ltd.
c/o Canadian Manda Group, P.O. Box 920, Station U,
Toronto, Ontario M8Z 5P9

CONTENTS

INTRODUCTION

The usual definition of a collector's doll is a doll for display rather than play. Obviously this includes antique dolls, once children's playthings but now so valuable that they spend their lives in glass cases. It also includes the beautiful work of modern doll artists, in porcelain, wax or cast resin, bought by collectors both in appreciation of their fine craftsmanship and as an investment. However, the borderline between child's toy and collector's doll is a fine one. For example, the modern commercial 'Sasha' dolls are sold as children's toys, but many collectors buy them for display and I certainly don't play with mine!

A doll's appeal is a matter of individual taste. I know ladies who collect rag dolls, and the simple felt dolls generally considered suitable for children often find their way to adults' dressing-tables. Conversely, an elaborately dressed costume doll, though obviously unsuitable for a small child, might give intense pleasure to a young girl who would 'display' it but not actually play with it. Toy or collector's item? — only the owner could tell!

The dolls in this book cover a fairly wide range, from simple rag dolls to waxed clay-headed dolls with 'real' hair and eyes. The individual reader will decide which of them are collector's dolls and which are toys, and in some cases only the quality of the workmanship or the elaborateness of the costume will make the difference.

My intention has been to write a book for the amateur dollmaker who has perhaps made simple rag dolls and would like to try something more ambitious. The materials used are all readily available, and the equipment needed can be found in any home. These dolls can all be made 'on the kitchen table'. Few of them are expensive to make, and even those which cost rather more, for example the Fashion doll, will be only a fraction of the store price of similar dolls.

The patterns are straightforward, and only basic sewing skills are required for the soft dolls. The modelled and waxed dolls can be made very simply or more elaborately, depending on your ability and inclinations. The variety of methods offered will enable you to choose techniques which suit your own skills when making the dolls, their faces and their wigs.

The large range of clothes patterns, most of them interchangeable, offer scope for dressing child and adult dolls in a variety of styles and periods. Many of the patterns are extremely simple, some more difficult, and some are recommended for experienced needlewomen.

Because my concern is with home-made dolls, I have not included porcelain or cast-resin dolls. The materials, kiln, moulds and other equipment needed for making them are expensive and specialised skill is necessary to achieve good results. However, you might find that having made dolls by the methods suggested in this book, you are ready to try your hand at more ambitious things and are prepared to invest in the equipment to do it . . . but that is another book!

The dolls are each given a 'difficulty rating' on a Scale 1–5; those marked 5 are recommended for experienced dollmakers.

Using the Patterns

The body patterns for the felt babies (Chapter 6), the clay and waxed babies (Chapter 12), the small character dolls (Chapter 8) and the costume dolls (Chapter 9) are drawn actual size, as are the clothes patterns for the costume dolls — and the children's-toy patterns (Chapter 6).

The rest of the patterns for both dolls and clothes are drawn on grids. To use these, rule a sheet of paper into 1in squares and re-draw the pattern pieces. Transfer the markings for folds, darts etc onto the wrong side of the fabric with soft pencil and mark the pieces for identification. Patterns may be drawn onto paper and pinned to the fabric, or drawn on thin cardboard to use as templates. The latter method is recommended if several dolls are to be made from the same pattern.

The rag-doll and the large felt-doll patterns include a seam allowance of 1/2in, as do the clothes patterns for these dolls. For the small dolls, such as the costume dolls, a seam allowance of ¼in is recommended for both the dolls and clothes.

All the patterns can be enlarged or reduced by drawing them onto paper with larger or smaller squares, but remember to adjust the seam allowances accordingly.

Knitting and Crochet Abbreviations

Knitting
    k–knit
    p–purl
    st st–stocking stitch
    sl–slip stitch
    psso–pass slip stitch over one
Crochet
    dc–double crochet
    ch–chain
    ss–slip stitch

1
SOFT DOLLS

Since I was at school I have designed and made hundreds of soft dolls, ranging from simple cuddly toys to elegant ladies with elaborate period clothes. Over the years I have experimented with many different materials and methods, making dolls for my own pleasure, for friends and to sell; and have found that the appeal of even simple rag dolls is in no way limited to children.

My earliest dolls were mainly traditional rag dolls made in cotton or calico with wool hair — but when I began to use felt I started to make dolls which had more character. They could be child or adult dolls, simple or sophisticated, and I tried out many different ideas for making their faces and wigs. I found that some methods suit one type of doll better than another and, sometimes, what seems like a good idea simply doesn't work — or I can't make it work! I tried making dolls with pressed-felt faces, with disastrous but funny results and I experimented with Victorian doll's-body patterns, with many seams and gussets, which made some weird and wonderful bodies!

This chapter includes many of the methods I have used for making soft dolls, not only those needed for the dolls illustrated in the book, so that you can choose the ones which suit your own skills and the type of doll you make. Many of the ideas are very easy, and these are recommended for beginners where relevant. I have also referred to the dolls in the book when they illustrate the various techniques, so that you can judge if a particular eye or nose makes the right effect for your own doll.

Consider, too, using the soft dolls as an alternative to the modelled dolls in the next chapter. For example, the head used for the Ballerina would fit as well onto the Fashion doll's body in place of the waxed-clay head — making an attractive felt fashion doll. Or the Pierrot could be made as a felt doll, using the Sailor's patterns cut in white felt. Most of the body patterns in the book are interchangeable or easily adapted within the size groups, so an enormous variety of soft dolls is possible, needing only your imagination to invent them!

This is not a book of rules, merely a guide.

Dollmaking is a highly personal craft and each dollmaker has her own tastes and talents, but I hope that the variety of methods described here will offer something for everyone, encourage experiment and produce satisfying results!

Materials

With the exception of the rag dolls (Big and Little Sisters and Emily) the patterns for the dolls' bodies are designed for felt.

I use felt for several reasons; the colour is soft, the texture pleasant and it does not fray. Felt will stretch and mould with stuffing to make rounded limbs, tummies and bosoms without the need for complicated darts and gussets. (Cotton fabrics do not stretch, so will not give the same three-dimensional appearance and will result in smaller dolls, which will not fit the felt-doll's clothes patterns.)

It is important to use only a good-quality felt, as cheap felt is thin and patchy and tears easily. Good felt is strong, much thicker and can be washed.

Before cutting, press felt with a steam iron to shrink it slightly, remove any creases and prevent excess fluffing. It stretches rather more from selvedge to selvedge than down the length, so ensure that the body-pattern pieces lie in the same direction. If, for example, one of a pair of legs was cut across the felt and one down the length, when stuffed, one would be longer and thinner than the other. It does not matter which direction you cut in, as long as you are consistent. If you use felt squares, check the stretch by pulling gently before cutting. Felt has no right or wrong side so it is economical to use, but much more economical bought by the yard — 36in or 72in wide. Pre-cut squares are only suitable for small dolls.

I have tried tee-shirt cotton and stockinette which I found too stretchy, and thin soft leather which produces very good results but is too expensive for all but special period dolls. I reserve leather for the bodies of dolls with elaborately modelled clay heads (it is unsuitable for the heads on soft dolls as the gathers will not ease out).

For rag dolls I recommend unbleached calico. It is cheap, easily available, with a pleasant colour and texture. Occasionally you find a closely woven fleshy-pink cotton which is suitable, but most pink cottons are too brightly coloured. Flesh-coloured calico is sold for making rag dolls but again it is usually too strongly coloured, though it can be faded by washing and mild bleaching. Creamy-pink winceyette and Viyella (a wool-cotton mixture) can also be used, especially for cuddly child dolls. If you are using cotton, white can be dyed with cold tea to a more natural colour. The rag

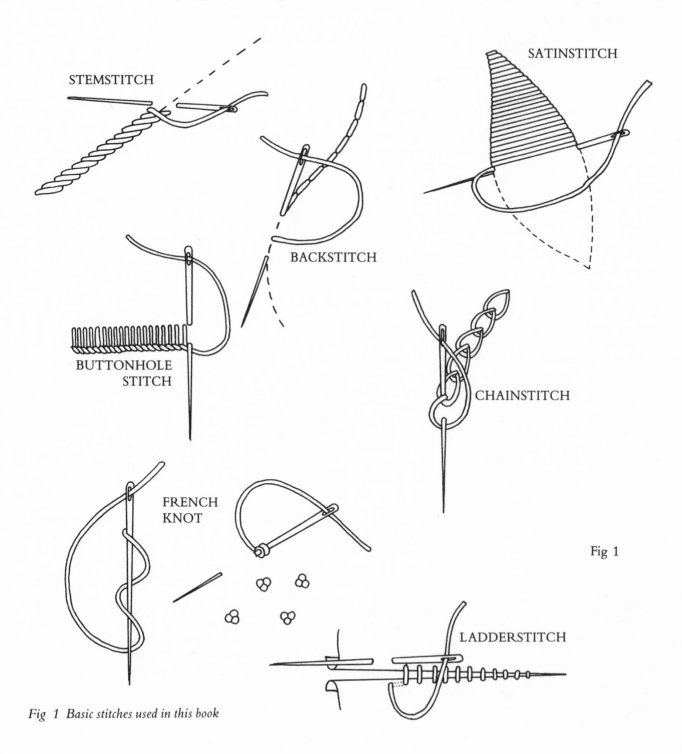

Fig 1 *Basic stitches used in this book*

STEMSTITCH

SATINSTITCH

BACKSTITCH

BUTTONHOLE STITCH

CHAINSTITCH

FRENCH KNOT

Fig 1

LADDERSTITCH

dolls can of course be made in felt if you wish, but because of felt's stretchiness they will make up quite a lot larger, and the clothes patterns will have to be altered.

If you are using new fabric, especially calico, wash it before use to remove the starchy dressing. Iron it when slightly damp to remove the creases, and pull it squarely to the grain. When cutting patterns, ensure that the pieces lie on the straight grain of the fabric, except for pieces marked to be cut on the bias, eg Big and Little Sisters' heads.

When making coloured dolls, choose felt or fabric which is a soft warm brown, not too dark, so that the features do not become obscured. For character dolls, consider also using chamois leather (an Eskimo or North American Indian?), velveteen (Baby Bunting or Mrs Rabbit?), white cotton (a clown or pierrot?) or silk (a 1930s flapper?).

Sewing the Bodies

Whether you use a sewing machine or hand-sew the dolls is a matter of personal preference. If you machine the pieces, use a short tight stitch to make strong seams; if hand-sewing, use small back-stitching. It is advisable, especially on children's dolls, to sew all the seams twice, as the doll is exposed to some strain, particularly during stuffing. The seam allowance on the large felt-doll patterns and on the rag dolls is ½in — but slightly more or less will have little effect on the finished doll (for the costume dolls and small character dolls, ¼in is recommended).

Use slipstitch to close the openings left for stuffing, making as neat a closure as possible. Heads and limbs are attached with firm stitches and strong button thread, working on the back of the doll.

Those dolls who have their fingers defined with stabstitching should have less well-stuffed hands. Work the centre line of stabstitch through the hand first, to divide the width of the hand into two halves, then work a line of stitching to divide each half. Turn the hand between each stitch to check that the needle comes out in the right place on back and front, and pull each stitch tight as you work. Fanny's hands which have separate fingers, should be sewn by hand on the inside. The fingers are oversewn with small tight stitches, working from the outside arm seams at the thumb to the little finger. Stabstitched fingers can be worked on any of the dolls, but separate fingers are impracticable on any doll smaller than Fanny, as it becomes almost impossible to turn them through.

All the dolls have feet with sewn-in soles. On the larger dolls, it is easy enough to machine-stitch the soles into the feet, though pinning or tacking first is recommended, but on the smaller dolls it is easier to oversew the soles by hand. If you wish, toes can also be defined by stabstitching.

The felt dolls all have heads made by the same method: a rectangle is seamed, then gathered at top and bottom and stuffed to make a ball. Strong button thread should be used for the gathering, which needs to be pulled up tightly — ordinary thread tends to snap under the strain.

The rag dolls have heads shaped with a gusset (for the Sisters) or darts (for Emily). The rag-doll head patterns can be used for the felt dolls if you prefer, but the stuffed felt ball, though simple, makes an effective head, nicely shaped and without seams or darts to spoil the face.

Turning-through

When the parts are sewn (and on rag dolls, clipped), they are turned through to the right side for stuffing. The tools you use to do this depend on individual preference and the size of the part. Large pieces are easily turned, with a knitting needle or something similar to poke out the corners. Tiny parts, such as Fanny's fingers, should be turned very carefully, using the blunt end of a darning needle, a cotton bud or some similar tool. Use a pair of tweezers to grip and pull through a fiddly part, or it may be easier to thread a needle with button thread, tie a large knot on one end, push the needle through and pull the thread.

Do not use anything sharp, such as the points of a pair of scissors — it is all too easy to poke a hole through the fabric. If you should have such a mishap, repair the hole immediately by oversewing on the wrong side. Generally, the smaller the part, the more tricky it is to turn through, but few of the dolls have such small parts, and even Fanny's fingers will turn with a little patience.

Stuffing

Good stuffing is essential to the finished appearance and feel of the doll. The cheaper acrylic stuffings tend to be heavier and more inclined to go lumpy than the better-quality acrylics or polyesters. Kapok, a vegetable fibre, is messy to use, tends to lump in time and is not washable. Foam chips and old stockings make such horrible fillings they are not even worth considering. I recommend terylene or the best-quality acrylic or polyester. These stuffings are white, clean, light and springy; and well-worth the extra cost.

Tools for stuffing are similar to tools for turning-through — knitting needles, paintbrush handles, thin dowelling and similar blunt sticks, anything which will push the stuffing in but not poke holes in the fabric.

All the dolls in the book require good, firm stuffing, some of them very firm. If dolls are understuffed, they do not look attractive, the limbs are floppy, the heads wobbly and the clothes will not fit properly.

When stuffing the limbs, begin with small pieces of stuffing packed well down and pinch the hands and feet to shape. Feet should have flat soles and rounded toes and heels. Hands which will have stabstitched fingers should not be stuffed too firmly. Once past the wrists and ankles, use larger pieces of stuffing, packed equally firmly. Turn the limb around as you stuff so that it is filled evenly, and roll and squeeze the limbs to shape them. If you get lumps which will not squeeze out, remove that part of the stuffing and try again, pulling the stuffing apart to fluff it up before re-using it. The bodies of child dolls need not be stuffed quite as firmly as the arms and legs, but the shoulders and hips should be well filled and the neck must be firm to support the head. Dolls which have rounded body parts, such as the Babies or the Ballerina, should have very firmly stuffed bodies. Push the stuffing into the front of the body, stretching the felt slightly as you work to shape the Baby's tummy or the Ballerina's bosom, and fill the rest of the body equally firmly so that the rounded part stays in place. The body is the part which a beginner is inclined to understuff — so if in doubt, pack in some more.

The head must always be stuffed very firmly. Begin by easing and stretching out the gathers at the lower edge and stuff the bottom half of the head, moulding rounded cheeks as you work, so that the gathers virtually disappear. The felt will stretch as you stuff, so keep packing it in until the head will hold no more and the gathering at the top will only just pull up. If you are a beginner, you will probably be surprised at the amount of stuffing which disappears inside the doll. Check that the head is symmetrical and evenly stuffed, otherwise it looks as though the doll has toothache! (This is particularly important with rag dolls, especially the Sisters.)

If you wish, wires (pipecleaners are suitable) can be inserted in the small-dolls' limbs during stuffing to make them bendable. Bend back the ends of the wires so that they cannot poke holes in the felt. Dowelling rods can be used to support legs on a standing doll and can be inserted between head and neck (though this is not necessary if the doll is properly stuffed). As you close the tops of arms and legs, push in a little more stuffing as you

work, and as the head is ladderstitched to the neck, poke as much stuffing as you can into the neck on your way round.

If, when the doll is assembled, you find that you have understuffed and the body feels thin or the head is floppy, cut a slit up the centre of the back body, pack in more stuffing until the doll is really firm, and close the slit with ladderstitch.

Assembly

When the various parts of the doll are stuffed, and the openings stitched closed, brush them with a soft clothes brush to remove any stray fluff. Using strong button thread in a colour to match the body (a good selection of colours is available at most haberdashery or notions departments), stitch the legs, arms and head to the body.

Sew the legs to the back of the doll. Use small tight oversewing stitches and start from the outside of the top of the leg, working into the crutch. Repeat with the other leg — ensuring that both feet face the same way! Little Sister and the Toddler Twins have simple arm joints, oversewn to the back of the body in the same way as the legs (Fig 2a). Start at the shoulder, and work down the side of the body.

The other dolls have rounded tops to the arms. To attach these, depress a socket with your fingers in the sides of the doll at the shoulder. The ridge which forms over the top of the shoulder can be tacked to hold it while you sew the arm in place. Oversew the top of the arm from front to back where it meets this ridge (Fig 2b). This joint will enable the arms to be raised, as well as giving the doll more realistic shoulders. Though it is not quite as strong as the previous simple joint because less of the arm is actually attached to the body, it is perfectly adequate for most dolls.

On felt dolls, when attaching the head to the neck, centre it carefully so that the bottom gathers sit evenly inside the neck. You might find it helpful to tack a circle of stitching around the bottom of the head to use as a guideline for the ladderstitching. Ensuring that the head seam is to the centre-back, work small ladderstitches, pulled up tightly every three or four stitches, through the bottom of the head and the top edge of the neck, poking in more stuffing as you go round. On a child's doll it is advisable to work this seam twice, making the second row of stitching slightly above and below the first, so that the head is very secure.

The beginner who finds it difficult to attach the stuffed felt-ball head may prefer to use Emily's darted head, pattern D1, as an alternative.

Big and Little Sister rag dolls also have heads

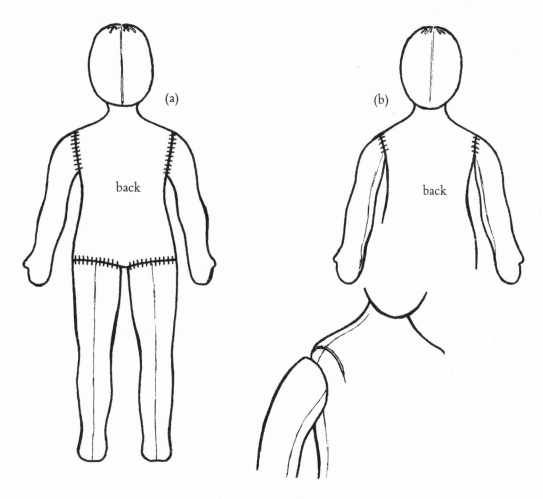

Fig 2 Methods for arm and leg assembly on soft dolls

which are ladderstitched to the bodies, but as this is a straightforward edge-to-edge seam it is easy to work. Ensure that the side seams on both parts line up, so that the head is sewn on straight. Emily rag-doll's head is very simple, as the neatened lower edge of the head is pulled down over the neck and oversewn in place before the head is stuffed. Ensure that the head seam is to the centre-back so that the darts in the bottom of the head are evenly placed. The neck and head are then stuffed from the top, and the top of the head is gathered and pulled up as for the felt dolls.

Some of the dolls in the book have stitched elbow and knee joints, enabling their arms and legs to bend. (I have described the method for this in the relevant instructions, eg Polly.) These joints can be used on any doll, but should be worked during stuffing rather than after. They are not very attractive joints, so I recommend them only for dolls whose clothes will cover them.

Articulated Joints

To make articulated shoulder joints which will enable the doll's arms to swing freely, use four fairly large, flat, strong buttons, of the type with four holes in the centre.

Before the body is turned through, lightly sew one button into the corner of each shoulder on the side seams. The arms should be cut from the rounded-top arm patterns — before turning through, stitch one button lightly to the top on the inside of each arm. Turn the body and arms through to the right side. Using strong button thread, pass the needle through the arm button and arm into the body and body button and back again. Work back and forth through the buttons in an X, joining them very securely. The thread between the buttons is all that attaches the arms to the body, so it must be strong.

Stuff the body and legs in the usual way and close the openings at the tops of the arms. Very firm stuffing is recommended for all dolls with articulated joints.

Legs can be jointed in the same way, but to do so it is necessary to cut the legs with rounded tops and attach them to either side of the body. The pattern given for the Fashion doll (Fig 88) is cut in this way, and if you wish, the other felt-doll patterns can be adapted for this type of leg joint.

As an alternative to buttons, the disc joints sold for soft-toy making can be used. These joints use cardboard discs and cotter pins rather than buttons and thread, and are therefore strong. They are inserted in the same way as for soft toys.

Making Faces

The shape of the human head is slightly different in babies and children — and in adults. Babies and young children have rather rounder-shaped heads, adults' are more egg-shaped. The eyes, though, are placed about halfway down the face, and though there are no rigid rules in dollmaking, a doll's face usually looks more pleasing if the natural human proportions are copied (see Fig 6).

When planning the doll's face, it is much easier if the wig is pinned to the head before the features are marked. Whether you are using wool, fur fabric or a bought wig, this will enable you to mark the hairline and to position the features so that the whole head is in balance. The beginner often places the doll's eyes too high on the face, leaving too long a nose and chin — a mistake which can be avoided by trying the wig first.

The actual face, and the methods used to make it, will depend on whether the doll is to be a child or adult, how simple or elaborate it is to be, your own skills and the methods you use.

Soft dolls usually have disproportionately large heads, so the eyes too are usually large. Child dolls generally look better with their eyes set rather wide apart, small noses and small mouths. Adult dolls, having longer heads, should have longer noses and larger mouths. The finished expression is all-important: many a beautifully made doll is rejected because it has a simpering or smirking expression which irritates its owner — remember that if you make a smiling face it's a permanent smile!

Eyes

The eyes are the most important facial feature, and to some extent will determine the doll's character. They should be carefully chosen to suit the type of doll. A simple child's toy needs only simple eyes, but an elaborately dressed lady doll would be far less attractive with felt-circle eyes.

Several methods are described here and you may have your own; choose whichever suits the doll and your own talents. If you are good at embroidery but not at painting, then embroidered eyes are for you. It is often worth experimenting with two or three different methods if you are making a special doll to find the one which makes the effect you want.

The simplest eyes are made from buttons. Shiny-black shank buttons, round or oval, flat or faceted (old jet buttons are excellent) can be bought in any good haberdashery or notions department and make effective eyes. Try them out on the face, using two or three different sizes to gauge the effect — usually the smaller ones look better. They are suitable for simple dolls (see the Toddler Twins, Polly and the Babies), but can also be used for characters (see the Sailor) or for more elaborately costumed period dolls.

Consider also using painted buttons. Choose round or oval, white-plastic shank buttons and paint the eye and eyelid onto the button with enamel paints. These eyes can look very realistic.

To paint eye buttons, wedge them into a piece of plasticine, modelling clay or Blu-tac to hold them while you work. Begin by painting the eyelid — mixing flesh colour and matt-white enamel paints to match the felt. When the eyelid is dry, paint the iris in blue, brown, grey, green or violet gloss enamel. When this is dry, paint a black-gloss pupil in the centre of each eye, and finally a small touch of white in each pupil as highlight. If you wish, the eye can be outlined in grey or brown and fine lashes painted on the eyelid. Use a very fine, good-quality paintbrush, and let each stage dry thoroughly before proceeding with the next.

Eye buttons should be sewn right through the head, both for safety's sake on children's dolls and also so that, pulled tight, they depress a socket in the face around the eye. Use strong button thread and a slim darning needle, mark the position of the eyes lightly in pencil before starting, and sew back and forth through the head, through the shank of the button, pulling tightly as you sew. Painted eyes must be sewn in straight — if they show any tendency to swivel, smear a little UHU or similar glue behind them, and press them into place as the glue dries. As the eye buttons are sewn in, sockets will also form on the back of the head as the stitches are pulled tight, but these will be concealed by the wig.

Glass and plastic eyes sold for soft-toy making look promising at first glance, but are in fact of little use to the dollmaker. The smallest size of glass eyes, sold in pairs with a wire stalk between them, can however be used for the small character dolls. Cut the wires to about one inch behind the eye, glue the wire and the back of the eye and push them firmly into the doll's head. Check before buying that you have a good pair of matching eyes; they tend to be irregular and you may need to buy two or three pairs to get one usable set. Obviously these eyes should never be used on a child's toy — they are not safe. The larger plastic safety eyes can be used for simple dolls, though they tend to look too much like teddy bears' eyes. To insert them, the head must be opened at the top and the stuffing removed. The shanks are pushed through the face and secured by washers on the inside — the head is then re-filled and re-gathered. Putting the eyes in before the head is made up is not feasible, as it is impossible to gauge the best position for them. I have experimented with setting these eyes into white-felt 'whites', but find them unsatisfactory because they sit on the outside of the head, rather than being 'set in' as the button eyes are. For the same reason I reject the stick-on 'googly' doll's eyes, also sold in craft shops.

Embroidered or appliqué eyes, or a combination of the two, can look most attractive. Simple felt shapes, glued or, better, sewn to the face have been used for the rag-doll Sisters' eyes and Thomas and Harriet's mouths. Plain black circles are really only suitable for very simple dolls, and the placement of them is critical. Try out several sizes in various positions to judge the most pleasing effect — usually they look best set wide apart. Buttonholestitch (or glue) them to the face. When cutting small pieces of felt like this, paint the back of the felt with glue before you cut, to stop the piece becoming fluffy around the edges. More elaborate felt eyes can be made by cutting the white, iris and pupil in appropriate colours and shapes, assembling each piece with blanketstitch, then stitching the completed eyes to the head. Outlined with stemstitch and with embroidered lashes and a few white stitches to make a highlight

in the pupil, such felt eyes can look very pretty.

Embroidered eyes can be worked straight onto the face, or onto a piece of white felt or fabric which is then appliquéd to the face. Mark out the eye lightly in soft pencil first (mistakes can be removed with a pencil rubber), and when the size, shape and position are correct, embroider with two or three strands of embroidery silk. The iris and pupil can be worked in satinstitch or buttonholestitch and the outline in stemstitch. Work eyelashes, and a white highlight in the pupil to finish. Embroidery is the technique traditionally used for rag-doll faces (*see* Emily), and if done well it is probably the best.

Covered-button eyes are also embroidered, but as they are three-dimensional they look very realistic. Choose commercial button forms of the appropriate size; take care not to buy them too large as they will be larger when made up (15mm diameter is used for the dolls in this book). Cover the button forms with closely woven white cotton, and mark the eye lightly in pencil as a guide for the embroidery. Use satinstitch or buttonhole to work the iris and pupil, ensuring that you do not leave too large an area of white around them, which would make a startled expression. Cut small felt semi-circles for the eyelids, and sew the straight edge across the front of the eye with buttonholestitch in brown thread, covering the white at the top of eye but not so low that the doll looks sleepy. Gather around the curved edge of the felt and pull up tightly behind the eye (Fig 3). Covered-button eyes, having shanks, are sewn into the head in the same way as other button eyes, but I recommend glueing their backs to hold them firmly in place. These eyes are suitable for any doll, safe enough for a child's toy and very effective.

Acrylic eyes, which are used for the modelled dolls, can also be used for felt dolls. They are how-

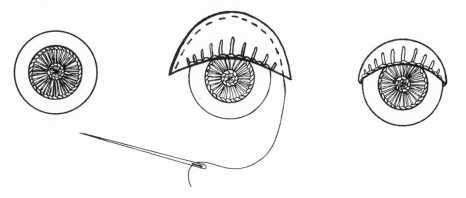

Fig 3 Making embroidered covered-button eyes

ever rather expensive, and the method is tricky, so I do not recommend them for beginners. The eyes are oval in shape with flat backs and are available in a variety of sizes — 16mm being most suited to the dolls in this book. Gauge the position of the eye carefully and mark lightly with pencil. Cut two squares of felt, approximately 1½in each side, and glue an eye to the centre of each square. Round off the corners of the felt squares. Using small sharp scissors, cut horizontal slits in the doll's face at the marked eye positions. Slip the eyes with their felt backings into the slits, taking care not to tear the slits. Using a wooden toothpick or similar tool, smear glue inside the felt eyelid above the eye and around the felt backing. Position the top edge of the slit carefully over the eye and hold in place as the glue dries (you may wish to push in a little stuffing to round out the eyelid). Repeat for the lower edge of the eye. As you can imagine, this method is very fiddly, and unless it is done well the result is not pleasing. The eye must be held securely in place, and the felt eyelid must be stretched just enough to curve over the eye but not too much. The method is completed by embroidering or painting an outline and lashes around the eye.

Eyelashes can be embroidered onto the face around any of the eyes mentioned here. Brown thread is usually better than black for more realistic eyes, black for simple button or felt-circle eyes. The embroidered covered-button eyes have blanketstitched lashes on the eyelid, and look better without further lashes. As an alternative to embroidery, lashes can be painted on with felt pens or make-up pencils — though neither of these is washable and they will smear if the face gets wet.

False eyelashes cut down from life-sized ones have been used on Fanny and the Ballerina. Use the cheapest lashes you can buy — one is usually sufficient for both eyes. Snip them to size and shape. Glue them to the edge of the eyelid on the covered-button eyes, and when the glue is quite dry, curl them upwards with your finger. False eyelashes give the doll a rather haughty expression and are really most suitable for adult-lady dolls, but occasionally they look right on a pretty Victorian or Edwardian little girl, and they are fun to use.

If acrylic eyes are set in at just the right angle, false eyelashes can be used with them too. If the angle is wrong, the lashes hang down, obscuring the eye completely — but if they will sit properly, they look very effective. Glue them carefully to the edge of the upper eyelid and, if you wish, glue small pieces to the lower eyelid.

Most dolls look better with eyebrows, though they should be small and light for babies and young children. When the eyes are fixed in place, mark the eyebrows lightly in pencil and embroider them with two or three strands of thread, in stemstitch or chainstitch. Keep them very small for babies, just a few stitches in light brown, slightly larger for children, and curved but light for lady dolls. Men dolls need stronger eyebrows, less curved and worked in the same colour as the hair. Eyebrows can also be painted in felt pen or make-up pencils. Take care not to place them too high or the doll will have a surprised expression.

Noses

Once the eyes are made, the other facial features can be decided on. The type of doll, and the type of eyes used affect the choice of nose and mouth. For example, if you have used acrylic eyes, a felt bobble nose would look ridiculous.

The simplest nose is merely indicated by dots for nostrils, either painted or embroidered with French knots. Although this method is often used on rag dolls I dislike it because it tends to make the doll look like a piglet! Equally simple but more attractive is a small curved line, painted or embroidered in two or three strands of pink thread. Judge the position of the nose carefully (about halfway between eyes and chin is usually right) and mark it lightly in soft pencil. Curve the line upwards or downwards as you prefer, depending on the character of the doll. An upward curve is usually more appropriate to a child, downward for an older face (see the rag dolls).

Felt bobble noses look cute, and can be made large or small as you wish. Cut a circle of felt to the size required, gather around the outside edge and pull up the gathers tightly around a little stuffing. Ladderstitch the nose securely to the face. To make a tiny bobble nose, suitable for a baby or young child, gather up a very small circle without any stuffing. When using bobble noses, do try out several sizes and shapes — a larger or smaller nose can make a considerable difference to the expression. The bobble nose does not have to be round. On some dolls a kidney-shaped nose is more effective. Cut a kidney-shaped or oval piece of felt, and gather and stuff it (or not) in the same way.

Several of the dolls in the book have inserted bead noses. This gives the face an appealing expression and a real profile! Choose light-coloured beads, wood or plastic, of the size you require. Polly and the Ballerina have fairly small bead noses, Thomas and Harriet have larger ones. For babies, you need very small beads. To insert the nose, cut a slit in the doll's forehead, under the hairline directly above where the nose is to be. Spear the bead on a knitting or darning needle and coat it with glue. Ease it down into the face, just under the felt and position it carefully. Holding the nose, gently draw out the needle. Pinch the doll's face over the nose so that the felt sticks to the bead, and leave it alone while the glue dries. Close the slit in the head with neat oversewing. This technique can also be used with a wedge-shaped piece of balsa wood, which makes a nose with a shaped bridge. To insert a balsa wood nose, spear it firmly on the point of a darning needle, coat with glue and push carefully into the face as before.

When positioning the nose, place it higher for a baby or child, lower for an adult; make sure that it is in the centre of the face and well glued so that it cannot move! Mark the nostrils lightly with brown felt pen.

Mouths

The mouth is of less critical importance to the expression than the eyes and nose, but a good one will enhance and a bad one mar the face. Some dolls look better with no mouth, or just the merest suggestion of one, others need a well-shaped, strongly defined mouth to suit the character. The three most commonly used methods are painting, embroidery and appliqué.

Gauge the position of the mouth and draw it lightly on the face in pencil. It is usually placed halfway between nose and chin. If you are going to paint it, draw the outline first with felt pen or make-up pencils, then fill in the shape with colour. Choose the colour carefully, avoiding bright reds and pinks. Children's mouths look better in softer, lighter colours, pinks or rusty pink, old rose or coffee pink. Felt-pen colours are usually garish; so lip pencils in natural colours are better. For a lady doll, the mouth can be coloured in a lipstick colour to harmonise with the clothes. For a man doll, choose a colour as close to natural as possible.

The same rules on colour apply to embroidered mouths. Draw the outline on the face, and work satinstitch to fill in the shape. For children keep it small; often just a few stitches are enough (see the Toddler Twins). Lady dolls look well with shapely mouths (see Fanny), with a second layer of satinstitch worked over the first to make the lips look full. If you wish, the lower lip can be coloured one shade lighter than the upper lip to give a pouting effect.

A combination of the two methods, with the outline embroidered in fine thread and then filled with painted colour, also works very well (see Polly).

Appliqué mouths can be cut in felt, trying out several different shapes, and glued to the face. They look better if a line of stitching is worked across the centre to define the lips. Choose the colour carefully. Most felt colours are too bright, but peach or soft pink usually look effective (see Thomas and Harriet).

When shaping the mouth, a slight turn-up at the corners makes a happier expression than a turn-down, but be chary of making broad smiles. A smiling doll can so easily become a smirking doll and very irritating! The exceptions of course are pierrots which should look sad, clowns which are either happy or sad according to type, and similar character dolls.

Finishing

The finishing touches to the face, coloured cheeks, freckles and beauty spots, are most easily made with make-up. Traditionally, rag dolls have little pink stars embroidered onto their faces to colour the cheeks, but I prefer to use blusher for rag dolls as well as felt dolls. Use a powder blusher in a soft natural pink or tawny shade and brush it onto the doll's cheeks. How much you use will depend on how strongly you wish to colour the face, and it can be applied to look natural — as with the Sailor and Ballerina — or very 'dolly' as with Emily rag doll. Brush the blusher well in, then rub over with a piece of silk to set it.

Freckles (see Polly) are most easily applied with a brown felt pen or eye pencil with a sharp point. Use a light golden-brown and dot carefully over the nose and cheeks — don't overdo it or it will look like measles, not freckles! Beauty spots for a lady doll can be painted on with brown felt pen or eye pencil or embroidered with French knots — the painting method looks more realistic. Put a beauty spot near a pretty eye or mouth, as a real one would be.

With the exception of black buttons, black felt circles and acrylic eyes, most eyes look more realistic with a white highlight in each pupil. If you have not embroidered these, they can be touched in with white paint, poster, enamel or acrylic as you prefer, and a fine paintbrush.

Fanny has a 'twinkle' in her eyes, made by glueing a small diamanté stone into each pupil. As the light catches her eyes, this gives her a roguish expression. Lady dolls with stabstitched or separate fingers can have the fingernails coloured with felt pen — either in a natural-pink colour or a nail-varnish colour, according to the doll's character. Some (though not all) nail varnishes will take on felt and fabric — try a test on a scrap first.

For lady dolls who have made-up faces, eg the Ballerina and Fanny, use ordinary cosmetics. Powder eye-shadows, eyeliner pencils, lip-pencils and face-shading powders can all be used in the same way as on your own face. Do not use the cream shadows as they smear on fabric. If in doubt, use scraps to test first, and if you are inexperienced with make-up use magazine advertisements for cosmetics as a guide. Beautiful dolls' faces can be made with make-up and it is worth trying a little on most girl and lady faces.

Mistakes in felt pen and make-up pencil can be removed from the face by painting bleach onto the affected part and blotting with tissues. Use a fine paintbrush and paint carefully with neat bleach. As soon as the colour disappears, blot firmly with tissues and leave to dry thoroughly before trying again. This procedure is not recommended for any doll which a young child might play with — sucking bleached felt is not good for you!

Wigs

The choice of materials and methods for making a doll's wig is governed by the same factors as the choice of eyes. A simple doll looks most effective with a simple wool or fur-fabric wig, an elaborate doll is enhanced by a 'real-hair' wig. If the doll is to be a child's toy and will be washed, then the wig should also be washable and must be firmly stitched to the head rather than glued.

The simple felt dolls in the book (the Toddler Twins, Polly and the Babies) have cap wigs made of fur fabric. Chapter 6 describes how to make the wigs for each doll. They are cut as a rectangle of fur fabric, seamed to make a cap to fit closely to the doll's head, trimmed to shape and stitched in place. A large variety of fur fabrics is available in both long pile and curly types, in many colours which are suitable for dolls' wigs. They can be cut, brushed to style and washed, and in natural hair colours they look surprisingly realistic. I find the light-blonde colour particularly suitable for child dolls, and the darker auburn or brown shades look attractive on more sophisticated dolls. Because the pile is knitted into the backing, the fur fabric is very strong — the hair can be brushed and pulled quite roughly without coming out, which makes it the ideal choice for wigs for children's dolls. The long-pile type makes shoulder-length hair if left untrimmed, so it can be styled with a fringe, a side or centre parting and brushed into bunches. It can also be sprayed with hair lacquer, dampened and

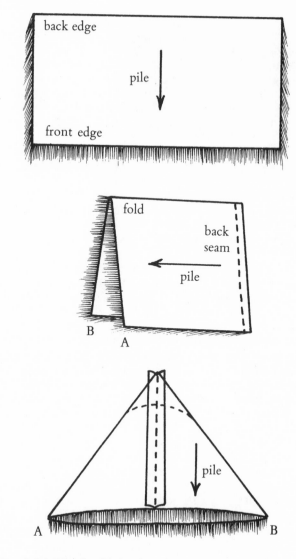

Fig 4 Making fur-fabric wigs

curled with small rollers or hair grips.

When cutting a fur-fabric wig, cut through the back of the fabric, snipping with small scissors so that you do not cut the pile. Pull the pile gently apart. I recommend sewing, rather than glueing the wig to the head, with small blanketstitches around the edge. Fur fabric has also been used for the Sailor's wig and beard. A strip, blanketstitched to the face under the chin, makes the beard, and the cap wig is made in the same way as the children's. This is the wig method I recommend for the beginner — it is even easier than wool hair and attractive results can be obtained very simply. Do give some thought to the choice of colour though; the natural hair colours look best, and avoid black or very dark brown which look harsh and attract fluff. If you are making a coloured doll, the obvious choice is a brown curly pile for boys or girls, and this also looks good for all boy dolls. The long straight pile, curled or not, looks attractive on girl dolls. For babies I recommend light-blonde shades — darker colours tend to make the baby look older — and straight pile which can be trimmed close; the curly type is too bushy for babies, making their heads look too big.

The next group of wigs are those made from yarns of all types — including the traditional rag-dolls' wool hair. Wool is of course not the only type of yarn which can be used; dishcloth cotton, in its natural colour or dyed, string, flax, linen thread, hessian thread, and thin strips of felt can all be considered, though these things are usually more suitable for character dolls. I have seen a little-girl rag doll made in creamy-white linen, its hair made of linen thread in the same colour, and dressed in a smock of the same creamy-white linen with white leather shoes: the effect was unnatural but very beautiful, and the doll was most certainly a collector's item, not a toy.

Wool, however, is the yarn most generally used for dolls' hair. There is an enormous variety of knitting and tapestry wools available, including the crinkly types of knitting wool and the chenilles which both make unusual and attractive wigs. Tapestry wools seem to have the best selection of colours, including many natural hair colours. I particularly recommend mohair wool: because the fluffy strands cling together on the doll's head, they do not separate to reveal bald patches (the most common problem with wool hair) and the wig does not have to be too thick, which means it is easier to style. It also looks more realistic than the ordinary knitting wools.

Interesting crinkly effects can be made using wool unravelled from a knitted garment, and most wools can be brushed to separate and fluff up the fibres, or be set with small rollers or hair grips to curl them. I suggest rolling the hair, then steaming it over a kettle to set the curls, rather than damping it before rolling. Wool is the ideal hair for styling into plaits, as long as it is not applied too thickly to the head, and it will twist into ringlets (*see* Emily) or make a bun or chignon on the back of the head (*see* the Ballerina). For short, curly hairstyles, especially suitable for boys, the wool can be sewn in loops all over the head — time consuming but effective; or for crew-cuts it is hooked and knotted through the scalp (as in rugmaking) and trimmed to shape.

Embroidery silk also makes effective dolls' hair. Because one is limited by the length of the skein, it is more suitable for small dolls — but the range of colours is extensive and the texture is pleasant. On smaller dolls, two or three skeins are sufficient to make even elaborate hairstyles, but for a larger doll, where the silk thread must be unwound and re-wound on a larger template, a great many skeins would be needed to make long hair, and the cost would become prohibitive.

Embroidery silk can be brushed to separate the strands, twisted into ringlets like wool hair, or curled around a paintbrush handle (using sugar water, or a solution of glue and water, as a setting lotion) to make curls. It is particularly suitable for the small character dolls or the costume dolls, because it is easy to work with and can be styled very elaborately and held in place either by sewing to. the head or glueing.

Equally suitable for small display dolls is the mohair or crêpe dolls' hair sold in craft stores. This is of little use for larger dolls because it is inclined to separate and pull out, and it looks very unrealistic used in larger quantities, but for small dolls the texture is perfect. It is usually better glued to the head and simply styled, especially under a head-dress of some sort, though with care and patience it can be used to create very elaborate styles. The white animal wool (sold in chemists' shops) or sheeps' wool from the hedgerow, are similar in texture to the mohair dolls' hair, can be used in the same way and are recommended for old ladies and character and costume dolls. White animal wool looks particularly effective as powdered hair for Georgian costume dolls.

I cannot recommend the commercial acrylic dolls' hair which is sold in various sizes and colours with a stitched parting, although it is cheap. It looks quite attractive, some of the colours are pleasant, it has a good sheen and the texture is fine, but it pulls out in handfuls and is unsuitable on larger dolls. I have however used it successfully on small costume dolls (*see* the Victorian lady) where the parting is glued to the head and the hair firmly plaited and secured. Even used in this way it is inclined to be wispy and fly-away and embroidery silk is a better alternative for all practical purposes.

Finally we come to the 'real-hair' types, home-made or bought. By 'real hair' I mean anything which looks like real hair, which includes all the man-made fibres like acrylic, Kaneklon and Dacron, and human hair. It is fairly simple to make dolls' wigs from clean cast-off life-sized wigs. Study how the wig is made, where the natural crown or parting occurs, and try it on the doll's head to judge the effect. Most modern wigs are made from long fringes of hair stitched around to form a cap shape, usually on some kind of stretchy backing. Very often you can simply cut out a piece from the crown of the wig and stitch it to the doll's head around the cut edge of the backing. Alternatively, it might be better to cut long strips of fringe and sew these to the head in a spiral, starting at the lower edge and working up to the crown. As the hair is firmly stitched either to its backing or in a fringe, these wigs can be brushed and styled as they would normally be. Long switches of hair, like false pony tails, can be used like the wool or other yarns. Stitch a firm centre parting through the middle of the switch before cutting off the end binding which holds the hairs together. Human-hair wigs and switches can be styled by any of the methods you would use to style your own hair — curlers, setting lotion, heated rollers or tongs — but most man-made fibres react badly to heat, so do test before making curls in the wig.

Wigmaking is a craft which is often taught at evening classes or on dollmaking courses, so if you wish to become expert at making 'real' wigs for dolls, try joining one of these, or ask your local hairdresser if she can recommend a wigmaking class.

Wigs made for dolls are available from specialist stockists. They range from fairly cheap acrylic wigs to those made of human hair, very beautiful but expensive. The large range of colours and styles, on stretchy or non-stretch bases, can be sewn or glued to the doll's head. When buying wigs, measure around the circumference of the doll's head at the hairline to get the size required. Acrylic wigs have been used for Thomas and Harriet, the effect of 'real hair' making something special of essentially simple dolls. The bought wigs are pre-styled in the same way as life-sized wigs, and can be brushed and combed. Human hair can be treated like your own hair, but, again, the cheaper man-made fibres are best left alone — heat and sometimes washing can spoil them. Check with the stockists when you buy the wig and take their advice.

Hairstyles

The hairstyles described here are for use with yarn, wool, embroidery silk, mohair, animal wool, acrylic or hair switches — they are all referred to generally as 'hair'.

To make partings, measure the length of hair required over the doll's head and use a book, a piece of stiff cardboard or something similar to wind the strands around. Cut through the strands when sufficient have been wound to cover the head evenly — but not too thickly. A common mistake made by beginners is to use far too much hair,

making a thick unmanageable thatch which is impossible to style.

The parting is best machine-stitched in matching thread, but if hand-stitching, use a small tight backstitch. The parting can be made through the hair alone, but it is stronger if a backing of $\frac{1}{2}$in wide matching cotton tape is stitched to the underside at the same time. Measure over the doll's head from the nape of the neck to the forehead and cut the tape to this length. Lay the hair over the tape, spread it evenly and stitch through the hair and the centre of the tape. For a side parting, the tape is laid to one side of the centre (Fig 5a).

To apply the hair to the head, the tape can be glued on the underside, but on soft dolls it is better to stitch it to the head. Turn under both ends of tape about $\frac{1}{2}$in and pin the hair to the head. Stitch through the parting into the head with small tight backstitches. For added strength, both long edges of the tape can be hemmed to the head.

To make a fringe, measure over the doll's forehead, cut a piece of tape to this length and stitch a small parting as previously. Sew the fringe to the head in the same way, before the main hair is sewn (Fig 5c).

To make bunches or plaits, draw the hair to each side of the face and tie with thread. Secure the bunches to the face with stitches, then plait if required. To make a pompadour or cottage-loaf style, measure around the circumference of the doll's head at the hairline and cut a piece of tape slightly longer. Stitch the hair to the centre of the tape in the same way as for the parting style. Sew it to the head, through the tape (with the tape uppermost) around the hairline. Draw up all the hair to the back of the head and tie it into a bunch with thread. Coil the bunch into a bun and secure. To pad out this style, if required, use cottonwool or, better, waste hair (Fig 5b).

To make a chignon, plait a length of hair, securing the ends, then coil and stitch it to the back of the head. To make ringlets, the hair should be very long, either loose or in bunches at either side of the face. Divide the hair into equal sections. Take a section of hair, holding it at the end, and twist it until it springs back on itself, coiling to make a ringlet. Secure the end firmly by stitching it to the head. To make curls, wind the hair around a suitably small roller or paintbrush handle and secure with hair grips. Or make pin curls, which should be secured with hair grips, sprayed with hair lacquer and left to dry thoroughly. On small dolls, forehead curls can be made with embroidery.

Bunches, plaits and long hairstyles look attractive tied with ribbons, but do not rely on the ribbon to secure the style. Stitch the hair to the head, then tie the ribbons in place.

Fig 5 (a) Hairstyle with centre parting; (b) cottage-loaf hairstyle; (c) hairstyle with fringe

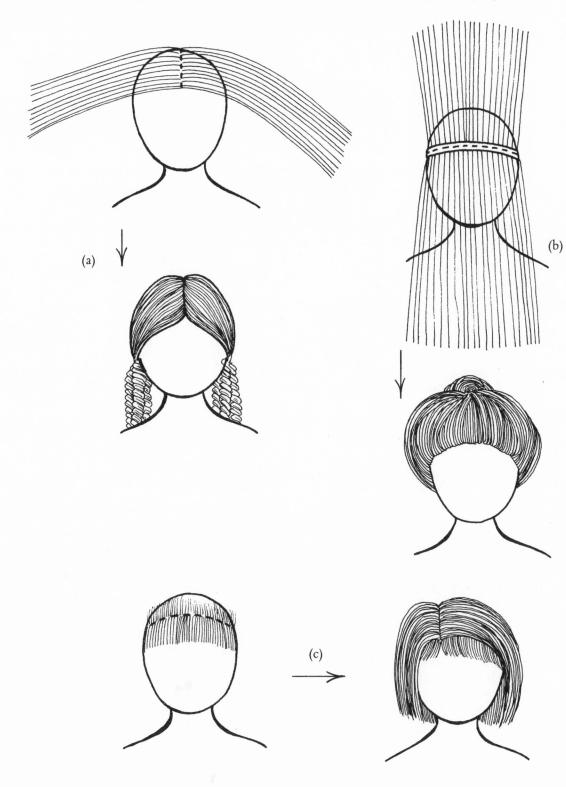

Fig 5

2
MODELLED
DOLLS

The methods described in this chapter for modelling dolls in self-hardening clay are those which I have evolved myself through trial and error. These dolls grew out of a desire to try something more ambitious than soft dolls, and a reluctance to invest in porclain or resin without experience with those materials. Without access to a kiln, self-hardening clay was the obvious choice of material and it is also easy and pleasant to use.

The initial major problem was one of weight, as a solid head would be impossibly heavy for anything other than a small doll. A hollow head was the obvious solution and once I came up with the idea of modelling the head around some kind of removeable core, it was simply a matter of experimenting to find the best core! A hollow neck was also necessary to give access to the core, and eventually I thought of using the neck of a bottle to support the core and modelling the neck in one piece with the head, so that there was a hole through the middle. The next problem was making a shoulder-plate to fit the body. Early attempts at shaping the shoulder-plate over a cardboard tube did not sit properly on the body and made ridges under the clothes. At last it dawned on me that I should make the body first and mould the shoulder-plate over the body — which also meant that it was easier to gauge the size of the head accurately. I learnt that it was better to join the neck into the shoulder-plate when the clay was almost dry (rather than still wet when everything could be squeezed out of shape) and I discovered that acrylic eyes could be used successfully in clay heads.

I have always had difficulty drawing and modelling hands, but, working patiently step-be-step and using my own hand as a guide, I can now produce quite acceptable hands. Experiments with modelling lower legs and feet, with and without shoes, proved straightforward — but this seemed pointless if they were to be covered by stockings and shoes, and I feel that modelled shoes look unrealistic with proper clothes. So, I decided to use felt legs on my own dolls, but I have included directions for modelled legs if preferred.

I have explained how my methods have evolved to encourage the beginner — nobody should be daunted by the prospect of modelling dolls in clay. It is not difficult, the technique is straightforward and patience is by far the most useful qualification. Simple shaping can produce attractive results, more easily than the beginner imagines.

If you do have a talent for modelling (whether you have discovered it yet or not) some very beautiful results are possible. Modelled dolls are rather special, each one is individual and unique. An elaborately modelled, beautifully dressed doll with 'real' eyes and hair, becomes dollmaking as an art form.

Body

The body of the doll should be made up before the head and lower arms are modelled — the modelled dolls have felt bodies which are made in the same way as the soft dolls. For a special doll you could use soft thin leather, rather than felt, stuffed very firmly with bran or sawdust. The body pattern for the Fashion doll (Fig 88) is particularly suitable for leather and would look very Victorian, especially with a wax-dipped head. Thin leather is better sewn by hand, as machine-stitching tends to tear when the body is stuffed.

The modelled lower arms have grooves around the elbow, which are used for attaching them to the felt upper arms (see Fig 12). With the felt upper arm inside out, push the clay lower arm inside it, elbow first (the seam in the upper arm should be to the inside, ie next to the body, when the doll is finished, so align it with the thumb). Smear glue around the elbow of the clay lower arm, then, tie strong button thread around the felt so that it sinks into the groove in the clay, and tie off tightly. Turn the felt upper arm right-side out, stuff, and close the top curved opening.

The arms are sewn to the body before the shoulder-plate is glued and seated. To attach the shoulder-plate, glue the underside liberally (UHU is ideal for this purpose) and seat it firmly onto the body. Hold it in place until the glue is dry. I find this method more effective than sewing the plate through holes drilled in the clay and it is completely secure.

If you are using clay lower legs cut the felt leg pattern off at the knee. Make up and attach the legs in the same way as the arms.

Materials

The self-hardening clay which I use myself and recommend is Das, but there are several varieties available. The smaller packet of Das is sufficient to model a head and lower arms for any of the dolls in this book, but if you wish to model legs as well you will need the larger packet. If you have access to a kiln and you are experienced with working in clay, you may prefer to adapt these methods to that material. Papier mâché made from pulped face tissues can also be used, but it will need rather more sanding in the final stages and several coats of gesso to give a really smooth finish.

The best type of core-ball is made from compressed cotton. These are available from some art and craft shops — but can be hard to find. Available in various sizes, they are made from a continuous length of tissue and are simple to remove from the head as they come out in one piece, unwinding as you pull. Polystyrene balls are usually easier to obtain, but are a little more difficult to remove — they have to be broken up into pieces inside the head and some care is needed to prevent the head being damaged. Being very light, the polystyrene ball can be left inside the head, but even this slight weight will make the head heavier and the drying-out will take a great deal longer. I have found that a firm ball of slightly dampened face tissues also makes a satisfactory core, but the damp tissue comes away in small pieces so it is time consuming (though not difficult) to remove. If you can find them, I recommend using the compressed-cotton balls.

The bottle used to support the core-ball should have a long thin neck without prominent ridges at the top (many wine or squash bottles are suitable). For extra stability, the bottle can be half filled with sand or gravel.

Tools used for modelling are a matter of individual preference. There is a large range of special modelling tools available at most places which stock Das, but these are not essential. You will need a small blunt knife for rough shaping the clay on the head and some shaping tools such as a skewer or toothpick, paintbrush handle and rounded knife blade, but your fingers will do most of the work and you will find odd things around the house to suit your needs. A fairly sharp knife is necessary to cut the clay and divide the fingers and a good-quality paintbrush which will not shed hairs is essential for smoothing the finished modelling. The best thing to use for rolling out the clay is an ordinary rolling pin. The clay will not damage it in any way and it can be scrubbed clean.

To keep the unused clay damp while you are working on the head, wrap it tightly in a polythene bag. If you cannot model the head in one session, cover it with a wet cloth and a polythene bag tied around the neck of the bottle, so that the clay remains workable.

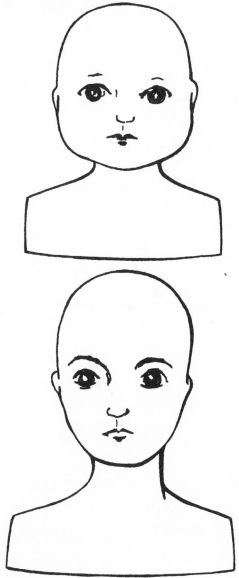

Fig 6 Relative proportions of child and adult modelled heads

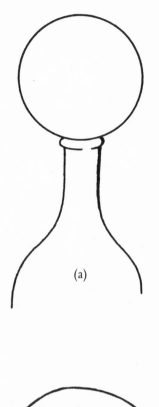
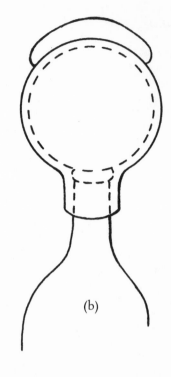
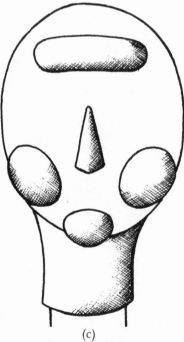
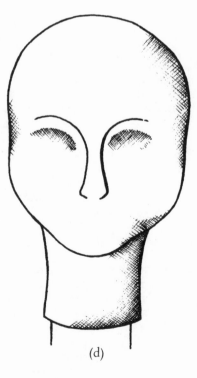

(a)

(b)

(c)

(d)

*Fig 7 (a) Place the core-ball on the neck of the bottle; (b)
cover with clay and build up the top of the head; (c) apply
pieces of clay to shape the features; (d) smooth the head and
neck*

Fig 7

You will also need petroleum jelly (eg Vaseline) to grease the neck of the bottle to prevent the clay sticking to it, a bowl of water to use with the paintbrush for damping the clay, and a clean damp cloth for wiping your hands. Work on a fairly large, flat surface such as the kitchen table and allow yourself plenty of time. Ideally you should finish the job in one session.

Modelling the Head

Grease the neck of the bottle liberally with petroleum jelly, dampen the core-ball slightly with water and place it on the neck of the bottle.

Roll out the clay to approximately ⅜in thick. Cut sufficient to cover the head and neck and put the rest in a polythene bag. Wrap the clay around the ball and the neck of the bottle, pressing firmly to shape head and neck. Cut away the surplus clay. Take a piece of clay, roll it into a ball, flatten it and put it onto the top of the head. Use a small blunt knife to drag the edges of this piece into the main body of clay. In the same way, use flattened balls of clay to build up the chin, cheeks and forehead, shaping the head roughly with the knife. Use a wedge-shaped piece, carefully centred, to form the nose. Press your thumbs into the clay to indent shallow sockets for the eyes. Working with your fingers and the knife, smooth and shape the head so that it is symmetrical. Check it from all angles to ensure that it looks right. Remember the difference in proportions between child and adult heads (*see* Fig 6). Ensure that the forehead does not recede, the eye sockets are not placed too high, the nose is a good shape both full face and in profile, the cheeks are evenly placed and shaped, the jawline is not too heavy and the chin not too prominent. Check also that the neck is the correct length and cut evenly along the bottom edge. This is all the shaping that is required for a simply modelled head, (*see* Amy, Sara and the Pierrot) but any of these dolls may have more elaborate modelling if you wish.

If the doll is to be fully modelled, press in the eyes before further shaping. The eyes used on Sophy, Oliver, the clay and waxed Babies and the Fashion doll are oval acrylic doll's eyes. They are available in blue, green or brown, in various sizes, and their flat backs make them ideal for this kind of modelling. As an alternative, you could try painted buttons (*see* Chapter 1) using fairly large flat ones so that the shape of the button can be concealed by the eyelid.

Gauge the position of the eyes carefully, then push them firmly into the clay, ensuring that they are evenly placed and facing forward. Use small rolls of clay, smoothed out and blended into the face for form the eyelids. Check that the eyelid covers the top part of the white of the eye and that both eyelids are symmetrical. Use small rolls of clay, smoothed out into the cheeks, to shape under the eyes.

You might prefer to make 'intaglio' eyes from balls of clay, or to press slightly rounded buttons into the eye sockets to shape the eyes which will later be painted as 'intaglio' eyes.

To shape the nostrils, push a paintbrush handle or something similar up each side of the nose — make sure that they are even and both the same size. Smooth tiny rolls of clay into the nose and face to shape the fleshy parts on either side of the nose around the nostrils. Cut a semi-circle of clay, and smooth it into the face below the nose to shape the top lip. Make a small roll of clay for the lower lip. Shape the lips carefully; the lower one rounded and quite full, the upper one curved or slightly pointed, adding a little more clay as necessary.

Ears are more easily modelled first and then applied to the head, though they are not essential as they are usually covered by the wig. Cut semi-circles of flattened clay, pinch to shape the earlobe and model the curved rim with a wooden toothpick or similar small tool. Fix the ears to the head with slip, smoothing the back and lower edges into the head. Check that both ears line up. I recommend making ears very small and only using them if you are sure that they will not interfere with the fitting of the wig.

Check the modelling thoroughly from all angles. When it is satisfactory, smooth the head and neck, first with wet fingers rubbed all over, then with a paintbrush and water. The smoother the finish at this stage, the less sanding will be required later. Leave the head on the bottle to dry.

For the shoulder-plate, roll out the clay to approximately ¼in thick. Measure across the width of the doll's shoulders, and from front to back over the shoulder to gauge the depth. The exact depth of the shoulder-plate will depend to some extent on the proposed costume — a low neck-line requires a deeper plate. Cut a rectangle of clay the required size and round off the corners slightly. Cut a circular hole from the centre of the rectangle to fit the lower end of the neck. If you have difficulty gauging the exact size, cut larger rather than smaller. Lay the shoulder-plate over the body, pressing gently so that the clay follows the contours of the felt body. Smooth the shoulder-plate with a paintbrush and water and leave it on the body to dry.

When both the head and the shoulder-plate are

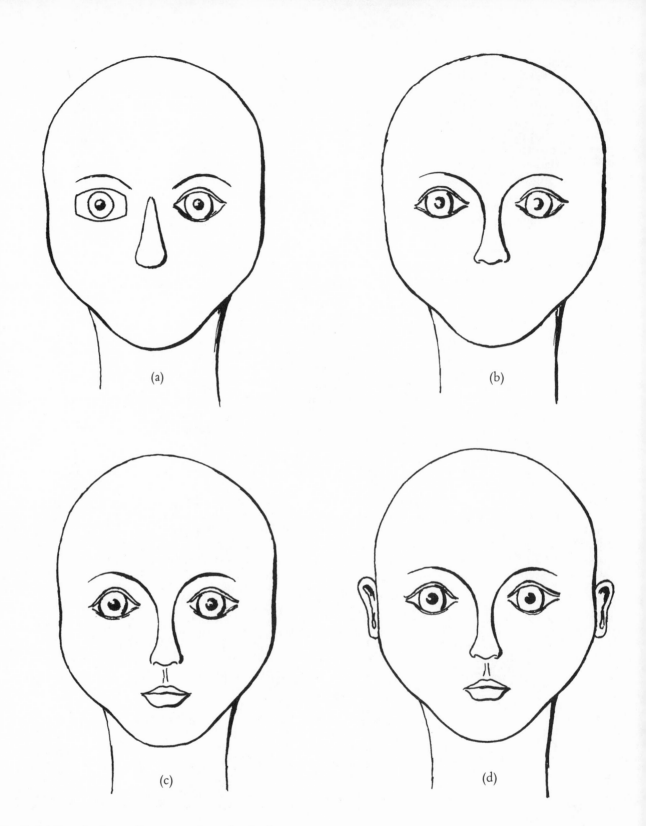

*Fig 8 (a) Press in the acrylic eyes, apply wedge for the
nose; (b) shape the eyelids and nostrils; (c) shape the mouth;
(d) attach modelled ears with slip*

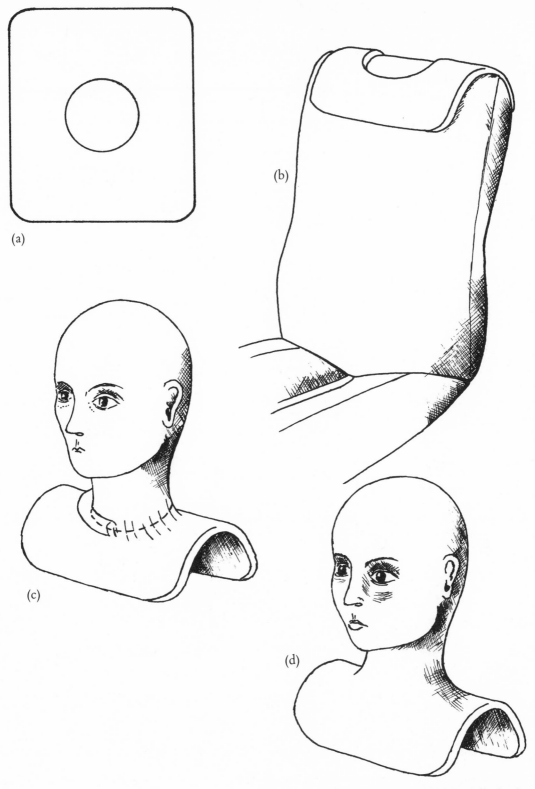

Fig 9 (a) Cut the shoulder-plate with a hole for the neck;
(b) mould the shoulder-plate over the body; (c) attach the
head to the shoulder-plate with clay roll; (d) completed head
and shoulder-plate

dry enough to handle lift the head carefully off the bottle, and the shoulder-plate off the body. Fit the lower end of the neck into the hole in the shoulder-plate. Make a roll of clay long enough to go around the neck and approximately ½in in diameter, then dip this in water so that it is very wet. Brush water onto the lower edge of the neck and the edge of the hole in the shoulder-plate.

Position the head carefully on the shoulder-plate (work with the pieces on the table, or, as I do, in your hands), wrap the roll of wet clay around the join and smooth it out into the neck and the shoulder-plate. Press small rolls of wet clay inside the neck to seal the join. When the two pieces are joined smooth with a paintbrush and water and leave to dry thoroughly.

Modelling the Hands and Lower Arms

Roll lengths of clay into 'sausages' thick enough to fit into the lower edge of the felt upper arm and long enough to make the lower arm and hand in one piece.

Pinch and roll the clay to narrow the arm at the wrist, and flatten and curve the hand into a spoon shape. For very small dolls, eg the costume dolls, this simple spoon shape, slightly indented for the palms, will suffice for the hands. Cut the clay into separate thumb and fingers with a sharp knife and trim them to the correct length. Roll the fingers gently to shape, trimming away surplus clay as necessary so that each finger is a small sausage. Add a little clay to the palm of the hand to shape a mound above the thumb, and press a hollow in the centre of the palm.

Use your own hand as a model to bend the fingers into a natural position. Cut a groove around the elbow about ½in from the end, for tying on.

Using wet fingers, then a paintbrush and water, smooth the arms and hands thoroughly. If you want to indicate fine detail such as fingernails, use a pointed tool such as a toothpick. More shaping at wrists and knuckles can also be worked to make the hands more realistic.

When the arms are smoothed leave them aside to dry. Check that you have made a pair of hands: one left, one right. As a general rule, dolls usually have unnaturally small hands, especially in relation to their heads. It is a matter of taste, but obviously large hands require wider sleeves, and can be inconvenient when dressing the doll. I tend to make larger hands for more realistic dolls, such as Sophy and Oliver, and smaller hands for elaborately costumed dolls such as the Fashion doll.

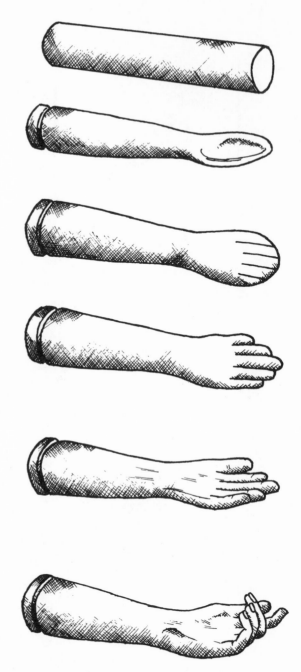

Fig 10 Stages for modelling arm and hand

Modelling the Legs and Feet

If you intend to model the lower legs and feet, cut the felt leg pattern to the knee and make up the legs in the same way as the arms. Seam the upper leg pieces, tie on the lower leg, turn through, stuff and close, then sew the upper leg to the body.

Roll lengths of clay into sausages thick enough to fit into the lower edge of the felt upper leg and long enough to model the leg and foot in one piece.

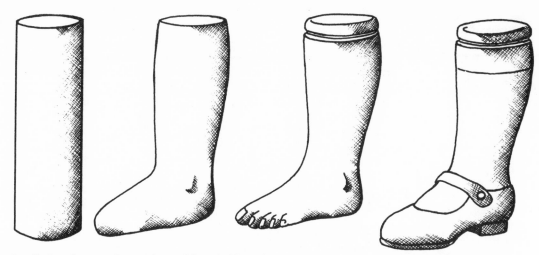

Fig 11 Stages for modelling leg and foot

Pinch and roll the clay to shape the ankle, and bend the foot forward. Flatten the sole of the foot and round off the toes and heel. Use a sharp knife to separate the toes, and gently shape them into small sausages trimming away the excess clay. Cut grooves about ½in from the knee for tying on. Hollow the arch of the foot, shape the ankle and, if you wish, indicate the toenails with a sharp pointed tool.

You can model the shoe rather than a naked foot. This is most easily done by rolling the clay out to approximately 1/16in thick, cutting out a sole, upper and strap, and making up the shoe on the foot, using a paintbrush and water to join the pieces. Cut a separate heel and attach it under the sole in the same way (Fig 11). A variety of clay shoes can be made (just like fabric shoes), with high or low heels, modelled bows, buckles or laces. Alternatively, boots can be modelled by cutting a clay upper and wrapping it around the leg like leather or fabric, but fixed to the leg and sole using a paintbrush and water. Laces can be modelled, or you can thread real laces through holes made in the clay upper.

Check that you have made a pair of feet: one left, one right. Smooth thoroughly and leave aside to dry. As with their hands, dolls' feet are usually very small.

Drying

Self-hardening clay dries fairly quickly and the head and shoulder-plate should be dry enough to join after about six hours in normal room temperature. To speed the drying process, leave them in a warm place such as in the airing cupboard or near a radiator. (I put my own in baking tins lined with wadding on top of the boiler.) As soon as the head and shoulder-plate are dry enough to handle join the pieces as described. Then leave them to dry thoroughly.

After approximately twenty-four hours the clay head will be dry, though the cotton core-ball will be damp as it has drawn the moisture from the clay. At this stage, remove the core-ball from the head. If you have used a compressed-cotton or wadded-paper-tissue ball, it will pull out easily. You may find that you cannot easily reach into the head with your fingers to pull out the core-ball, in which case a pair of tweezers will help. Compressed-cotton balls, once you have picked away the outside, will unwind in long lengths. Wadded tissues require patience to remove as they have to be picked out in small pieces. A polystyrene ball will not be damp, and will have to be broken up into very small pieces inside the head with a small screwdriver or something similar. Take great care that the head is not damaged. Once the core-ball is removed the inside of the head can dry thoroughly, which will take another six–twelve hours. Arms and legs should be turned occasionally to speed drying, but will be dry by the time the head is completely dry.

Sanding

When the clay parts are completely dry sand them carefully with medium-grade sandpaper. Work with small pieces of sandpaper, taking care to sand each part very thoroughly. If you have used acrylic eyes, be careful when working around them as they scratch easily. (They can be covered with pieces of tape to protect them during sanding and painting.) If necessary, use a craft knife with a sharp new blade to pare away any lumps or bumps which have been left in the modelling or to refine the shaping. When each piece is sanded as smoothly as possible, change to a very fine-grade abrasive paper such as flourpaper and sand each piece again. The better the finish after sanding, the better the final result will be, so don't skimp on this stage. When each piece has been very thoroughly sanded, finish by rubbing firmly all over with cloth such as a linen or cotton teatowel.

During the sanding process, smooth the edges of the shoulder-plate slightly rounded and check that the underside is also smooth so that it will sit well on the body.

Painting

There are two types of paint which I recommend for painting modelled dolls, both of which give a good finish and are readily available. The first is a paint especially formulated for clay or bisque dolls, available from specialist shops in two flesh shades (I prefer the lighter shade). It is painted on straight from the pot, can be thinned with water and the brush is washed out in water. It is easy to use, but is rather thick with a tendency to show brush marks, so it is better applied in two coats thinned with water rather than one thicker coat. This paint also dries fairly quickly. However, it does not give quite such a good finish as enamel paint.

The second type of paint recommended is Humbrol enamel which is available in small tins from hobby and art shops. The flesh colour is much too dark, and must be mixed with a fair amount of white to get a suitable shade. Use the matt colours (unless you want a shiny effect, perhaps for a pierrot) and mix a sufficient quantity to cover in one coat, as colour matching can be tricky. Paint on the first coat and leave it to dry. This will raise a suede-like grain in the clay. When the first coat is completely dry, rub the parts with a rough cotton cloth to smooth them, then apply the second coat of paint. If the second coat, as occasionally happens, is also suede-like, leave it to dry, smooth again and apply a third coat. Enamel paint takes longer to dry, requires mixing and is therefore not as easy to use as the other type, but the finish on a well-sanded head is very smooth.

It is essential to use a good-quality artist's paintbrush, which will not shed hairs, and to clean it thoroughly between coats. I recommend a soft flat brush about ½in wide for the larger areas, and a small fine brush to paint around the eyes, between the fingers and other fiddly parts. If you wish, a coat or two of gesso can be applied before painting, sanded finely when dry. Gesso is a liquid plaster available from art shops, which is applied like paint. However, if the pieces have been

thoroughly sanded, it is not necessary and will make only a slight difference to the finish.

The head and body may be assembled before the features are painted or after as you prefer. The type of paint used for the features is a matter of individual preference; oil, acrylics or enamels are all suitable but good-quality fine brushes are essential.

For simply modelled heads with painted eyes and mouths, mark the features lightly in pencil — mistakes can be removed with a pencil rubber. It can be very helpful to try the wig in place while marking the features to gauge the best effect.

Begin painting the eyes by painting the whole

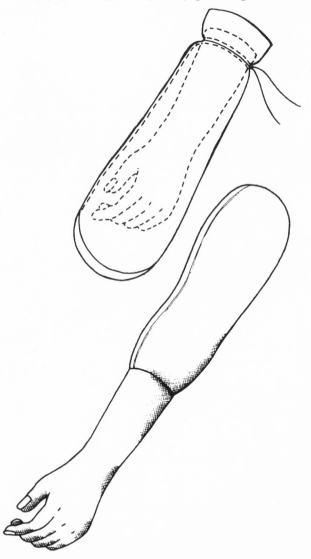

Fig 12 Method for tying on modelled lower arm to felt upper arm

area white. When this is dry paint in the eyelid, then the iris and pupil. Allow each colour to dry before applying the next. A touch of white paint in each pupil highlights the eyes, and outlines and lashes can be painted in as you wish. Choose colours carefully: softer greys and browns around the eyes for young faces, darker colours for older faces. The same rules apply to the mouth: soft natural colours for children, lipstick shades for ladies. Paint the outline of the mouth first then fill in the colour. Heads with inset eyes require less painting, but the eyes should be outlined and lashes (if you want them) painted around the eyes. The mouth must be carefully painted to follow the modelled shaping.

Eyebrows should be marked lightly in pencil, checking that the effect is pleasing. Similar colour rules apply: lighter for young faces, darker for older faces. Cheeks can be coloured by rubbing a little paint well in with your finger, freckles or beauty spots should be painted on with a fine brush, and fingernails can be coloured with paint or nail varnish. A coat of clear varnish (Das varnish is excellent) should be applied over painted eyes (and mouths) to seal the colours and make them shiny.

Modelled socks and shoes or boots usually look best painted in slightly shiny colours, or varnished. Paint them carefully and as realistically as possible. The sole of the shoe should be a different colour from the upper and any trimming such as buckles or bows should be clearly defined.

Painted clay can be polished slightly with a good-quality wax polish and a soft cloth, but be wary of making it too shiny.

Wigs

Several of the wigmaking methods described in Chapter 1 can be applied to modelled dolls, but my own preference is for 'real hair', which makes even simply modelled dolls look more attractive (*see* Sara). A wig cut from a discarded life-sized wig or an inexpensive acrylic doll's wig is far more suitable for this type of doll. An elaborately modelled doll with inset eyes obviously needs a 'real-hair' wig — anything less would look out of place.

To fix the wig to the head, try it in place and mark the hairline. Remove the wig and cover the head liberally with glue (UHU is excellent) then carefully re-fit the wig, holding it firmly in place as the glue dries.

Cheaper acrylic wigs are usually permanently styled, so choose carefully a style appropriate to the type of doll you are making. Human-hair wigs can be styled, to suit the costume, by any method you can use on your own hair.

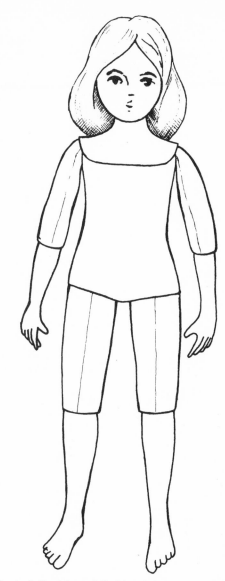

Fig 13 Basic doll with modelled head, lower arms and legs

If the doll has modelled ears, the wig will have to fit around them and this should be considered when choosing it. The types with small flat bases are generally more suitable for dolls with ears, especially boy dolls. Those with cap-shaped bases are more suitable for dolls without ears, unless the cap will fit behind them.

You might like to use the method described here to model a copy of an antique doll. Victorian dolls of porcelain, bisque or composition can be copied in self-hardening clay, using original dolls or good photographs as models. The antique dolls usually had a head and shoulder-plate and lower arms and legs attached to a stuffed-cloth body. To make your copy more authentic use a strong, firmly woven cotton or calico for the doll's body (adapting the patterns as required — Victorian doll pro-portions often seem very strange to the modern eye) and cut the upper arms and legs as simple tubes without shaping. Make up the arms and legs with stitched elbow and knee joints, and use bran or sawdust to stuff the body firmly.

On the antique dolls the shoulder-plate is sewn to the body through pierced holes, rather than being glued. Make two or three holes along the lower edges of the shoulder-plate, back and front, while the clay is wet. Use a long darning needle and button thread to sew the finished shoulder-plate onto the body.

When painting your doll, imitate the original material with enamel paints — white gloss for porcelain, matt pale-flesh colour for bisque. Copy the way in which the original doll's features were painted. For example, the heavy eyebrows on Bru and Jumeau dolls were painted with feathery brush strokes in two shades of brown and the fine eyelashes were painted in straight lines around the eyes.

If you wish to sign your work, the usual method is to incise your name or initials and perhaps the date on the back of the shoulder-plate while the clay is wet, using a small pointed tool or pen nib.

(above right) *The rag dolls: Big and Little Sisters, 18 and 15in tall, with their own miniature doll; and old-fashioned Emily, 21in tall (see Chapter 5)*

(below right) *Felt dolls: the Toddler Twins, 16in tall (see Chapter 6)*

(overleaf) *A group of felt children: Polly (wearing hat), Thomas and Harriet, all 16in tall; and the Babies, 11in tall (see Chapter 6)*

3
WAX DOLLS

Wax has been used in dollmaking for centuries, reaching a peak in the nineteenth century, particularly in England. There are three basic types of wax doll; Those carved or modelled in solid wax; those made of layers of wax poured into a mould, leaving them hollow in the centre; and those made of other materials with an outer coating of wax. The three methods are generally referred to as solid wax, poured wax and dipped wax.

Wax dolls are a great deal stronger than is generally believed, as the many antique dolls which have survived will testify. Though they will suffer if exposed to extremes of temperature such as direct heat, strong sunshine or severe cold, when properly cared for, a wax doll is no more fragile than a modelled-clay doll. Wax dolls should be dusted from time to time with a soft clean paintbrush, and, if necessary, cleaned with a little face cleansing lotion on cotton wool.

Wax has a translucent almost flesh-like quality which can make a doll look uncannily real, and many of the greatest modern doll artists have chosen to work in this medium, producing exquisitely beautiful dolls which rival the best of those made in the last century.

For the amateur dollmaker, wax is readily available, relatively easy to use and, with a degree of skill, will produce impressive results. Hot wax is, however, potentially dangerous and I most strongly recommend that the following safety precautions be followed.
1 Never work when small children and pets are around.
2 Always use a double boiler or a pyrex jug or basin in a saucepan of hot water. Do not heat the wax directly.
3 Heat the wax slowly — do not be tempted to turn up the heat to speed things along.
4 If possible, use a wax thermometer to check the temperature.
5 Never leave melting wax unattended.
6 Do not let the temperature of the wax exceed 260°F (126°C).
7 If the wax should catch fire, use baking soda to put it out. Do not try to douse a wax fire with water.
8 Allow yourself plenty of time when working with wax — it can be a lengthy process.
Providing that these precautions are observed, there is no danger in using wax for dollmaking.

Professional dollmakers use many different types of wax — mixing them with various additives and colours often to their own secret formulas — but for the purposes of the amateur dollmaker, beeswax, candlewax or a mixture of the two are perfectly adequate. I use natural beeswax as I live in the country and it is freely obtainable from a bee-keeping friend. It can also be bought from craft shops and saddlemakers, as well as candlemaking suppliers, though it can be expensive to buy. In its natural state, beeswax must be melted and strained through muslin to remove the impurities before use. It produces a rather yellowish-coloured doll — very old-fashioned looking.

Candlewax, either bought by the pound from craft shops or obtained from melted candles, produces a harder, more brittle wax, but is the most easily obtainable, the cheapest and the most easily coloured. Beeswax and candlewax can be mixed to tone down the yellowness of the beeswax and soften the candlewax, producing a very satisfactory medium.

The best, though most expensive, wax to use for dollmaking is bleached beeswax. This is a soft, creamy-coloured, purified beeswax which is obtainable from specialist candlemaking suppliers. If you wish to colour the wax, use the discs of coloured wax which are sold especially for the purpose rather than pieces of wax crayon or lipstick which will not mix satisfactorily. The colour should be thoroughly stirred into the melted wax with a wooden spoon, very little at a time, testing the colour with strips of white card until the required flesh tone is achieved. I recommend using equal amounts of red and brown colours (in very small quantities), rather than pink, for a natural flesh tone. Alternatively, you can use the wax without added colour, and paint the completed head to colour the cheeks etc. When the colour of the wax seems satisfactory, drop a spoonful into a saucer of cold water where it will immediately harden into a disc, showing the colour of the finished doll.

Melting Wax

Always use a double boiler, or a pyrex jug or bowl in a saucepan half filled with water. There are double boilers designed for wax melting available from candlemaking suppliers, though a domestic double boiler is equally efficient. If you use a bowl or jug inside a saucepan, ensure that you do not splash water into the wax, and that the pan does not boil dry. *Never melt wax in a pan directly over the heat.* Have by you a tub of baking soda in case of fire.

Break up the wax into small pieces (doing this inside a polythene bag will prevent mess) and put it into the boiler, bowl or jug over a low heat, adding more wax as it begins to melt. The amount of wax you will need depends on the type of doll you are making, and the size of the vessel you use. As a rough guide, 1lb of wax will melt to approximately ¾pt. The dipped-wax dolls in this book required 1lb of wax, melted in a 1pt pyrex jug.

A wax thermometer is a very useful investment if you plan to make any quantity of wax dolls. Available from candlemaking suppliers, these thermometers clip to the side of the melting pot and take the guesswork out of judging the best temperature to use the wax. Alternatively, use a sweet-making thermometer. *Melt the wax slowly — do not be tempted to turn up the heat.* If you are melting wax to pour, do not fill the vessel more than three-quarters full. For dipping, fill it two-thirds or less full to allow room for displacement of the wax when the head and limbs are dipped. When the wax is melted to the correct temperature for your purpose, turn off the heat.

After use, liquid wax may be poured into a basin lined with aluminium cooking foil and allowed to cool. The wax can then be stored, wrapped in the foil, for future use.

Wax Modelling

Modelling in wax is no more difficult than modelling in clay. Beeswax is the most suitable as it is softer and more malleable than candlewax. When the wax is completely melted, pour it into a bowl of lukewarm water where it will form a soft lump which can be removed after a few minutes when it has cooled. Break off pieces of the wax, work them to make them soft and pliable and then use the wax to model the head and limbs in the same way as described for clay modelling in the previous chapter. A solid wax head will be heavy and therefore only suitable for a small doll eg the costume dolls. However, a larger head can be modelled over a compressed-cotton core-ball as previously described. Instead of damping the core-ball with water, spear it on a knitting needle and dip it into the hot wax. Position the waxed ball on the greased neck of the bottle and build-up the head in the same way as a clay head. Modelling tools and acrylic eyes may also be used with wax — metal tools or a small knife can be heated to help blend added pieces into the main body of wax.

The main difference between modelling in clay and in wax is that clay parts are joined with slip, whereas wax parts are joined by melting the wax. The shoulder-plate is modelled in the same way as for the clay doll, but it is joined to the neck by melting the wax. While the wax is in this soft pliable state care must be taken not to spoil the modelling. Bore sewing holes in the shoulder-plate (not too close to the edge) for attaching it to the body, as wax will not glue satisfactorily. Model the lower arms and legs in wax (with grooves) and tie them to the upper arms and legs in the same way as for clay-modelled limbs. When the modelling is completed, dip the head and limbs into very hot water to smooth the surface of the wax, then dip into cold water to harden it. Leave the pieces in a cool place for a few hours to harden thoroughly.

The beginner often has difficulty making the wax soft and pliable enough to work with. Natural beeswax is usually easy to work but other types of wax may not be sufficiently soft. If this happens, return the wax to the melting pot and when it has become liquid again stir in a teaspoonful or two of petroleum jelly (eg Vaseline). This will give a much softer wax which should work easily. Warm hands and a warm atmosphere will also help.

Another possible problem is that both the hands and the tools can become very sticky during modelling. Frequent washing of the hands and tools in warm water and a light dusting of talcum powder from time to time will counteract this. Keep metal tools heated while you work, ideally using a small electric hotplate — though always wipe the tool before replacing it on the hotplate to avoid burning drips of wax. If this is not available use a candle, but put the tool into the side of the flame rather than the top and wipe it to avoid transferring carbon to the wax.

The core-ball is left inside the modelled-wax head — trying to remove it would probably destroy the head. The surface of the wax can be smoothed if necessary by rubbing it carefully with a little turpentine on a soft cloth. The features can be painted with oil, acrylic or water colours as you prefer, but good-quality brushes are essential. If you use oil colours, mix them with turpentine to speed the drying, which can take a long time on wax. Acrylic paints are water based, so mistakes can be removed easily as with water colours. You might prefer to paint the features with a drawing pen rather than a paintbrush. To colour the cheeks it is usually better to rub the colour in with the finger rather than painting it on. As with the clay dolls, a coat of sealer or varnish painted over the eyes and mouth will protect the colour and give a realistic shine.

Carving Wax

Carving a doll's head and limbs from a solid block of wax requires some skill and, as the head is solid and therefore heavy, it is a method only suitable for small dolls. A clean ½pt milk or fruit-juice carton provides good mould for the wax block as it has a waxy coating on the inside which makes it easy to peel the carton away. Melt the wax as previously described — a mixture of candlewax and beeswax is most suitable as this method requires a harder though not brittle wax. Pour the melted wax into the carton at a temperature of approximately 150°–160°F (65°–71°C) (ie just after it has melted). As the wax cools, a depression will appear in the centre. Prod a hole in this depression with a piece of dowelling to remove air bubbles, and then top up with hot wax. Put the wax into the fridge for a few hours to harden, then peel away the carton.

A sharp craft knife is probably the best tool to use for carving, and a piece of elastoplast wrapped

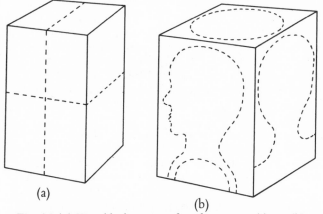

(a)

(b)

Fig 14 (a) Wax block cut into four for arms and legs; (b) wax block marked for carving head and shoulder-plate

around your thumb will help prevent accidents. Score the outline of the head on the wax block, and carve away the excess wax at the corners, working around the marked outline. As you carve, turn the piece continually to check that the profiles and the back of the head are a good shape. Carve the head, neck and shoulder-plate in one piece, and bore sewing holes through the shoulder-plate. If you work over a bowl or tray the wax shavings will not make a mess. When the piece is completed dip it into hot water to smooth the wax and cold water to harden. It may be further smoothed by rubbing gently with a little turpentine on a soft cloth.

Use the materials and methods described for modelled wax to paint the features with a fine brush or drawing pen. Carved-wax arms and legs may be made by the same method. If a ½pt carton is used to mould a block, this can be cut into four pieces to use for arms and legs. Grooves should be scored in the usual way for tying the limbs on to the body.

Poured Wax

This is a technique which requires some special equipment for mould making, and a great degree of skill. It is the method most often used by professional wax-doll artists and has the advantage that several dolls may be produced from the same mould. As the method is complex and requires a high degree of skill and experience to achieve good results, it does not really have a place in this book, but for the sake of the more intrepid reader who may like to experiment, I shall outline the method briefly.

Firstly, the mould must be prepared from an existing head or an original model. This might be a two- or three-part mould in plaster or a one-piece mould made from flexible rubber which is painted onto the model. The mould is cured and then coated with a release agent like Vaseline. The melted wax, usually bleached beeswax with additives for strength and colour, is poured into the mould in a slow steady stream. After a few minutes, the still-liquid wax in the centre of the mould is poured out, and the wax left in the mould is allowed to cool. This procedure is then repeated a number of times depending on the size of the doll, building up a wax 'skin' which is hollow in the centre.

As you can imagine, the process is lengthy and fraught with problems and is probably not one which the amateur dollmaker would care to attempt. However, those dollmakers whose work is now so much admired were all beginners once, and if you like a real challenge, this might be the method for you!

Dipped Wax

This is the method used for Baby William and the Fashion doll, and it is a much easier proposition.

Beeswax (natural or bleached) or a mixture of beeswax and candlewax can be used. It is heated to a temperature of 150°–165°F (65°–74°C) (ie just after the wax has completely melted). If you have no thermometer, judge the temperature by dropping small flakes of wax into the melting pot. At first these flakes will float for a second or two before melting, but as the wax gets hotter they will dissolve immediately. At this point the wax is ready for dipping. *Turn off the heat.*

The two waxed dolls in this book are clay-modelled dolls with acrylic eyes, made and painted as described in Chapter 2. The lower limbs are attached to the upper limbs before dipping. The parts where the felt joins the clay can be protected with masking tape to prevent seepage. The baby's head is also attached to the stuffed body before dipping (this join can be protected in the same way), and the body is held while the head is dipped.

Shoulder-plate heads (eg the Fashion doll) should be dipped before being attached to the body, and to do this it is necessary to make a support for the head. Glue and bind a length of ½in thick foam rubber around one end of a length of dowelling (or the handle of a wooden spoon) and wedge this well into the head. Check that this is very firmly wedged and will not drop off. This will give you a handle to hold well clear of the hot wax and it also blocks the hole in the underside of the shoulder-plate so that wax cannot seep inside the head (Fig 15).

Ensure that the vessel you use for the wax is no more than two-thirds full to allow for displacement, and that it is large enough to accommodate the head up to the lower edge of the shoulder-plate. When the wax has reached the right temperature, remember to turn off the heat before dipping.

Hold the handle firmly and, with the face uppermost, lower the head into the wax so that it covers the shoulder-plate. With a controlled movement, lift the head out of the wax. As the face is uppermost, any drips or blobs should run to the back of the head, and at this temperature the wax will begin to harden immediately. If you wish to practise this operation before dipping the head, try spearing a ball of hardened waste clay and dipping this a few times so that you can see how the wax will behave. Dip the arms (and legs) in the same

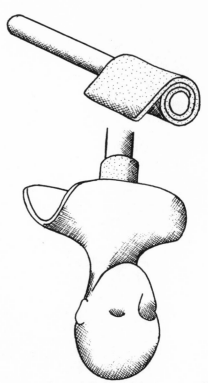

Fig 15 Support for modelled head during wax dipping

way, holding the felt upper limb while you dip the modelled lower limb.

The thickness of the wax coating will depend on the size of the doll and the effect you wish to achieve. For a small doll, eg the costume dolls, one coating is usually sufficient, and more might obscure the features. Larger dolls may be dipped several times, allowing each coat to dry thoroughly before dipping again. The thicker the wax coating, the more the finished doll will resemble poured wax, but build-up will occur in areas of undercutting such as the nostrils and lips. This build-up may be removed, when the wax has hardened, by very careful paring with craft knife and gentle rubbing with turpentine on a soft cloth. Such refinement should be done very carefully to avoid removing the wax right down to the painted clay. A wooden toothpick or cotton bud with a little turpentine can be used to get into small areas like the nostrils.

Both William and the Fashion doll were dipped once in natural beeswax, which has given them a smooth, slightly translucent finish, allowing the painted colouring under the wax to show through clearly. Natural beeswax is rather too yellow to use for a thick wax coating, though this can be counteracted to some extent by painting the face in a very pale whitish pink, rather than a more natural flesh colour. Bleached and carefully coloured bees-wax is the best for a thick wax coating. When the wax coating is satisfactory leave the pieces to harden for an hour or so before removing the support from the head.

Using a craft knife, scrape off any wax which has seeped onto the underside of the shoulder-plate and cut away the wax from inset eyes. Work very carefully around the eyes, as a false move could scratch the eye or the wax. Use a wooden toothpick to remove the small pieces, then clean the eyes with a little turpentine and a cotton bud. Small blobs and runs in the wax can be smoothed out by rubbing gently with turpentine on a soft cloth. Any large blobs should be pared gently with the craft knife, then rubbed. Rub the head with a piece of nylon stocking for a final smoothing. If you prefer a gloss finish use a very little baby oil rubbed onto the wax with a nylon stocking. For a matt finish use a little turpentine on the nylon stocking (quickly and carefully wiped on) and allow it to dry thoroughly. A dusting of talcum powder, brushed on with an artist's paintbrush, will give the wax a pearly effect. (These finishes also apply to modelled-wax dolls.)

If you have used a thin wax coating, the doll's colouring and features should show through clearly from the painted clay beneath and will need no further colour. On a thick wax coat you may prefer to use surface colour. Use the oil paints, acrylics or water colours as recommended before, or, if only a little extra colour is needed, try make-up pencils.

If you wish, the finished head may be sealed with an acrylic spray varnish, but many doll artists would argue that this spoils the effect of the wax. However, if the doll's eyes are painted, they should be given one or two coats of gloss varnish to protect the colour and to give them a realistic shine. Paint or nail varnish can be used to paint fingernails.

In the event of an unsatisfactory dipped-wax coating, re-heat the wax until it is hot (not exceeding 260°F (126°C) and dip the head into the hot wax. The wax coating will melt off and the head should be wiped clean with a soft cloth such as butter muslin. Allow both the head and the wax to cool thoroughly, then begin again. The beginner often finds drips and runs in the wax coating, which is usually caused by using the wax too hot

(and, therefore, too liquid). It is also important to use a smooth controlled movement when dipping, to avoid splashes. If you have difficulty, I suggest practising with balls of clay, apples or any other odds and ends until you achieve the knack. Obviously, blobs on the back of the head do not matter as any imperfections here are concealed by the wig. The aim is to get a smooth coat which will require the minimum of refining on the doll's face.

The dipped-wax method has been used in the past on many materials ranging from composition to fabric, but for the best results the material should be porous. Papier mâché and self-hardening clay are excellent. Commercial plastic dolls can be dipped, though the wax is likely to chip off in time — beeswax is best for this because of its good adhering properties. Wax coatings can also be used to improve an imperfectly smoothed finish or to soften a badly modelled face — they can often work astonishing transformations.

Wigs

Before glueing a wig to a wax doll's head, score the scalp slightly to provide a rough surface. Glues such as Copydex and UHU are suitable. The wig suggestions offered for clay-modelled dolls also apply to wax dolls; the more realistic 'real-hair' wigs are the most effective.

Alternatively, you may care to try the Victorian method which involves implanting the hair into the scalp. This is only practicable on dolls with a thick layer of wax on the head. The scalp can be dipped several times to build up a sufficiently thick coating. Human hair is the best material, and you will need a reasonably large amount of it. The simplest method is to use a sharp craft knife (which is kept heated on a hotplate or in a candle) to cut small slits, one at a time, in the scalp. Insert a small bunch of hair into each slit, pressing and sealing the wax over the ends of the hairs with the hot knife. Work from the hairline back to the crown of the head, cutting the slits and inserting the hair so that it lies flat against the head.

As you can imagine, this is both fiddly and time consuming. A full head of hair for a lady doll would be quite an undertaking, but a baby doll does not need a lot of hair and might be a good subject for the beginner to try this method on. If well done, it is a very effective and realistic technique.

4
DOLLS' CLOTHES

A doll's clothes, particularly those of a collector's doll, are an important element in its appeal. This is an area of dollmaking which is often neglected and some well-made and attractive dolls are spoiled by being dressed in badly designed clothes made in unsuitable fabrics. Many of the rules which apply to life-sized clothes can be applied to dolls' clothes.

I never decide how to dress a doll until it is made, and then I take into account such things as the colour of the hair and eyes, whether the doll is a child or an adult, and whether it has a modern or old-fashioned look — I try different colours and fabrics to gauge those which best suit the individual doll. Sometimes the style is chosen first and a suitable fabric found to make up that style; sometimes the fabric is chosen first and then the design is selected to suit the fabric. Once the clothes are decided, the underwear, stockings, shoes, hat and accessories can all be planned to harmonise in colour, period and style.

I am an inveterate hoarder of fabrics, trimmings and bits and pieces and whenever I see a suitable print or piece of lace I buy a half-yard or a yard for future use. This is a policy I recommend to any serious dollmaker, as it is intensely frustrating to go back to a shop where you saw the 'perfect thing' a month ago, only to find they no longer have it. Jumble sales and antique shops are a useful source of old fabrics, especially suitable for period dolls; and I cheerfully scrounge odds and ends from friends. I rarely use scraps from my own dressmaking — what looks right on a life-sized lady hardly ever looks right on a 20in lady doll. And, on the whole, scraps are very little use for dolls' clothes. It is far better to buy a half-yard of something that looks really good than to spoil your work by economising on the clothes.

Anything you use for dolls' clothes should be lightweight and any patterns should be small. Patterns with overlarge flowers look perfectly horrible, hiding the style so the garment looks shapeless and the doll is swamped. Often something which looks quite delicate on the bolt will look overpowering when held against the doll —

judge this by looking at about 6sq in of the fabric rather than the whole width. As a general rule, simple styles in plain or tiny-print fabrics are most suitable, and over fussy or large trimmings should be avoided. The clothes should be in complete harmony with the doll, enhancing rather than detracting from the doll's personality.

When dressing modern dolls, take life-sized clothes as your models, simplifying where necessary — blue jeans and tee shirts can look just as good on a doll as on a person, and smocks, dungarees, hand-knitted cardigans or stretch-towelling 'babygros' are perfect for modern-child dolls. It is amusing to dress a child's doll in miniature versions of its owner's clothes. As a gift to a bride, you could make a portrait doll with appropriately coloured eyes and hair, dressed in a miniature copy of the wedding dress complete with headdress, veil and bouquet. If you can, use the same fabric, but if this is not available or suitable, match it as closely as possible.

When dressing period dolls some costume research is advisable. A good reference book will supply details of the style, colours and fabrics fashionable at any period and will enable you to design costumes which look absolutely right for child or adult dolls. Some costumes are too bulky or fussy to translate well to this scale, but most of them can be simplified in the cutting and the correct period effect can be made by trimming with the appropriate braid, lace or ribbon (see the Fashion doll).

Colour becomes more important in a smaller scale as style is less immediately apparent. A simple dress in the right colour will look far more effective than a more elaborate one in the wrong colour. As with life-sized clothes, the colour is chosen both to suit the individual's own colouring and to make the designed effect. For example, simple modern-child dolls look well in primary colours, but a Victorian-lady doll needs something more subtle and sophisticated.

Remember also the purpose for which the doll is made. Children's dolls should have clothes which can be taken off easily whereas collector's dolls will probably not be undressed unless the clothes need cleaning. So, although silks and velvets look beautiful, they would be most impractical for children's dolls, and soon spoilt by wear and tear. Save your best fabrics for dolls which will spend their lives sitting safely on a shelf or in a display case.

Materials

Even within the limitations imposed by scale, there is an enormous variety of fabrics suitable for making dolls' clothes. The obvious first choice is dress fabric, but look also at lightweight furnishing fabrics, household linens such as napkins or pillowcases, scarves, handkerchiefs and old clothes. Generally, natural fabrics such as cotton and silk are more useful than man-mades, as they gather and hang better. Non-crease man-made fibres rarely make good dolls' clothes; they look hopelessly wrong on period dolls and even on modern dolls they are bunchy and clumsy. The cotton/polyester fabrics, although they will not gather quite as well as pure cotton, are useful, readily available and reasonably priced. Cotton/polyester is quite suitable for a modern doll, but for the more old-fashioned types it is worth the effort of searching out pure cotton. Lightweight wool, needlecord and velveteen make excellent dresses, providing the pattern does not require too much gathering, and furnishing cottons can also look very effective in a suitable style. Wool and cotton mixtures, such as Viyella and Clydella, flannel and winceyette are useful for dresses, shirts and nightwear — they gather neatly and hang well and some of the Viyella designs, particularly the tiny flowers, have a charming old-fashioned look. Cotton lawn is probably the most useful of all fabrics, suitable for anything but the most elaborate costumes, and silk, though expensive, makes beautiful clothes.

Period costume dolls are the exception to most rules, as the look of the fabric is the all-important element and sometimes even a thick furnishing fabric can be used effectively. The choice of fabric must be dictated by the type of doll you are dressing, but as a general rule, avoid anything thick or heavy, crease-resistant, stretchy (such as Crimplene) or anything which frays badly.

UNDERWEAR

The perfect fabric for underwear is white cotton lawn. It is fine, lightweight, and gathers and hangs beautifully. It is ideal for pintucking, can be starched for extra crispness, and is light enough to hang well under any dress, even silk. Polyester/ cotton can also be used, but it is heavier and therefore bulkier — useful if you wish to give fullness to a skirt, but it could spoil a slim line. This also applies to old sheets or pillowcases, which are made of thicker cotton. Handkerchiefs can be useful, especially for small dolls, as they have ready-made hems.

For a boy's pants and vests, tee-shirt cotton is ideal. As it is stretchy, the garments will fit closely and can be put on and taken off easily. Old vests, ranging from cherub-type wool/cotton baby vests to the lacy-cotton ladies' vests, are also good for dolls' underwear and will suit most periods and types of doll.

For corsets, soft satin is usually the best choice, lined with lawn and boned with 'whalebones' salvaged from old clothes or collar stiffeners. Stockings, tights and socks can be made from pieces of the life-sized things; cotton or pure-wool socks for period dolls, nylon only for modern ones. Tubular-gauze finger-bandage makes good cotton stockings for small dolls or socks for larger ones. Alternatively, stockings and socks can be knitted on small needles in fine cotton, silk or wool yarn.

FOOTWEAR

Dolls' shoes and boots can be made in felt, though I recommend this only for very simple dolls. More sophisticated dolls need more realistic footwear. I have found the range of elbow patches available at most department stores a useful source of supply for shoe materials. These oval patches come in real and imitation leather and suede in a good range of colours. One pair provides sufficient material for most shoes, two pairs are needed to make a pair of boots. Thin leather from old gloves or handbags is excellent, and soft plastic (imitation leather) is also good. Old suede clothes can be used if the suede is not too thick and jumble sales will often produce a suede or leather jacket which will provide sufficient material for dozens of shoes. Offcuts of leather can be bought at most craft shops, but choose pieces which are soft and thin. Slippers and shoes can also be made in fabric if this is appropriate to the doll, but it is advisable to line fabric shoes with lawn to prevent them stretching and fraying.

There is a good range of plastic shoes and Wellington boots (available from dolls'-wear stockists) which are ideal for children's dolls. More expensive leather shoes and boots can be bought from the specialists if you do not wish to make your own (these shops also sell socks and stockings).

HATS

Dolls' hats can be made in fabric, felt or straw. For larger dolls, fabric hats or bonnets should be stiffened with Vilene iron-on interfacing so that they are not floppy, and the fabric is usually chosen to match or complement the dress. For felt hats, the best source of materials is life-sized originals — again, jumble sales are a good hunting ground. Hat felt is thicker than ordinary felt and can be steamed over a block or mould to shape it. The type used for the dolls' bodies is too floppy for most hats, though it can be used double thickness and backed with iron-on interfacing.

Straw hats and bonnets can be made by cutting up old straw hats (if the straw is fine enough) or make them yourself, from hat-straw or plaited raffia. Hat-straw is available in several widths and colours to suit any size doll. Natural raffia is available from garden or craft shops and artificial raffia, which comes in a large range of shiny and matt colours, is available from craft shops.

Knitted bonnets or bobble hats (perhaps with matching mufflers) look charming on babies or children and are appropriate for both modern and old-fashioned dolls. The specialist dolls'-wear shops stock dolls' bonnets and hats, and some commercial dolls (eg Sasha) include straw hats among their accessories.

JEWELLERY

Jewellery is most suitable for adult dolls, particularly fashion or costume dolls, though a little girl might wear a pearl necklace or earrings and a gilt bracelet. Broken life-sized jewellery is an obvious source of materials, or new costume jewellery. A life-sized earring is often suitable for a doll-sized brooch or pendant. Gilt or silver chains are usually fine enough for dolls' necklaces and bracelets, and small bead necklaces can be cut and re-strung to fit. The tiny pearl beads sold in haberdashery departments can be threaded for necklaces and bracelets or stuck-on as earrings, and a small pretty button will make an attractive brooch. Small crosses or lockets, bracelet charms and rings are often suitable for doll-sized jewellery. Toy shops also sell dolls' jewellery — these items are often made in plastic and do not look very realistic, though some of the 'Sindy' pieces are worth considering.

TRIMMINGS

The range of laces, braids and ribbons in any good haberdashery or notions department is extensive, and suitable trimmings for most dolls' clothes are not hard to find. For period dolls and costume dolls where cotton lace or silk ribbon is desirable, the specialist shops are the best suppliers. Look also in the ranges of lampshade trimmings — the silky braids and fringes are excellent for Victorian and Edwardian clothes and the gold metallic lace, though it is becoming hard to find, is perfect for period costumes. For those who cannot embroider, the sew-on embroidered motifs available from haberdashery departments make lovely embroidered trimmings and in the same place you will find beads, sequins and rhinestones for ladies' costumes. Miniature buttons, (perfect for even the smallest dolls) can be bought from the specialist suppliers who also stock miniature buckles. Tiny beads and pearls also make effective buttons on small garments. Flowers and feathers for trimming dresses and hats can be found in cake-decoration suppliers, art and craft shops, and some florists, as well as specialist shops. Jumble sales are a good source of materials — old lace or tiny buttons can be cut from a garment, even if the fabric itself is useless. It is also easy and inexpensive to make pretty trimmings, such as scallops, bows and flowers, out of ribbon. Consider bias bindings (especially satin or patterned ones) for trimmings — also, bands of coloured tape or ribbon which can look attractive on simply styled dresses.

ACCESSORIES

Most dolls can have some accessory; from miniature toys for child dolls to handbags, fans or parasols for adult lady dolls. Miniature versions of the doll can be dressed to match — and handkerchiefs are particularly useful for dressing these. A boy doll could have his own little teddy bear made in fur fabric or felt. Consider also a hoop and stick (an embroidery frame and length of thin dowelling) for a Victorian boy, a plaited-raffia basket for a little girl, or a knitted or crocheted shawl for a lady doll. Tiny handkerchiefs (hemmed or lace edged) can be tucked into pockets, miniature perfume bottles, pencils and felt purses can fill handbags. A trunk full of clothes and accessories makes a charming addition to a lady doll, and babies can have their own carrying-pillows or cradles.

Toy shops sell small items such as paint boxes, dustpan-and-brush sets, feeding bottles and hairbrushes which are all suitable for dolls.

Methods

Whether you sew dolls' clothes by hand or machine is a matter of preference. I use an old hand sewing-machine for seams but finish hems and facings by hand. If you are a beginner you will probably find it easier to make small clothes by hand, using a sewing-machine only for straight seams. I recommend pressing clothes as you work, as with life-sized garments. A sleeve-board is invaluable for this, making it easy to press awkward pieces such as inside skirts, armholes etc.

It is worth pressing all fabric before cutting-out, to remove the creases — if the fabric is twisted, stretch it gently to pull it back to the true grain. As with life-sized dressmaking, lay out the pattern pieces carefully to match any design in the fabric and check that the grain is consistent on all pieces. Use small sharp scissors for cutting-out, large ones will not cut neatly into small corners.

It is worthwhile finishing all seams neatly on the inside. French seams are useful on very fine fabrics, but overcast or turn under the raw edges of thicker fabrics. Armholes and waist seams can be bound with bias binding or blanketstitched to neaten them.

Many dolls' clothes can be lined with fine silk or lawn — most look and hang better for being lined, especially dresses, jackets and coats. If stiffening is required, eg on period costumes, back the fabric with lightweight iron-on Vilene before cutting.

I recommend fitting all garments on the doll while you are making them. The actual size of the doll might vary because of firmer or looser stuffing and the clothes will look better for being an exact fit. When dressing dolls with several layers of clothes work from the body outwards, fitting the dress over the underwear and a coat over the dress. Always try the dress on the doll to pin up the hem so that you can gauge the most attractive length.

Fastenings should be appropriate to the type of doll. The clothes of simple dolls are best fastened with press-studs which are easily managed by children. More sophisticated dolls might have buttons and loops or worked button-holes, or zips. Period ladies' clothes look best with hook-and-eye fastenings. Casings at wrist, knee or waist can be drawn up with elastic or narrow ribbon tied in bows.

Most cotton clothes look better if they are lightly starched (a spray starch is ideal) and velveteen and needlecord benefit from being steamed over a kettle after they have been pressed.

UNDERWEAR

To make simple pants in stretch-cotton or nylon fabric, cut a pattern to fit the doll, with the fold at the crutch, as shown in Fig 16. Sew both side seams and neaten around the legs. Turn a casing at the top edge and thread with elastic. Girls' pants might have narrow lace edging at the legs. A

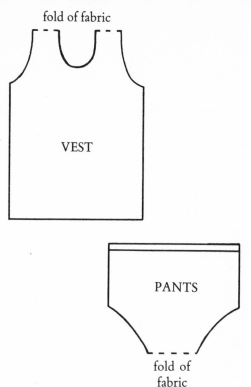

Fig 16 Simple vest and pants

simple stretch-fabric vest should be cut with the fold at the shoulders. Cut out a hole for the head and check that it fits easily, sew the side seams, neaten the armhole and neck and hem the bottom edge.

For pantalettes, cut out the two legs, turn a casing on the end of each leg and add a lace or broderie-anglaise trim (Fig 17). Thread elastic through the casings, pull and secure at each end. Sew each leg seam, then the centre seam joining the legs from front to back. Thread elastic through a casing turned around the top edge. Alternatively, pantalettes might have button-fastened bands at the knee (with or without frills) and a button-fastened waistband. You could also use narrow-ribbon drawstrings at knee and waist, tying them in bows. Trimmings for pantalettes include lace or broderie anglaise, ribbon-threaded lace, pintucks and small ribbon bows.

Petticoats can be full length or from the waist. To make a full-length petticoat, cut a bodice from the dress-bodice pattern, scooping the neckline a little lower and stitching any bodice darts. Hem the armholes and neckline with small rolled hems or face them with bias binding or fabric. Gather the top of the skirt to the lower edge of the bodice. Trimmings for petticoats should be similar to those used for pantalettes, and fastenings should be as unobtrusive as possible. Waist petticoats can have elastic casings or waistbands fastened with a small button and buttonhole. Pintucks and self-fabric frills make pretty trimmings for petticoats

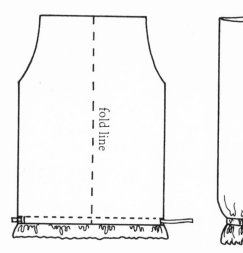

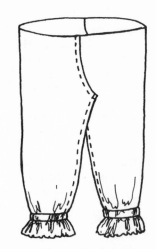

SOCKS

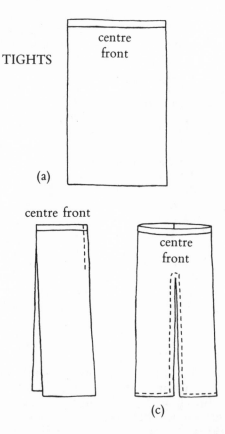

Fig 17 Making pantalettes

worn under full skirts but flat lace or broderie anglaise are better for slimline clothes. Ribbon-threaded lace or broderie anglaise with tiny ribbon bows also makes an effective trimming, and on most dolls a little petticoat frill peeping beneath the skirt hem looks very pretty.

For more elaborate dolls try more adventurous underwear, such as combinations (*see* Amy) made in silk or lawn, trimmed with lace and fastened with tiny buttons; or a chemise made from the upper half of the combinations pattern (suitably lengthened) and worn with pantalettes. Most period lady dolls could wear a corset (*see* Fanny) with suspenders made from shoulder-strap clips or simple elasticated lace garters.

For socks, stockings and tights cut pieces from the real thing, using the top finished edge as the top edge of the doll's version. For socks and stockings, fold the back and bottom edges to make a bag, then make a strong seam, trimming it as closely as possible and turning through (*see* Fig 18). For tights, cut a rectangle wide enough to fit around the doll's waist and long enough to fit from waist to toe. Sew the centre-back edges together from the waist to the crutch, then cut up the centre-front from the feet to the crutch to make two legs. Sew a seam from one foot, up the leg, through the crutch, and down the other leg and foot. Reinforce the seam, trim it as closely as possible and turn through.

Stockings knitted in fine yarn can be worked as simple rectangles, then seamed down the back and under the foot. Babies' bootees can be made like socks from stretch towelling, trimmed with ribbons tied in bows around the ankles.

Consider wide stretch lace for stockings — whip

Fig 18 Making socks, stockings and tights

44

the two long edges together to form a tube and then sew across the bottom to form the foot seam.

SHOES

When making felt, suede, leather or plastic shoes, cut a sole, upper and strap, if required, for each shoe. Stitch the upper's centre-back seam on the inside, then stitch the upper to the sole. Ease the fullness around the toe and work either on the inside with oversewing stitches or on the outside with small blanketstitches. Stitch straps to the instep and fasten with small buttons or buckles (watch-strap buckles can be useful), or to the heel, with holes punched at the ends for ribbon ties (Fig 19).

Line fabric shoes with a firmly woven fabric (eg lawn), and back with iron-on Vilene any fabric inclined to fray. Stitch the centre-back seams in the uppers and linings, then (with right sides facing) sew the lining to the upper around the top edge. Clip the curves, turn through and press. Tack the outside edges together, and stitch the uppers to the soles on the inside. Neaten this seam with blanketstitching, then turn through.

To make boots, cut an upper and a sole for each boot. Stitch the toe of the uppers, then turn back and stitch the front and top edges (*see* Fig 19). Sew the upper to the sole as for shoes. Punch holes on each side of the front and put the boot onto the doll's foot to lace it. Thread the laces with a darning needle. Russian braid, fine cord or narrow ribbon can be used for bootlaces.

Soles for boots and shoes can be cut in 1/16in cork (available from craft shops) and glued to the undersides. Small heels can be cut in cork or balsa wood, painted or covered to match the shoe and glued in place. For the best effect a cork sole should have a matching cork heel. Trim shoes and boots with ribbon bows or rosettes, buckles, buttons

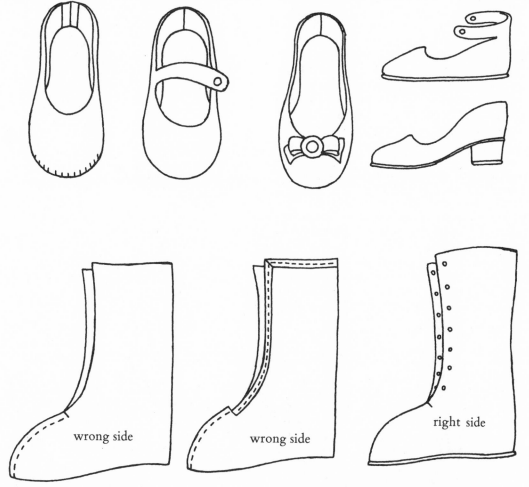

Fig 19 Making shoes and boots

and tassels. On larger shoes and boots, metal eyelets (sold in haberdashery or notions departments) can be punched into the lace holes. Cardboard or thin-cork insoles can be fitted and glued inside the shoe to shape it.

HATS

A variety of hats can be made in fabric or felt to suit most child or adult dolls. Make a beret with a circle of fabric gathered onto a band; add a peak to make a cap or trim with a pompom (Fig 20). For a mob cap, cut a circle of cotton fabric, hem the outer edge (or trim with lace), then sew a casing for elastic or a row of gathering. A similar circle gathered onto a wide brim makes a sun bonnet tied with ribbons under the chin.

Make a skull cap with four triangular panels seamed together (see the Pierrot); add a circular brim to make a hat (on larger hats, the brim should be stiffened so that it is not too floppy). Cut the panels larger and add band and peak to make a baker-boy cap. Hat felt can be steamed over a dome-shaped mould to form a cloche hat — or stitch it to a circular brim.

Bonnets are simple to make in fabric or felt. The brim is an elongated D shape long enough to fit over the doll's head from chin level and deep enough to shade the face and reach the back of the head. The back of the bonnet is a circle with the bottom edge cut off. Stitch the brim to the edge of the back piece, trim and fasten with ribbons under the chin. A steamed-felt cloche with a semi-circular brim will also make a good bonnet.

To make straw hats and bonnets, coil and oversew hatstraw or plaited raffia, working from the centre outwards. 'Invisible' nylon thread is useful for these hats as it is strong and hardly shows. The same material and method can be used to make baskets. Knitted caps, berets and pull-on hats should be worked in fine yarn on small needles, adapting patterns for babies' and children's knitted hats.

Trim hats with ribbon (flat, ruched or in bows), braid, flowers, feathers, and pompoms. Fine elastic is useful for securing a hat under the back hair or chin. Lady dolls might have hatpins — glass-headed dressmaker's pins for small dolls or pearl beads glued onto darning needles for larger dolls. Edwardian hats look elegant with a little fine veiling to pull down over the face, and Victorian bonnets look pretty lined with frilled lace.

ACCESSORIES

There are innumerable small accessories which are

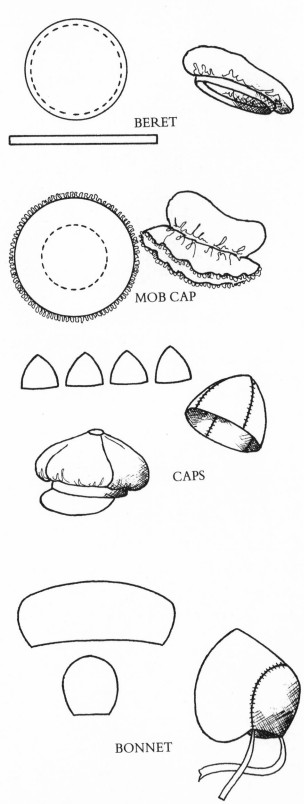

BERET

MOB CAP

CAPS

BONNET

Fig 20 Making simple hats

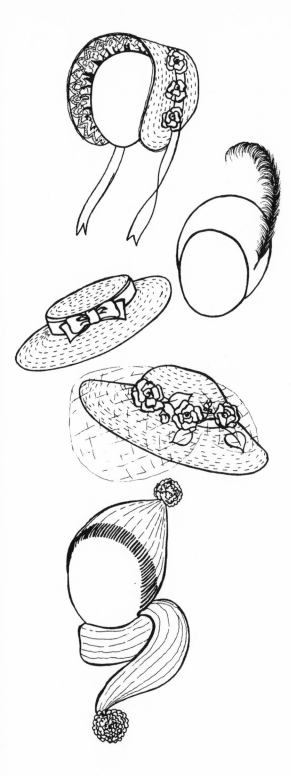

simple to make and add interest to the doll. Fine-lawn handkerchiefs should have tiny rolled hems, lace borders with mitred corners and perhaps an embroidered flower or initial. Gloves are very fiddly to make, but try knitted mittens for a child doll or mittens made from scraps of lace edging for a lady doll. Handbags can be made to suit any doll — rectangular, draw-string or flap-over styles of braid, felt, fabric or ribbon, with cord, ribbon or chain handles.

Lady dolls might have fans of pleated stiffened lace, feather boas made of lengths of marabou trimming, and parasols with whittled-dowelling or paintbrush-handle sticks and fabric covers. Shawls can be knitted or crocheted in fine yarn, or made from fabric, with silky lampshade-fringe trimming. Artificial flower posies make a pretty accessory, and children's dolls might have edible extras, eg the Sailor's kit bag could be filled with small chocolate bars or a child doll might hold a real lollipop.

The most interesting accessories, however, are extra clothes, whether it is just a nightdress or pair of pyjamas in a cardboard suitcase or straw basket, or a whole wardrobe in a leather-covered trunk.

Fig 21 A selection of hat styles

5
THE RAG DOLLS

Rag dolls are among the oldest toys in the world. The remains of simple cloth dolls have been found in graves from Greek, Roman and Egyptian times and it is reasonable to assume that the mothers of many ancient civilisations made such 'babies' for their children. The materials required were easily obtainable and the skill needed was minimal. Obviously, because of their perishable nature, very few have survived intact from much earlier than the nineteenth century, but those that have bear a remarkable resemblance to modern rag dolls.

In its simplest form the rag doll is cut in two pieces, back and front, including the head, arms and legs. The two pieces are stitched together, then stuffed, and the features are usually embroidered. The hair, generally wool but sometimes flax, hemp or string, is sewn to the head and the doll is simply dressed in fabric scraps. The original bran or rag stuffings were fairly heavy, resulting in a rather stiff doll with a very flat, two-dimensional appearance. More sophisticated versions use softer stuffings and darts, seams and gussets to give shape to the head and body. The modern rag doll usually has rather longer legs and a larger head than her nineteenth-century ancestor, but she is still made of calico, with embroidered features and wool hair. The three rag dolls in this chapter, Big and Little Sisters and Emily, are all simple traditional rag dolls. They are very easy to make, even if you have never made a doll before.

Because they are very unsophisticated, the choice of materials is important. Unbleached calico, with its creamy colour and pleasant texture makes a more attractive doll than white cotton, which gives a rather ghostly look — pink cotton is rarely pale enough. Wash the calico in hot water to remove the finish and shrink it slightly, then iron it damp to remove the creases.

I recommend mohair wool for the hair. Ordinary double-knitting wool, which is often used, looks unreal and separates to reveal bald patches (however thickly you put it on!). Mohair is fluffy and the strands of wool cling to each other, cover-ing the head completely and looking more realis-tic, as long as the colour is right. Although mohair wool is more expensive it goes further, so one ball is sufficient for both Big and Little Sisters. Also, because you do not need to put on a thick thatch of hair, it is much easier to style.

The dolls' faces can be appliquéd, embroidered or painted, depending on your skills (or use a com-bination of these methods). The position of the eyes on such a simple face is critical, so leave the features until after the doll's hair is styled (and, if you wish, after she is dressed).

The black felt-circle eyes used for the sisters are very simple — cut them out and move them around the face until they look right (they will not necessarily look best in the most 'natural' place). Emily's embroidered eyes are a little more difficult, use felt circles to decide on their position and then draw them onto the face lightly in pencil. Use two or three strands of embroidery silk to work the buttonholestitch eyes and stemstitch outline.

For the nose, work a small curved line upwards or downwards (depending on the doll's character) in stemstitch or backstitch rather than French-knot 'nostrils'. Gauge the mouth's shape and position with different felt cut-outs, then embroider it in satinstitch, or outline it in stemstitch and colour with felt pen.

If you have a talent for embroidery, this is the doll to use it on. A beautifully embroidered face looks most attractive on rag dolls, but do re-member that the placement of the features, espe-cially the eyes, is all-important. If these are in the wrong place the doll will look odd or even ugly, however fine the workmanship.

Fabrics for the rag-dolls' clothes are equally important. The less sophisticated the doll, the less sophisticated its clothes should be. Big and Little Sister's dresses are very simple to make, and look best in small cotton prints, plain colours or ging-ham. Primary colours look particularly good on these dolls and are in keeping with their childish characters. They would also look attractive in

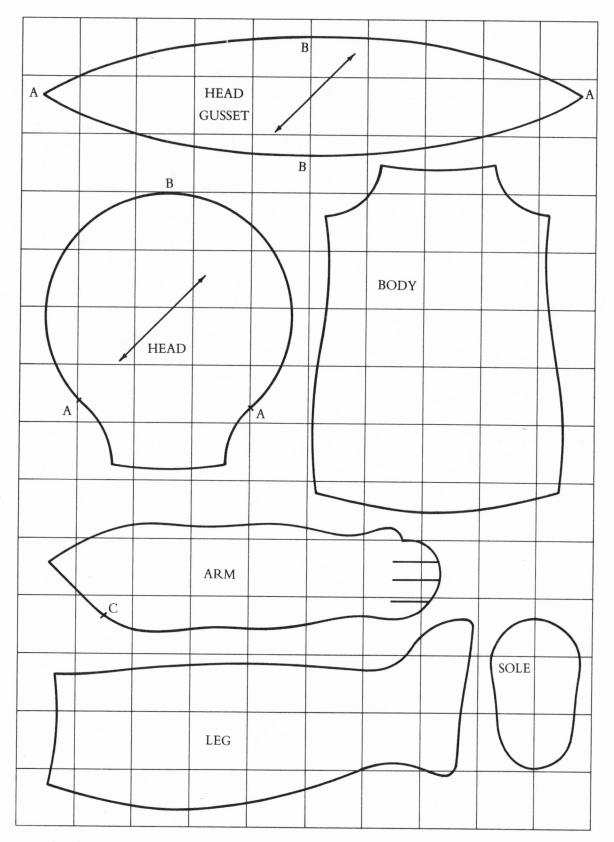

Fig 22 Body pattern A

plain navy-blue with red hair-ribbons, or in golden yellow with green ribbons. You will have your own tastes, but I strongly recommend that you keep it simple.

Emily, being an old-fashioned girl, looks best in tiny flower prints and soft or dark colours. Try a print-fabric dress and plain pinafore, perhaps coffee and cream, or pink and cream. She would also look well in a dark-brown dress with a white or cream broderie-anglaise pinafore. Wherever possible use 100 per cent cotton rather than the polyster/cottons, especially for period dolls.

If you prefer to dress Big or Little Sister as a boy doll, (perhaps to make brother and sister dolls) see the clothes patterns for the boy Toddler Twin (Fig 29) and Thomas (Fig 34) which will fit Big Sister and can easily be shortened to fit Little Sister.

Full instructions follow for the three rag dolls, but if you are a beginner you will find it helpful to read through Chapter 1 before you begin.

Little Sister

(15in tall)

Difficulty: 1/Colour picture page 33
Body pattern A/Fig 22

1/2yd unbleached calico (36in wide)
1oz mohair wool for hair
scraps of black felt for eyes
black and pink thread for features
terylene stuffing

Cut two heads and one head gusset on the cross grain of the fabric. Cut two bodies, four arms, four legs and two soles on the straight grain of the fabric.

Seam the head gusset to the heads, matching points marked A and B on both sides. Turn through, turn in the raw neck edge and tack in place. Seam the body pieces together to form a bag, leaving the neck edge open. Turn through, turn in the raw neck edge 1/2in and tack in place. Seam the arm pieces together in pairs, leaving edge C open. Clip between thumb and fingers and turn through. Seam the leg pieces together in pairs, leaving the top of the leg and the sole of the foot open. Stitch the sole into the foot on each leg and turn through.

Stuff the legs firmly, turn in the raw top edges, matching the front and back leg seams, and over-sew closed. Stuff the arms firmly, turn in the raw edges and oversew closed. Stuff the body slightly less firmly, working the stuffing well into the hips and shoulders and leaving the neck edge open. Stuff the head firmly, moulding with your hands

as you stuff to shape the face. Make sure that the head is evenly stuffed and not lop-sided. Ladder-stitch the head to the body, pushing stuffing into the seam as you stitch, so that the neck is firmly stuffed and the head does not flop. Oversew the arms and legs to the body using strong thread and working on the back of the doll (choose the better side of the head as the face — *see* Fig 2a).

Cut sufficient 18in lengths of mohair wool to cover the head, and machine or backstitch a centre parting in matching thread. Pin the hair to the doll's head and backstitch in place along the parting. Divide the hair into two bunches and stitch the bunches to the doll's head at either side of the face (*see* Fig 5a). Plait the bunches, twist them into ringlets or cut them to the required length.

For the eyes, cut two circles of black felt 1/2in across and try them on the face to gauge the most pleasing effect. Blanketstitch (or stick) the eyes in position. Work three long straight stitches in black thread for the eyelashes. With pink thread work two or three small stitches for the nose, and a small mouth in satinstitch. Use a little powder blusher to colour the doll's cheeks.

LITTLE SISTER'S CLOTHES

1/4yd white cotton (36in wide) for pants and petticoat
1/2yd broderie-anglaise trim (1in wide) for petticoat
1/2yd cotton print (36in wide) for dress
approx 12in gauze finger-bandage for socks
1 square of black felt (12 x 12in) for shoes
1/2yd narrow black ribbon for shoelaces
1/2yd ribbon (1in wide) for hair ribbons
1/2yd narrow elastic
1/2yd narrow ribbon to match dress fabric

(above right) *Fanny, 24in tall, a large felt character doll (see Chapter 7)*

(below right) *Felt character dolls: the Sailor and the Ballerina, both 20in tall (see Chapter 7)*

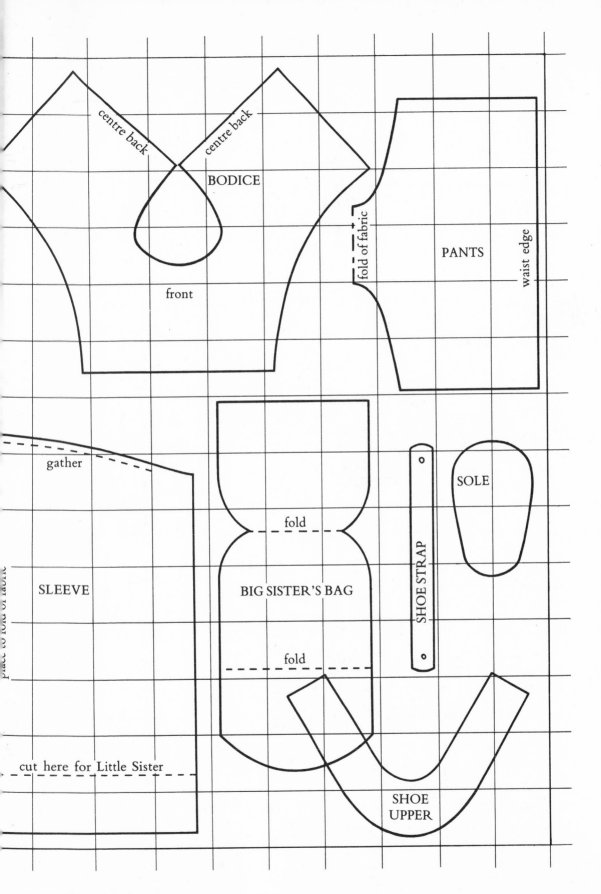

and Little Sisters' clothes patterns

Fig 23 Big and Little Sister rag dolls

Cut the pants in white cotton, with the crutch to the fold of the fabric. Seam both sides and turn a small hem around each leg. Turn a casing at the top edge and thread narrow elastic to fit the doll's waist.

For the petticoat, cut a piece of white cotton 17 x 6in. Seam the short edges together and turn a narrow hem along one long edge. Stitch the broderie-anglaise trim to the hemmed edge. Turn a casing at the top and thread narrow elastic to fit the doll's waist.

To make the dress; cut two bodice pieces (one as a lining), two sleeves and a rectangle 22 x 8in for the skirt. Stitch the bodice pieces together, right sides facing along the centre-backs and around the neck. Clip around the neck, turn through and

(above left) *Small felt character dolls: the Pedlar, 11in tall; the Country Boy and Girl, 11in tall (see Chapter 8)*

(below left) *William, a waxed, clay-modelled, Victorian baby, 11in tall (see Chapter 12)*

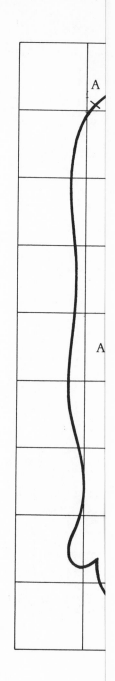

Fig 22a Arm pattern A1

press. Gather the sleev bodice sides, then stitch Stitch the sleeve seams f the shoulder seam, lea open (this becomes pa the bodice and skirt are

Gather the top edge c doll. Pin the skirt to the matching the centre-fr using the open top edge of the waist seam. Stitch

Fig 24

centre-back seam in the skirt, leaving the top 2in open. Try the dress on the doll, pin the sleeve and skirt hems in place, then remove and stitch the hems. Fasten the back opening of the dress with two or three small press-studs. Sew the matching narrow ribbon to each sleeve seam — when the dress is on the doll, tie these ribbons in bows around each wrist to form sleeve frills. To make the socks, cut two 6in lengths of tubular-gauze finger-bandage. Turn each length through to form a double thickness with both raw edges together. Seam the raw edges closed through both thicknesses and turn the seam to the inside.

Cut the shoes from black felt — one sole, one upper and one strap for each shoe. Sew the back seam on the upper on the inside, then, working on the outside, blanketstitch the upper to the sole. Try the shoe on the doll's foot, stretching it gently if necessary to fit. When the shoe is a good fit, blanketstitch around the top edge of the upper to prevent further stretching. Stitch the centre of the strap to the back of the shoe and punch two small holes for the ribbon laces. Thread the laces and tie them into bows when the shoe is on the foot.

Stitch the hair ribbons to the bunches at either side, tie bows, and trim the ends to the required length.

To make Little Sister's rag doll, see the patterns and instructions on pages 75–7. Make the doll in calico with wool hair and the dress in a fabric to match Little Sister's dress.

Big Sister
(18in tall)
Difficulty: 1/Colour picture page 33
Body patterns A & C/Figs 22 & 42

Big Sister rag doll uses the same head pattern as Little Sister, pattern A (Fig 22), but the body, arms, legs and soles are cut from pattern C (Fig 42).

The materials are the same as those for Little Sister (page 49) and the method is the same, except for the arms and shoulder joint. The arms are cut out and seamed together in pairs as before, but the top curved edge AA is left open to be stuffed and then oversewn closed, forming a rounded top to the arm. To attach the arm to the body, depress a curved socket in the shoulder with your fingers and oversew the top of the arm over the shoulder from front to back (see Fig 2b). Make the rest of the doll as for Little Sister.

Big Sister's hair is applied in two layers to make the head appear slightly larger. She wears her hair loose, so the under layer is glued to her head to prevent her from being bald when held upside down. Cut the first layer and stitch it to the head as for Little Sister. Lift one side of the hair and cover the head lightly with glue (UHU is excellent) then smooth the hair down over the glue and hold it for a few minutes as the glue dries. Repeat with the other side of the head. Make sure that the back of the head is covered and that the hair falls evenly all the way round. Cut the second layer and stitch it on in the same way, over the first parting, but leave it to fall loose. As long as the parting is firmly stitched, the hair can be brushed or combed gently and trimmed neatly to the required length.

BIG SISTER'S CLOTHES

The materials required for Big Sister's clothes are the same as for Little Sister, and the patterns (Fig 24) are the same, with the following exceptions. The petticoat is 18 x 7in and the dress skirt is 25 x 9in. The dress sleeve is longer (see pattern) but otherwise the clothes are cut and made up in exactly the same way as for Little Sister.

The socks require 8in of gauze finger-bandage each, and the shoes should be made from the patterns given for Sara's shoes (Fig 75) with the shoe strap from Little Sister's shoe pattern (Fig 24). Tie the hair-ribbon in a large bow at the top of the head, around a small bunch of hair.

Make Big Sister's shoulder bag from a scrap of quilted material, bind the edges with bias binding, then make a ribbon strap and a small loop-and-button fastening on the flap.

Emily
(21in tall)
Difficulty: 2/Colour picture page 33
Body pattern D/Fig 47

½yd unbleached calico (36in wide) for the body
2oz mohair wool for the hair
Black, brown and pink thread for the features
terylene stuffing

Using body pattern D, cut out two body pieces, four arms, four legs and two soles on the straight grain of the fabric. The head pattern D1 (Fig 47a) is also cut on the straight grain of the fabric.

Stitch the darts on the head, then seam the two short edges together and turn through. Turn in the raw neck edge ½in and tack in place.

Do not stitch the body darts marked on the pattern (these are for Fanny). Stitch the body pieces together to form a bag, leaving the neck edge open, then turn through. Seam the arms together in pairs, following the outline shape of the

Fig 25 Emily rag doll

stitches. Continue stuffing through the top of the head into the neck so that it is very firm, then stuff the head, moulding and shaping the stuffing as you work. Work a gathering thread (using button thread) around the top of the head about 1in from the edge, pull it tight and fasten off. If this thread pulls up easily, there is not enough stuffing in the head, so release the thread and add more stuffing until it is an effort to pull up the gathers. The gathers will be completely concealed by the doll's hair.

Depress a curved socket in the shoulder with your fingers and oversew the arm to the body over the shoulder from front to back. Repeat for the other arm, making sure that both thumbs face forward. Oversew the legs to the body on the back of the doll, using strong thread.

To make the hair, cut sufficient 24in lengths of mohair wool to cover the head fairly thickly. Machine or backstitch a centre parting in matching thread. Pin the hair to the doll's head and backstitch in place. Divide the hair into two bunches and secure each bunch to the doll's head with a few stitches at either side of the face. Divide each bunch into four sections and twist each section into a ringlet. Secure the end of each ringlet by stitching it in place, and trim any loose ends.

Draw the doll's features lightly onto the face in pencil, (mistakes will rub off with a pencil rubber or a piece of bread) and, when satisfactory, work them in embroidery thread. The eyes are two circles of buttonholestitch; the inner circle black, the outer circle brown (or blue, green, grey or violet). Make the eye highlights with a few white stitches or a touch of white paint. Work six or seven small stitches in fine thread to make the nose. Outline the mouth in fine thread and fill it in with satinstitch. Use a little powder blusher, rubbed well in, to colour the doll's cheeks.

EMILY'S CLOTHES

1/2yd cotton (36in wide) for dress
1/2yd cotton (36in wide) for pinafore
1/2yd white cotton (36in wide) for petticoat and pantalettes
1 1/2yd broderie-anglaise trimming (1 1/2in wide) for petticoat and pantalettes
1yd of narrow elastic
1 pair of first-size baby socks
1 square of leather or felt (12 x 12in) for boots
1/2yd of fine black cord or ribbon for bootlaces

Cut two pantalette pieces from white cotton, make casings at the end of each leg and trim with

finger ends, and leaving the top of the arm AA open. Clip carefully between the fingers and thumb and turn through. Stitch the legs together in pairs leaving the sole of the foot open. Stitch the sole into the foot on each leg and turn through.

Stuff the legs firmly and oversew the top closed, tucking the raw edges inside and matching front and back seams. Stuff the arms quite firmly, except for the fingers which must be loose to allow for stabstitching. Oversew the top of the arm closed, tucking the raw edges inside. Following the lines marked on the pattern, stabstitch the fingers on each hand. Stuff the body firmly, working the stuffing well into the hips and shoulders.

Pull the neck edge of the head down over the neck, ensuring that the head seam is to the centre-back, and oversew the seam with small firm

56

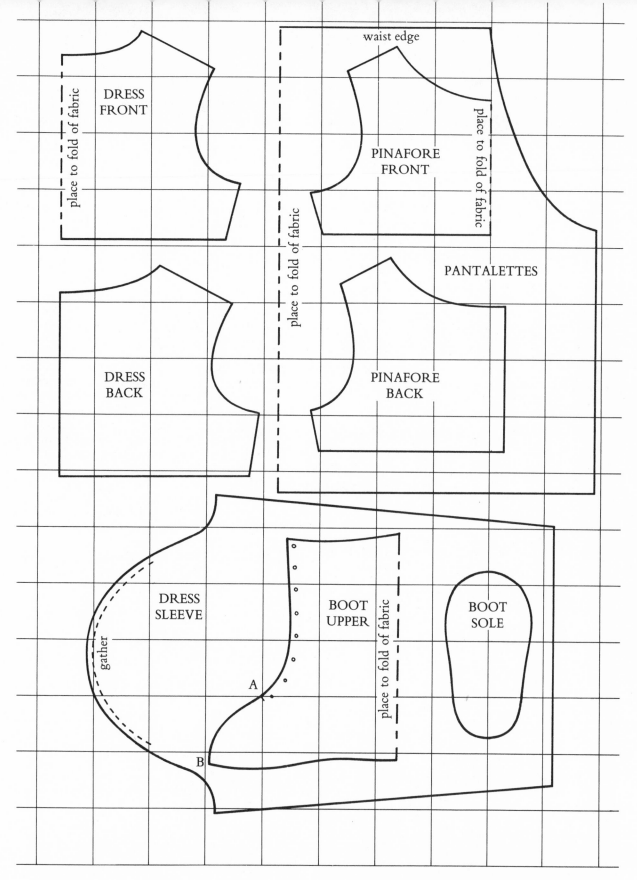

Fig 26 Emily's clothes patterns

broderie-anglaise. Thread narrow elastic through the casings to fit the doll's leg and secure both ends. Seam each pantalette leg, then join them together. Turn a casing at the top edge and thread elastic to fit the doll's waist (*see* Fig 17).

Cut a piece of white cotton 8½ x 20in for the petticoat. Seam the short edges together and make a narrow hem along one long edge. Stitch broderie-anglaise trimming to the hemmed edge. Turn a casing at the top edge, and thread with narrow elastic to fit the doll's waist.

To make the dress, cut two sleeves, a bodice front and two backs from the pattern, plus a piece 23 x 11in for the skirt. Stitch the bodice shoulder and side seams. Stitch the sleeve seams and gather the sleeve heads. Set the sleeves into the armholes. Gather the top edge of the skirt evenly to fit the lower edge of the bodice, matching centre-fronts and backs. Stitch the waist seam. Stitch the centre-back seam in the skirt, leaving the top 2in open. Turn back the edges of the open centre-back seam in bodice and skirt to form facings. Bind the neck edge with a bias-cut strip of dress fabric. Fit the dress onto the doll to pin sleeve and skirt hems; remove and stitch the hems. Fasten the back of the dress with three small press-studs.

To make the pinafore, cut the bodice front and backs from the pattern plus a piece of 26 x 10in for the skirt. The pockets are 2½in square. Stitch the bodice shoulder and side seams. Face the neck and armholes with bias-cut strips of fabric or bias binding, or roll narrow hems. Gather the top edge of the skirt evenly to fit the lower edge of the bodice, and stitch together. Turn a ½in hem down each side of the centre-back. Make a 1in hem along the bottom. Turn a small hem on one edge of each pocket, then fold under and press the other three edges. Position the pockets carefully and stitch in place. Fasten the back of the pinafore with two or three small buttons and worked button-holes. Make a handkerchief from a 3in square of lawn, hemmed and trimmed with lace.

Emily wears a pair of first-size white baby socks with the toes shortened an inch or so to fit. The boots are made in soft leather or felt. Cut one upper and one sole for each boot. Stitch the seam AB on the inside of the boot, right sides together. Oversew the sole to the upper, also on the inside. Turn a narrow hem around the top edge of the boot and down both open front edges, then turn through to the right side. Punch the lace holes on both sides as shown on the pattern and put the boot onto the doll's foot to lace it. Use a darning needle to thread the bootlaces and tie them in bows at the top (*see* Fig 19).

6
THE FELT CHILDREN

The five children and two babies in this chapter are all fairly simple to make, particularly the Toddler Twins, who are suitable for childrens' toys (though they also appeal to adults). Their button eyes, bobble noses and fur-fabric wigs are completely safe and, provided they are stuffed with good-quality polyester, they are washable. Their hair can be brushed and combed, their arm and leg joints are strong and they can be dressed and undressed easily.

Polly also has a fur-fabric wig and button eyes, but her wistful expression and old-fashioned clothes give her a stronger adult appeal. Polly's face has a profile made by inserting a bead nose under the surface; and her freckles and colouring are painted onto the face with felt pens or make-up pencils. She also has knee and elbow joints so that she can be posed quite naturally.

Thomas and Harriet are a rather Victorian pair. They have 'real-hair' wigs, shaped noses, and naturalistic eyes, embroidered on button forms. Their clothes are more elaborate and their bodies more detailed. The fingers are indicated by stabstitching, the arms are jointed at shoulder and elbow and the legs at hip and knee. These two are more suitable for an older child or adult.

The two babies are basically the same but wear different clothes. They are sweet but simple, with fur-fabric wigs, button eyes and bead noses. You can choose to make a sitting or lying baby, depending on how you attach the legs, and they too are washable.

All the childrens' clothes patterns are interchangeable, and will fit any of the dolls, so you can dress them as simply or elaborately as you please.

Use only the best-quality felt and stuffing to make these dolls. Cheap felt is thin and will tear when you insert noses or mould a rounded body. Stuffing should be polyester or terylene, not the cheap acrylics which are heavier and lumpier, or kapok which will not wash — and definitely not foam chips!

Eye buttons should be black and shiny with shank at the back. Alternatively, you could use white shank buttons and paint on the eye and eyelid (I hope some enterprising button manufacturer will eventually think of this!). Always use strong button thread and a darning needle to attach the eye buttons very securely, right through the head. For the noses, wood or plastic beads both work well, but do not use a dark colour which will show through the felt skin.

Fur fabric is available in great variety. I have used a long pile for these dolls — blonde for the Toddler Twins and babies, and auburn for Polly — but the curly type also makes good doll's hair. Choose natural hair colours and avoid black which looks very harsh and also shows fluff (I have made a punk toddler with green hair — amusing, but not very attractive!).

I have given my suggestions for fabrics and colours for clothes with each doll, but you will have your own tastes. I would, however, point out that the clothes are an integral part of the dolls' appeal and the choice is important. Polly, for example, would be a very different doll dressed in pink flowery cotton! None of the clothes need more than ½yd of 36in wide fabric, so it is not expensive to buy the right thing, rather than relying on rag-bag scraps.

Full instructions follow but you might find it helpful to read Chapter 1 before beginning.

Toddler Twins
(16in tall)
Difficulty: 1/Colour picture page 33
Body pattern A/Fig 22

½yd felt (36in wide) for bodies
2 pieces of fur fabric (approx 12 x 6in each) for wigs
4 black buttons (½in diameter) for eyes
black, brown and pink thread for features
terylene stuffing

The boy and girl twins are made in the same way and the quantities given will make them both. Using body pattern A, cut two bodies, two soles,

Fig 27 The Toddler Twins

four legs and four arms for each doll. The heads are made from felt rectangles, 9 x 5in.

Seam the body pieces together to form a bag, leaving the neck edge open. Turn through, fold under the neck edge ½in and tack in place. Seam the arm pieces together in pairs, leaving edge C open. Clip between the thumb and fingers and turn through. Seam the leg pieces together in pairs, leaving the top of the leg and the sole of the foot open. Stitch the sole into the foot on each leg and turn through.

Stuff the legs firmly, turn in the top edges, matching the front and back seams, and oversew closed. Stuff the arms firmly, turn in the open edges and oversew closed. Stuff the body slightly less firmly, but work the stuffing well into the hips and shoulders, leaving the neck open.

Seam the head piece together along the two shorter edges and turn through. Run a strong gathering thread around one edge of the head piece and pull it up tightly, easing the gathers out evenly. Stuff the head very firmly, moulding it into shape as you work. Run a gathering thread around the other edge and pull it up tightly. If this thread pulls up easily, there is not enough stuffing in the head; release it and add more stuffing until it is an effort to pull up the gathers. Select the least puckered end of the head to be the chin and ladderstitch the head to the neck, ensuring that the head seam is to the centre-back and pushing stuffing into the neck as you go so that it is absolutely firm. The gathers on the top of the head will be completely concealed by the wig. Oversew the arms and legs to the back of the body, using strong thread.

To make the wig, use a long-pile or a curly fur fabric in a natural hair colour. Cut fur fabric from the back, using sharp small scissors and taking care to snip only through the backing and not the pile of the fabric — pull the pile apart gently.

To make up the wig see Fig 4. Cut a strip of fabric 9 x 3½in with the pile of the fabric overhanging one long edge — this will be the front edge of the wig. Fold the fabric in half and stitch the back edges together to form a centre-back seam. Flatten the wig out as shown so that the back seam is uppermost and in the centre. Stitch a curved seam to round off the point and trim the fabric close to the seam. Still inside-out, pull the wig onto the doll's head and trim the front corners into a rounded shape to suit the doll's face. Remove the wig and turn it rightside out. Pin it in place on the doll's head, but do not stitch the wig until the eyes are sewn in.

Gauge the most attractive position for the eyes and mark it lightly in pencil. Remove the wig and sew the eyes right through the head with strong thread, pulling it tight to depress sockets around the eyes. If the doll is for a child, make sure that these buttons are sewn very firmly. When the eye buttons are sewn in replace the wig, pin it to the head and oversew or blanketstitch all around the edge with small stitches.

The doll's nose is made from a circle of felt about 1¼in across (but larger or smaller if you prefer). Run a gathering thread around the edge of the circle and pull up around a little stuffing to form a ball. Ladderstitch the nose to the face. Embroider the doll's eyebrows in lightbrown thread, the mouth in pink and work three long black stitches above each eye for lashes.

Brush the fur-fabric wig to style and trim to the required length. Both the Toddler Twins have fringes; the boy's hair is trimmed short, the girl's is longer. If you wish, colour the cheeks with a little powder blusher.

60

THE TODDLER TWINS' CLOTHES

½yd cotton (36in wide) for girl's dress and pants
scrap of white piqué for dress collar
½yd of ribbon (1in wide) for hair bow
¼yd cotton (36in wide) for boy's shirt
½yd fabric (36in wide) for dungarees
3 small shirt buttons
2 dungaree buttons
½yd trimming for pants

To make the girl's pants, cut two pant pieces, hem the leg ends and trim with lace or broderie anglaise. Seam each leg, then stitch them together. Turn a casing at the top edge and thread elastic to fit the doll's waist. Gather each leg with doubled shirring elastic to fit.

To make the dress, cut a yoke front, two yoke backs, two sleeves, two sleeve bands and a skirt in cotton fabric and four collars in white piqué. If you prefer, the sleeve bands could also be in white piqué.

With right sides facing, sew the collars together in pairs. Clip the curves, turn through and press. Stitch the yoke front to the backs at the shoulder seams. Gather the top edges of the skirt to fit the yokes and seam them together. Gather the lower edges of the sleeves to fit the sleeve bands and stitch them together. Stitch the sleeve seams, including the sleeve bands. Turn up the sleeve bands and hem. Gather the tops of the sleeves to fit the armholes and stitch in place. Stitch the centre-back seam in the skirt, leaving the top 2in open. Hem under the open edges of the back seam to form facings. Stitch the collars to the neckline of the dress so that they meet at the centre-front. Bind the raw edges of the neckline with bias binding. Turn up the skirt hem and stitch in place. Fasten the back of the yoke with two small press-studs.

To make the boy's shirt, cut two fronts, one back, two sleeves and two collars from cotton fabric. With right sides facing, sew the two collars together, clip the curves, turn through and press. Stitch the shirt fronts to the back at the shoulder seams. Gather the heads of the sleeves slightly and stitch them into the armholes, easing to fit. Stitch the sleeve seams from the wrist through the armhole, and down the sides of the shirt. Turn back the fronts of the shirt to form facings and hem in place. Stitch the collar to the neckline, enclosing the raw edge. Turn deep hems at the sleeve ends, then turn them back to form cuffs and press. Turn a small hem on the bottom edge of the shirt. Work three small buttonholes down the left shirt front to match three buttons on the right.

Cut two dungaree pieces and two straps. Sew the centre-front seam from the top of the bib to the crutch. Sew the centre-back seam from waist to crutch. Match together these centre seams, then stitch up one leg, through the crutch and down the other leg. Turn small hems at the ankles and face the top edge with matching bias binding. Fold the straps in half lengthwise, right sides together, and stitch along one short edge and the long edge. Turn through, turn in and oversew the open edge, then press flat. Stitch the straps in place at either side of the centre-back and work button loops on the other ends. Sew buttons to each side of the bib front. Cut a small pocket from scrap, hem the top edge, turn the other edges under, and stitch to the centre of the bib.

Both dolls wear socks cut from childrens' socks and red-plastic 'Cinderella' shoes, size 2 (if you prefer to make their shoes, see the patterns given for Thomas and Harriet Figs 33 & 34). Finally, stitch the centre of the hair-ribbon to the top of the girl's head and tie into a bow; and hem a square scrap of cotton into a handkerchief to tuck into the boy's bib pocket.

As with the rag-doll Sisters, these simple dolls look most appealing when simply dressed. They represent modern children so primary colours and childish prints are most suitable. The girl's dress and pants and the boy's shirt look best in cotton or cotton/polyester fabrics in plain colours, gingham or small prints. The dungarees could be made in denim, cotton drill or needlecord.

The boy twin's teddy bear and the girl twin's doll are made from the patterns in Figs 40 & 41. The teddy is made in ginger felt with a ribbon bow. The doll is felt with wool hair and painted features. Her dress is made from a handkerchief.

Polly
(16in tall)
Difficulty: 2/Colour picture page 34
Body pattern A/Fig 22

Polly is made with the same materials and by the same method as the Toddler Twins, except that she has stitched joints at elbows and knees to allow her arms and legs to bend. As these joints do not look particularly attractive I suggest using them on dolls with clothes which cover them.

Stuff the arms to the elbow (level with the doll's waist), match the seams, then stabstitch through the arm from side to side before stuffing the upper arm. Repeat this process on the legs for the knee joints.

Polly's wig is made, like the Toddler Twins',

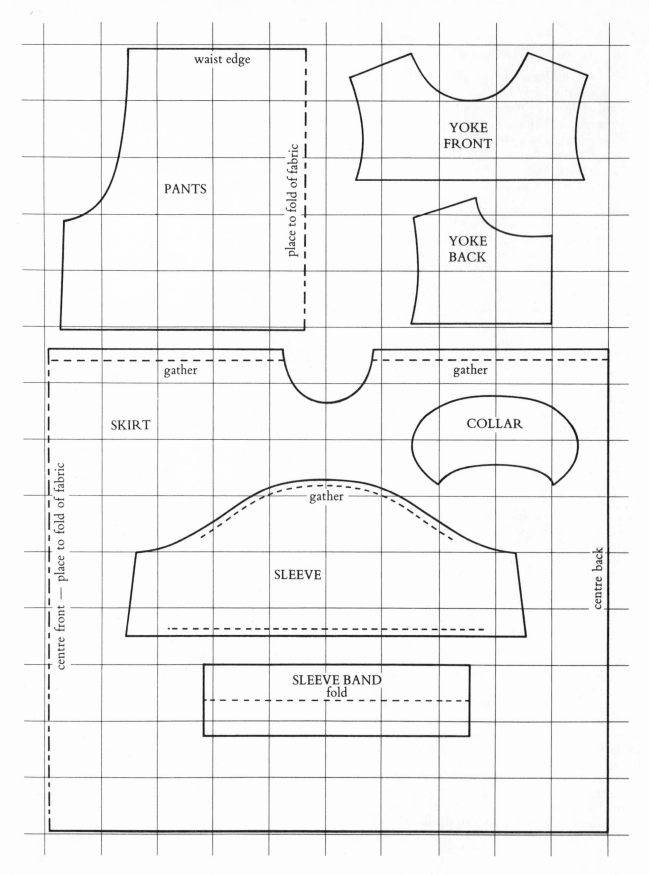

Fig 28 Girl twin's clothes patterns

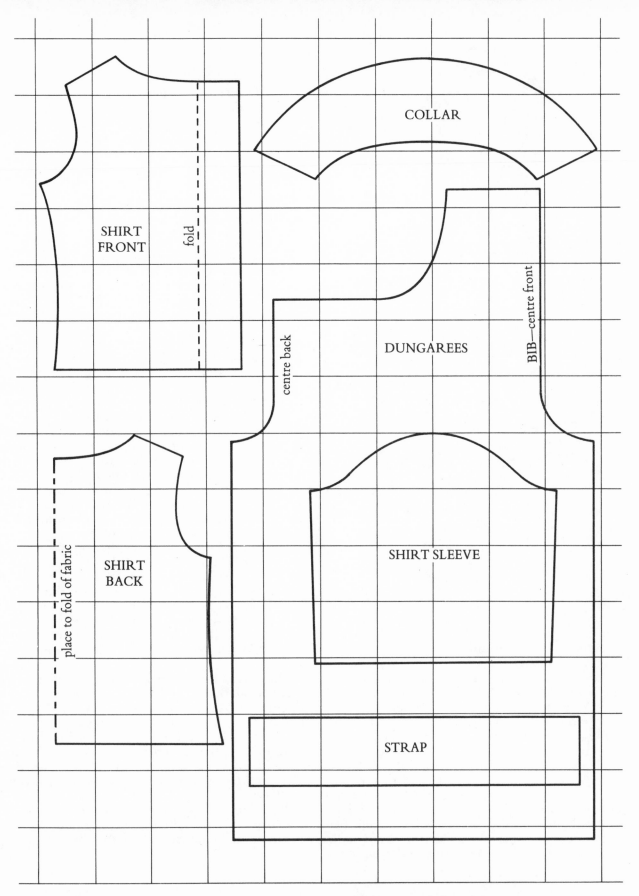

Fig 29 Boy twin's clothes patterns

Fig 30 Polly

*½yd white cotton (36in wide) for petticoat and
    pantalettes
½yd cotton (36in wide) for dress and collar
hat-straw or raffia (or purchased hat)
artificial flower for hat
1yd broderie-anglaise trimming (1in wide) for
    underwear
narrow elastic
½yd narrow braid or ribbon for trimming collar*

Cut two pantalette pieces from white cotton, trim
the legs with broderie anglaise and stitch casings.
Thread narrow elastic through the casings to fit the
doll's legs and secure both ends. Seam each pantalette leg then stitch them together. Turn a casing
at the waist and thread elastic to fit the doll (*see* Fig
17).

Cut a piece of white cotton 6 x 18in for the petticoat. Seam the short edges together and hem one
long edge. Stitch broderie-anglaise trimming to
the hemmed edge. Turn a casing at the waist and
thread elastic to fit the doll.

To make the dress, cut two collars, two sleeves,
two yoke fronts, four yoke backs and one skirt.
Stitch the yoke fronts to the backs at the shoulder
seams, then with right sides together, stitch the
two yokes together up each side of the centre-back
and around the neck. Clip the curves, turn through
and press. Gather the top edges of the skirt to fit
the yokes and stitch them together, turning back
the centre-back skirt edges to form facings.

Stitch the sleeve seams. Gather the sleeve heads
slightly and stitch them into the armholes, easing
to fit. Hem the sleeves at the wrist. Stitch the
centre-back skirt seam, leaving open the top 2in,
which should be hemmed to make facings. Work
two pintucks parallel with the bottom of the skirt,
and turn up the hem behind the lower pintuck.
Fasten the back of the yoke with two small press-
studs.

To make the detachable collar, seam the two
pieces together (right sides facing) leaving an
opening at AA to turn through. Clip the curves
and corners, turn through and press. Slipstitch the
opening closed. Trim with narrow braid or ribbon, mitring the corners at the back. Stitch a small
loop of trimming to the centre-front of the dress
yoke and pull the front ends of the collar through
the loop.

Polly wears long socks cut from a child's sock
and black plastic 'Cinderella' shoes size 2 (if you
prefer to make her shoes, see the shoe pattern for
Harriet Fig 33).

from long-pile fur fabric (*see* Fig 4) styled with a
centre parting and left untrimmed.

Before stitching the wig in place sew the eye
buttons into the head. Then cut a slit about 1in
long at the top of the doll's head above the hairline
to insert the nose. Coat a small wooden or plastic
bead (about ¼in diameter) with glue and spear it
on the end of a knitting needle. Push the bead into
place under the felt and pull out the knitting
needle. Oversew the slit closed. Embroider the
eyebrows in brown thread and the lashes in black,
then outline the mouth in pink and fill it in with felt
pen or embroidery. Mark the nostrils and the
freckles lightly on the face with brown felt pen.
Stitch the wig to the head as for the Toddler
Twins. Colour the cheeks with powder blusher.

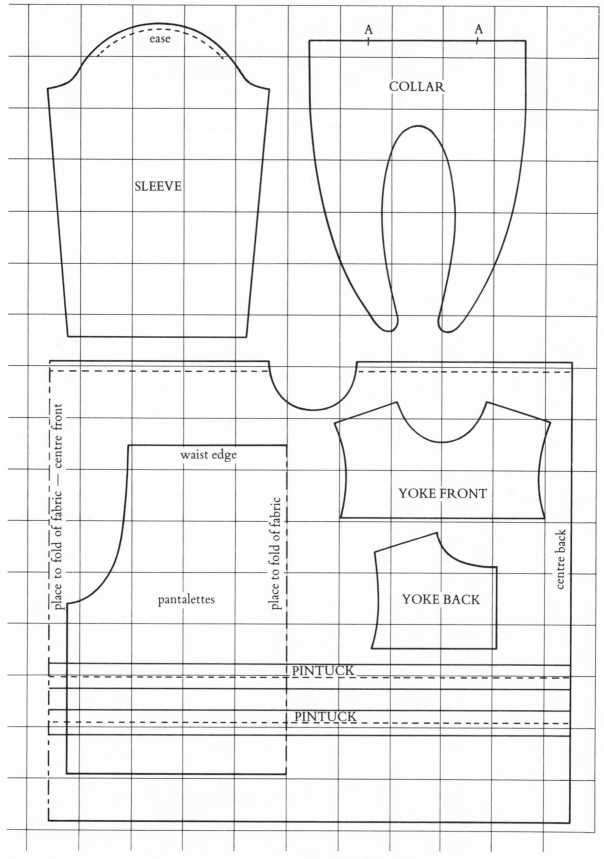

Fig 31 Polly's clothes patterns

Use hat-straw or plaited raffia to make the hat. Starting at the centre of the crown, coil and over-sew the hat-straw, shaping the crown to fit the doll's head then working outwards to form the brim. The crown will vary in size according to the fur fabric used for the wig. When the hat is the right size tuck the end under and stitch it firmly in place. Trim the hat with a band of ribbon and an artificial flower at the front. The straw hats sold for 'Sasha' dolls also fit these dolls.

Polly is an old-fashioned doll and looks best in plain but subtle colours in cotton or cotton/polyester fabrics. This dress would look equally good in navy blue with scarlet trimming or dark brown with cream trimming, but the style is not really suitable for patterned fabrics as the detail becomes obscured by the pattern.

Thomas and Harriet
(16in tall)

Difficulty: 3/Colour picture page 34
Body pattern A plus arm A1/Figs 22 & 22a

For Thomas and Harriet you need the same materials as for the Toddler Twins (page 59), plus four button forms (5/8in) for the eyes. They are made in the same way as the Twins and Polly (with or without knee and elbow joints), except for their arms, which are cut from pattern A1.

Seam the arms together in pairs leaving the curved edge AA open. Turn through and stuff, packing the hands fairly loosely and the arms firmly. Slipstitch the openings closed, tucking in the edges. Stabstitch the fingers as shown on the pattern, pulling the thread tight at each stitch to form the fingers. Depress a curved socket in the shoulder and attach the arm, oversewing over the shoulder from front to back. Make sure that both thumbs face forward.

Both dolls have acrylic wigs (from specialist shops) which are sewn or glued to the head after the eyes and nose are in place. If you prefer, fur-fabric wigs could be used.

For the eyes, cover the button forms with circles of firmly woven white cotton. Make a pupil in the centre of each eye with a small circle of black buttonhole stitch, then stitch another circle around this in brown or blue to make the iris. The eyelid is a semi-circle of felt; blanketstitch the straight edge to the eye then gather the curved edge and pull up behind the eye. Work the blanketstitches on the eyelid in brown thread to make the eyelashes (see Fig 3). The dolls' noses are 1/2in beads pushed under the felt from a slit in the forehead, as for Polly. Work the eyebrows in brown thread, and indicate the nostrils lightly with brown felt pen.

Fig 32 Thomas and Harriet

Cut the mouths from scraps of pale pink felt, glue them to the faces and stitch them across the centre. Colour the cheeks with a little powder blusher. When the faces are completed, glue (or stitch) the wigs to the heads.

THOMAS' AND HARRIET'S CLOTHES

1/2yd white cotton (36in wide) for petticoat and pantalettes
1/2yd cotton for dress
3/4yd broderie anglaise (8in wide) for pinafore skirt
1/2yd broderie-anglaise flat-and-frill trimming for pinafore yoke
1yd trimming (1in wide) for underwear
1/4yd cotton (36in wide) for shirt
1/4yd fabric (36in wide) for knickerbockers
2oz wool (4 ply) for sweater
5 shirt buttons
4 sweater buttons
black leather (or similar) for boots and shoes

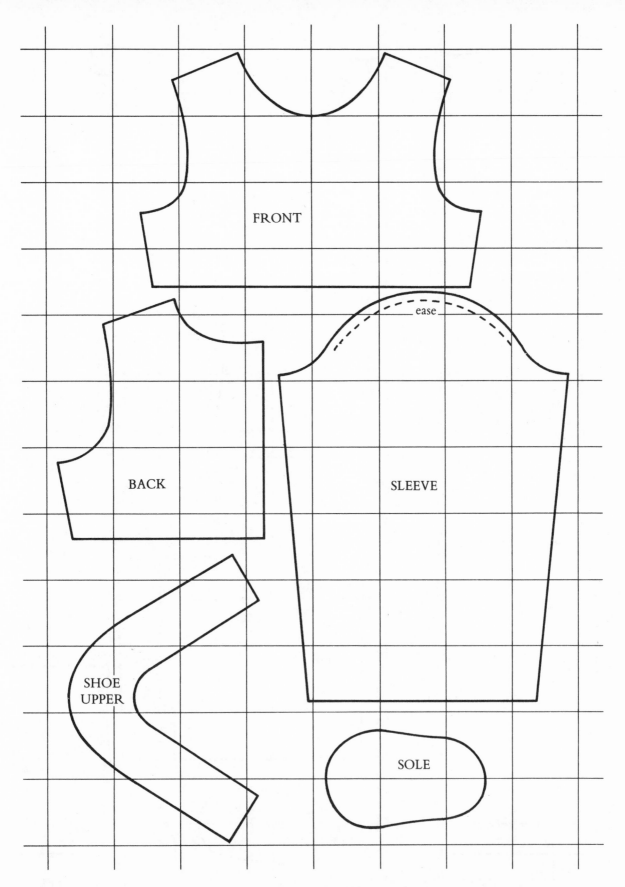

Fig 33 Harriet's clothes patterns

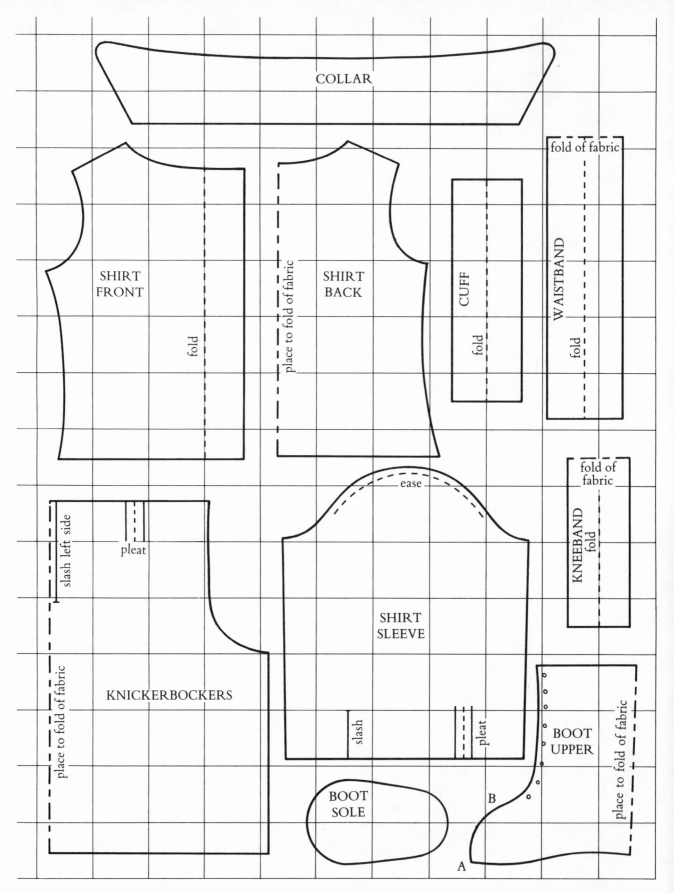

Fig 34 Thomas's clothes patterns

Harriet's pantalettes and petticoat are made in the same way as Polly's, using Polly's patterns (Fig 31).

For the dress, cut a bodice front, two bodice backs, two sleeves (from Fig 33) and a rectangle 10 x 21in for the skirt. Stitch the bodice front to the backs at the shoulder and side seams. Stitch the sleeve seams, gather the heads and stitch the sleeves into the armholes. Gather the top edge of the skirt to fit the bodice. With right sides together, matching centre-fronts and distributing the gathers evenly, stitch the bodice to the skirt.

Stitch the centre-back seam in the skirt, leaving the top 2in open. Turn under and hem the edges of the open back seam in bodice and skirt to form facings. Bind the neck with a bias-cut strip of dress fabric. Stitch sleeve and skirt hems and fasten the back of the dress with three small press-studs.

The pinafore skirt is a 25in length of 8in wide broderie-anglaise trimming, the scalloped edge forming the hem. Turn under and hem the two short edges and gather the top edge to fit around the doll under the arms. Bind the gathered edge with white bias binding. The yoke is made from the type of broderie-anglaise trimming which consists of a flat band with a gathered frill along one side. Working on the doll, fold this trimming to form the complete yoke with four mitred corners. Cut off the excess and hem the edges. Pin the lower edge of the yoke to the bound top edge of the skirt, matching centres, then oversew them together on the inside. This method automatically forms the armholes as shown. Fasten the pinafore with press-studs, or small buttons and loops.

Cut the long black stockings from a sock. To make the shoes, use black leather, plastic or felt. Cut one sole and one upper for each shoe. Oversew the back seam on the upper, right sides together, blanketstitch the upper to the sole and turn through. Cut straps from scrap and sew them to the inside of each shoe at the instep; then cut small slits in the other ends of the straps and stitch tiny black buttons or beads to the outside of each shoe. If using felt, blanketstitch all around the top edge of the shoe to prevent stretching.

To make Thomas' shirt, cut one back, two fronts, two sleeves, two cuffs and two collars from Fig 34.

Stitch the collars together, clip, turn through and press. Stitch the backs to the front at the shoulder and side seams. Hem finely (or face) the slashed openings in the sleeves and stitch the sleeve seams. Stitch the cuffs to the sleeves, pleating the fullness, turn up the cuffs and hem them. Gather the sleeve heads and stitch them into the armholes, easing to fit. Turn back and hem the front facings. Stitch the collar to the neckline, enclosing the raw edges. Make a small hem on the bottom of the shirt. Work three buttonholes on the left shirt front and one on each cuff, then sew on the buttons.

Cut two knickerbocker pieces (slashing an opening on the left side) plus a waistband and two kneebands. Gather the bottom of the legs and stitch on the kneebands, then stitch the inside-leg seams through the kneebands to the crutch. Turn up and hem the kneebands. Hem finely (or face) the slashed opening, then seam the two legs together. Stitch the top of the knickerbockers to the waistband, pleating the fullness. Turn over and hem the waistband. Fasten the waistband with a button and buttonhole or with two hooks and eyes.

Knit the sweater in 4-ply yarn, back and front alike, using size 14 (2mm) needles. Cast on 48 stitches. Work six rows k1, p1 rib. Change to size 13 (2¼mm) needles. Continue in st st until the work measures 5in from the beginning. Cast off. For the sleeves use size 14 needles and cast on 34 stitches. Work six rows k1, p1 rib. Change to size 13 needles. Work in st st increasing 6 stitches evenly along the first row. Continue until the work measures 3½in from the beginning. Cast off. Press the pieces.

To make up the sweater, oversew ¼in long shoulder seams and stitch the tops of the sleeves in to the shoulders. Sew the sleeve seams from the wrist through the armhole and down the side. Work button loops on either side of the back shoulders and stitch buttons to the front shoulders.

Thomas also wears long black stockings cut from a sock. His boots are made from thin black leather (plastic or felt would also be suitable). Cut one upper and one sole for each boot. Right sides together stitch the small seam AB, then stitch the sole into the upper. Stitch a narrow hem around the top of the boot and down both open front edges, then turn through to the right side. Punch the lace holes on both sides as shown on the pattern, and put the boots onto the doll's feet to lace them. Thread the laces (fine cord) with a darning needle and tie them at the top. If necessary, cut cardboard soles to go inside the boots (*see* Fig 19).

Harriet's felt doll is made from the pattern in Fig 41. Her hair is embroidery silk, her eyes are glass beads and she is dressed in a pink-silk frock with coffee-lace trimmings.

Thomas and Harriet, with their realistic eyes and hair, need to be dressed in more elaborate clothes than the previous dolls. Harriet's dress is simply cut and could easily be made in velvet, perhaps with a lace collar. Brown, crimson, dark-blue or green velvet would look very pretty with the broderie-anglaise pinafore, as would small cotton prints and plain dark colours in cotton, wool or Viyella. Thomas' shirt looks right in any plain-coloured or small-patterned cotton or Viyella, and his knickerbockers would look very plush in velvet or corduroy for 'best'. Although they belong to no specific period, there is a vaguely Victorian air about these two, which could be enhanced by dressing them in suitable fabrics and colours. Thomas can also be dressed in a sailor suit, using the patterns for the Sailor with the legs and sleeves shortened. Harriet could wear a more elaborate dress cut from the patterns for Amy who is the same size.

Babies
(11in tall)

Difficulty: 2/Colour picture page 34
Body pattern B/Fig 35

2 squares of felt (each 12 x 12in) for body
1 piece of fur fabric (approx 6 x 4in) for wig
2 buttons (3/8in) for eyes
brown and pink thread for features
terylene stuffing

Both babies are made in the same way, the materials and method given are for one. From Body pattern B, cut two bodies, two soles, four arms and four legs. Cut a rectangle 3½ x 7in for the head.

Seam the body pieces together to form a bag, leaving the neck edge open, and turn through. Turn the neck edge under by ¼in and tack in place. Seam the arms together in pairs, right sides together, leaving the curved edge AA open. Clip between thumb and fingers and turn through. Seam the legs together in pairs, right sides together, leaving the curved edge AA and the sole of the foot open. Stitch the sole into the foot and turn through.

Stuff the legs firmly, turn under the open curved edges and oversew closed. Stuff the arms firmly, turn under the open curved edges and oversew closed. Stuff the body firmly, moulding a rounded tummy as you work.

Seam the two short edges on the head piece, run a gathering thread around one long edge and pull it up tightly, easing the gathers to make them even. Stuff the head very firmly, gather and pull up the top edge. Select the least puckered end to be the chin and ladderstitch the head to the neck, pushing stuffing into the neck as you work so that it is firm, and ensuring that the head seam is to centre-back.

Ladderstitch the top of the arms to the body on the side seams, ½in below the neck, with the thumbs to the inside. Ladderstitch the top of the legs to the body — on the side seams; at right angles to the body for a sitting baby, in line with the body for a lying baby (Fig 36).

Cut a piece of fur fabric 6 x 2½in for the wig and make up in the same way as for the Toddler Twins (*see* Fig 4). Pin the wig to the head and mark the eye positions. Sew the eyes firmly through the head with strong thread, pulling tightly to depress sockets around the eyes. Insert a small bead nose from a slit in the forehead under the hairline, then sew the wig in place. Work a few small stitches in light-brown thread for the eyebrows and pink thread for the mouth. Mark the nostrils lightly in brown felt pen and colour the cheeks with powder blusher. Brush the hair to style and trim it to the required length.

THE BABIES' CLOTHES

¼yd cotton (36in wide) for angel top
1 small child's sock for tights
½yd fabric (36in wide) for pram suit
1 zip (4in) for pram suit
1 white face flannel for nappies
scrap of cotton and trim for bib

To make the babies' nappies, use a white face flannel. Cut it diagonally to make two nappies and hem the raw edges. Fold the nappy onto the baby in the usual way and fasten with a small safety pin.

Use the top edge of the sock as the waist edge of the tights. Cut the foot off the sock to give a piece 7in long. Cut this piece in half up to 2½in below the waist to form two legs. Stitch across one foot, up the leg, through the crutch, down the other leg and across the second foot. Reinforce the seam and turn through (*see* Fig 18).

For the angel top, cut two front yokes, four back yokes (one yoke is used as a lining), two sleeves and two skirts from Fig 38. Sew the four shoulder seams, then stitch the yokes together at centre-back and around the neck. Clip the curves, turn through and press. Stitch the skirts together at the side seams and slash an opening in the back. Stitch the sleeve seams and sew the sleeves into the armholes. Gather the top edge of the skirt and sleeves. Roll a small hem around the slashed opening on the back skirt. Pin the gathered skirt and sleeves to the yoke, distribute the gathers evenly and stitch in place. Oversew the lining yoke over the seam to neaten. Turn up sleeve and skirt hems. Fasten the back yoke with two small press-studs.

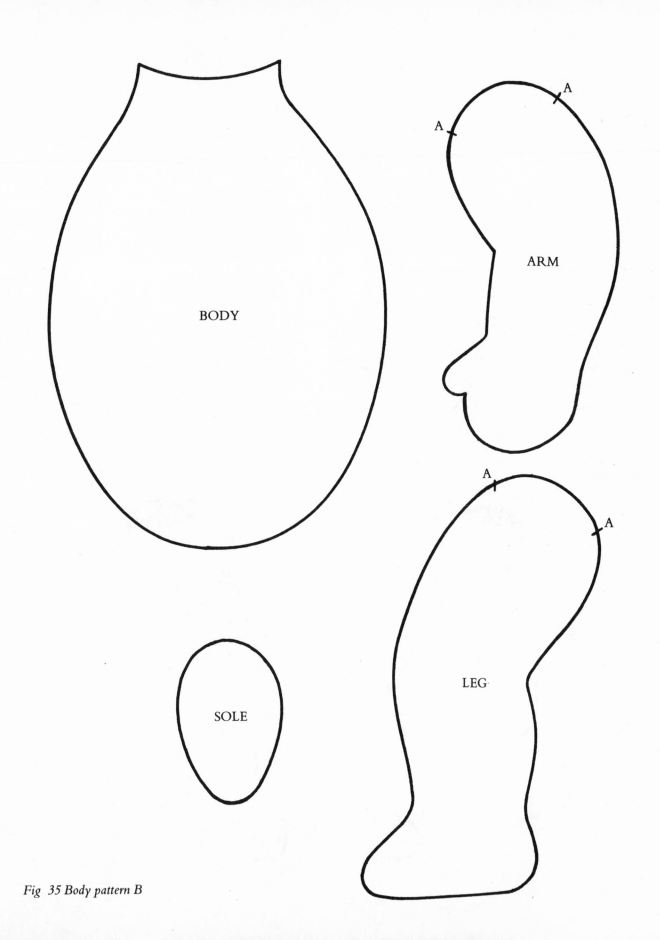

BODY

ARM

A

A

A

A

LEG

SOLE

Fig 35 Body pattern B

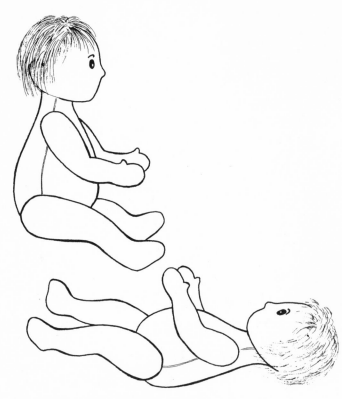

Fig 36 Assembly for sitting and lying felt baby

Fig 37 Felt babies

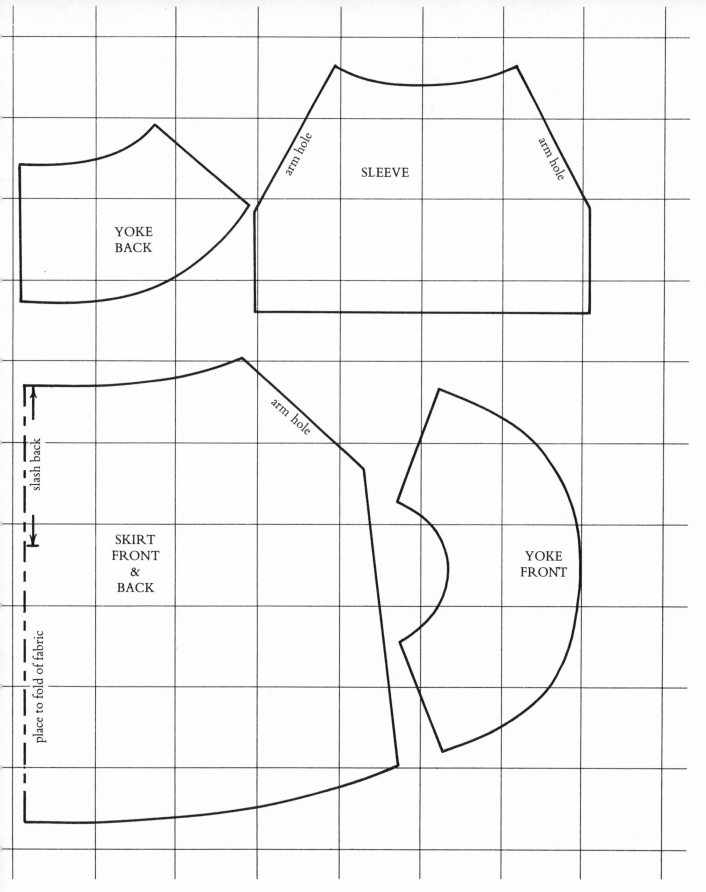

YOKE
BACK

arm hole

SLEEVE

arm hole

arm hole

slash back

place to fold of fabric

SKIRT
FRONT
&
BACK

YOKE
FRONT

Fig 38 Baby's angel top

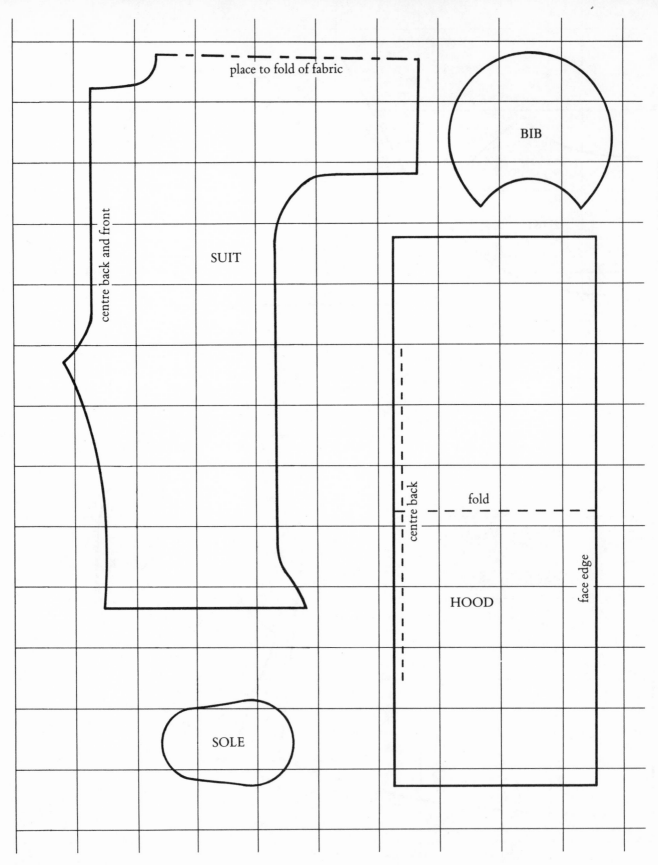

Fig 39 Baby's pram suit

Trim the front yoke with embroidery or an embroidered appliqué.

To make the pram suit, cut two body pieces, two soles and a hood from Fig 39. If you are using a fabric which frays easily, bind each piece with bias binding. Stitch the centre-back seam. Stitch the fronts together at the crutch and sew in the zip. Sew the side seams from wrist to foot. Sew the inside-leg seam from one foot, through the crutch and down the other leg. Stitch the soles into the legs. Face the neck and sleeve edges with bias binding. Fold the hood in half, and sew the back seam. Face the front edge with bias binding, gather the neck edge slightly to fit the pram suit and oversew it in place. If you are using a pile fabric you will need to ease the trapped pile out of the seams with a darning needle, and possibly, trim the pile so that the zip will move freely.

Cut two bib pieces in cotton fabric and seam them together around the outside, leaving the top edge open. Clip the curves, turn through and press. Bind the top edge of the bib with bias binding, leaving lengths at either side to form ties. Trim with lace edging.

Any fabric used for baby clothes can be used to make the angel top, including cotton, cotton/polyester, Viyella or lawn. It would look pretty in broderie anglaise as a 'best dress', perhaps with a matching bonnet (*see* Fig 87). The angel-top pattern can be adapted to make a nightgown by lengthening the skirt to 8in. Use cotton, Viyella or winceyette. Fasten the back yoke with ribbon ties.

The pram-suit pattern can be used to make a stretch-towelling babygro by omitting the hood, using press-studs to fasten the front, and facing the edges with bias binding. These babies can also wear the elaborate christening gowns, bonnets and bootees shown on the clay and waxed babies which are the same size (*see* Figs 85 and 87). For a baby's shawl use the pattern for the Ballerina's shawl in the next chapter.

Watch out for baby accessories in toy shops — potties, feeding bottles, baths etc are made for commercial dolls in this size (eg Tiny Tears).

Toys
(6in tall)
Difficulty: 1/Colour pictures pages 33, 34 & 51
Figs 40 & 41

These easily made little toys are dolls in their own right but they also make charming accessories. They are most easily made by the 'stitch-round' method where the pattern is drawn onto a double thickness of fabric and the toy is stitched round the drawn line before being cut out. It is then trimmed close to the stitching, turned through and stuffed.

I recommend felt or fleecy dressing-gown fabric for the teddy rather than fur fabric which would be too thick. Felt, cotton or calico are suitable for the doll, though felt will stretch to make a slightly larger doll. Use button or bead eyes for safety, but if they are not for children these toys can have glass eyes (the smallest size with wire shanks).

To make the teddy, draw the pattern onto doubled fabric and stitch round it, leaving the feet and the top of the head open. Cut out and trim the surplus fabric. Stitch the soles into the feet, clip the curves at underarm and crutch and turn through. Stuff the bear through the top of the head using small pieces of stuffing packed firmly. As you work mould a rounded tummy and twist the legs so that the feet point forward. Before closing the top of the head, push a bead into the face to form the snout. If you are using wired glass eyes, position them carefully, push the wires into the head and twist the ends together inside to secure them. Top up the stuffing and slipstitch the gap closed. Stabstitch through the head on the lines indicated to shape the ears. Run a gathering thread around the neck and pull it up tight. Tie a narrow-ribbon bow around the neck over the gathering thread. If using bead or button eyes, stitch them firmly in place. Embroider the nose and mouth in black thread or mark them with felt pen. Cut small oval felt pads and stitch them to the bear's paws.

To make the doll, draw the pattern onto doubled fabric and stitch round it leaving the top of the head and the feet open. Cut out, trim and stitch the soles into the feet. Clip the curves at underarms and crutch and turn through. Stuff firmly, and as you work pinch the hands and feet to shape and twist the legs so that the feet point forward. If you are using glass eyes, push them into the head and twist the wires together inside to secure them. A bead nose can also be inserted at this stage. Top up the stuffing and slipstitch the gap. Run a gathering thread around the neck (and the wrists if necessary) and pull it up tightly. Mark the features in felt pen (bead, button or embroidered eyes are possible). The hair is wool or embroidery silk stitched or glued to the doll's head.

Any pieces of fine fabric, lace or broderie anglaise and ribbon can be used for the clothes — handkerchiefs are particularly useful because of their ready-made hems. It is simplest to make and sew the clothes on the doll, though they could be removable and fastened with tiny press-studs. Tubular-gauze finger-bandage makes good stockings. The felt shoes or boots in Figs 54 and 55 can

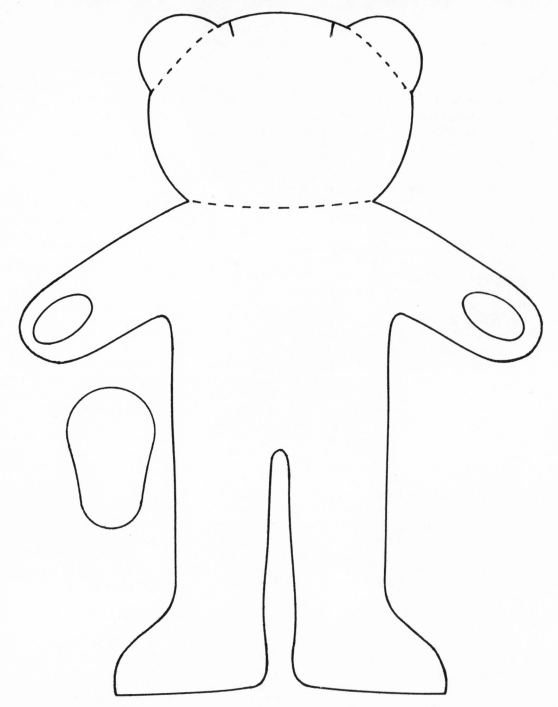

Fig 40 Toy teddy bear

be sewn to the foot or tied with fine ribbons. A small piece of ribbon or broderie anglaise wrapped around and stitched under the crutch will make simple knickers; and a longer piece can be seamed and gathered into a petticoat. If you enjoy working in miniature, you could make quite elaborate clothes for these tiny dolls, using any pretty scraps available. If you find this scale difficult to work in

use wide ribbon, gathered along one edge for a skirt, or folded and wrapped over the shoulders for a bodice.

The four miniature dolls shown in the colour illustrations are made from this pattern. Little Sister's doll is made in calico with wool hair in bunches. Her pants and petticoat are pieces of broderie anglaise, her dress a simplified copy of Little Sister's dress in the same print. The Toddler Twin's doll is made in felt and also has wool hair

76

and features drawn in felt pen. It wears tiny lawn knickers, a broderie-anglaise petticoat and a smock dress made from a handkerchief. Harriet's doll is rather more elaborate. She is made of felt, with a bead nose and glass eyes. The hair is embroidery silk styled into ringlets and a plaited bun (*see* Fig 53). Her pantalettes and petticoat are made of lawn trimmed with fine lace. The pink-silk dress has full sleeves, a gathered skirt and a coffee-lace bodice. All the dolls wear white tubular-gauze stockings and felt shoes.

The little pierrot is made in white felt and wears a miniature version of the Pierrot's suit in white

Fig 41 Toy doll

satin with black-satin ribbon cap and ruffles. The eyes are black beads, the features are marked with felt pen.

Children find these pocket-sized dolls very appealing and they make acceptable toys in their own right. It might be fun to make a whole family of them, lengthening the pattern an inch or so at the waist to make adult-size dolls, or using the Country Couple (Chapter 8) as parents and these dolls as children.

7
THE FELT CHARACTER DOLLS

The Sailor, the Ballerina and Fanny are made in felt using the same techniques as for the children in the previous chapter, so I shall refer back to those instructions where appropriate. The Sailor has a fur-fabric wig, button eyes and a bobble nose and is made in the same way as the Toddler Twins. The Ballerina has a mohair wool wig, shaped nose, and covered button-form eyes and is made the same way as Thomas and Harriet. Fanny is larger than the Ballerina but is made in the same way except for her hands which have separate fingers. She wears a 'real-hair' wig. The Sailor and Ballerina would both make suitable toys for older children, but Fanny is definitely an adult's toy!

These three dolls demonstrate that basic patterns can be used to make up a variety of very different characters — and your imagination is the only limit to their costumes. For example, a spaceman, a pierrot, a cowboy or a guardsman could all be made from the Sailor pattern. A peasant girl, a queen, a Victorian lady or a modern girl in blue jeans could be made from the Ballerina pattern. Only the eye, nose and wig methods need be changed to suit the character — it is the costume detail which gives the reality. For example, the Ballerina's shoes are miniature copies of the real thing, and the Sailor has a kit bag.

Fanny's body patterns are the right proportions for a large child doll. The arms and legs are plump and the head is over-large for an adult, but these childlike proportions somehow add to Saloon-girl Fanny's voluptuous charms! Fanny wears a boned satin corset, French knickers and classic saloon-girl dress. She carries a black-satin bag complete with purse, perfume and handkerchief.

Once again it is important to use best-quality felt and stuffing for these dolls, though the choice of clothes fabrics will of course depend on the character you make. For the Sailor and Ballerina I recommend fabrics as close as possible to the real thing: lightweight wool and white piqué for the sailor suit, satin and net for the ballet dress, in colours appropriate to a specific ballet (the doll illustrated is costumed for *Les Sylphides*). Fanny's costume is best made in satin or taffeta in any bright colour — scarlet, purple or emerald green — trimmed with black lace, and her underwear should of course be black!

The Sailor and Ballerina are basically the same size though taller than the children in the previous chapter, so the childrens' clothes patterns can be used with arms, legs and hems lengthened as necessary. The Sailor and Ballerina will also fit clothes made from patterns for Sara and the Pierrot (Chapter 10).

Sailor
(20in tall)
Difficulty: 2/Colour picture page 51
Body pattern C/Fig 42

½yd felt (36in wide) for body
piece of fur fabric (approx 12 x 6in) for wig and beard
2 buttons (½in) for eyes
brown and pink thread for features
terylene stuffing

Cut two body pieces, four arms, four legs and two soles from body pattern C, and a head rectangle 9 x 5in. Do not sew the darts in the body, these are for the Ballerina. Make up the head, body and wig as for the Toddler Twins (*see* page 59), making shoulder joints like those on Thomas and Harriet.

Sew in the eyes, make and sew on the nose and wig as for the Toddler Twins (*see* Fig 4). Work the eyebrows in fairly thick brown thread and the mouth in pink. Cut a strip of fur fabric and oversew it to the doll's chin for a beard. Stabstitch through the hands to indicate the fingers. Colour the face with a ruddy-coloured powder blusher.

SAILOR'S CLOTHES

½yd navy-blue wool (36in wide) for suit
¼yd white piqué for collar, vest and hat
1yd navy-blue ribbon (½in wide) for tie and hat-band

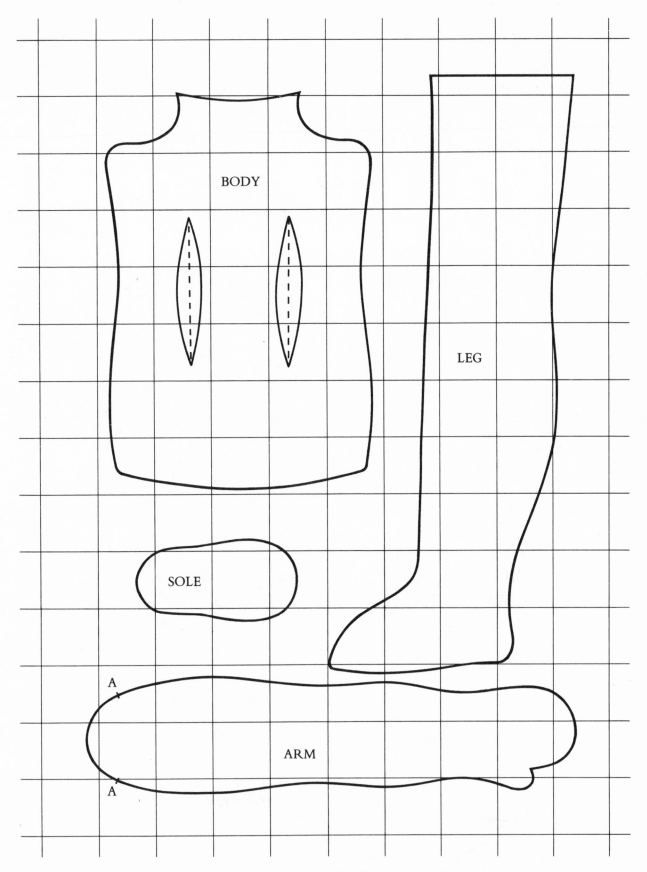

BODY

LEG

SOLE

A

A

ARM

Fig 42 Body pattern C

½yd fine piping cord for lanyard
½yd narrow braid for collar
small piece olive drill or canvas for kit bag
black leather for shoes

Cut the blouse back, blouse front, two sleeves, two trouser pieces and one waistband from the woollen fabric. Cut two collars and two vests from piqué. For the hat, cut two piqué circles of 5½in diameter and a 2in wide band to fit around the doll's head. From the centre of one piqué circle, cut out a circular hole (approximately 3in diameter) to fit the doll's head.

To make the trousers, hem (or face) the slashed opening on the left side. Seam each leg, then seam the legs together from centre-front through the crutch to centre-back. Stitch the waistband to the top edge of the trousers, turn under and hem in

place. Turn up the leg hems. Fasten the waistband with a button and buttonhole or two hooks and eyes. Press the trousers to make creases at back and front.

To make the blouse, seam the front to the back at shoulder and side seams. Stitch the sleeve seams and set the sleeves into the armholes. Face the neck with matching bias binding and hem the sleeves and bottom edge.

Sew the collars together, leaving AA open, clip the curves, turn through, press and slipstitch the opening closed. Sew on the narrow-braid trim. Oversew the collar to the inside of the neckline. Sew the vests together, leaving a gap to turn through. Clip the corners, turn through, press and slipstitch closed. Sew narrow-braid trim to one edge of the vest. Sew one side of the vest to the blouse, inside the neckline and sew a press-stud to fasten the other side.

To make the hat, stitch the two circles together around the outside. Seam the short ends of the band together and sew one long edge around the cut-out circle, easing to fit. Turn up the other edge and hem. If the piqué you are using is not very stiff, iron Vilene interfacing to each piece before making up. Print a ship's name on the ribbon band in gilt letters (hand written or rub-down lettering) and stitch the ribbon around the hat band.

Knot the ribbon tie and the lanyard under the collar and trim. To make the bag, cut a 3in diameter circle for the base and a piece 9 x 7in for the sides. Stitch the shorter edges together to form a tube and stitch in the base. Stitch a ½in hem round the top edge. Punch holes around the top and thread string through, knotting the ends.

Use the Pierrot's shoe pattern (Fig 77). Cut one upper and one sole in black leather for each shoe. Right sides together, stitch the back seam on the upper. Stitch the upper to the sole and turn through. Use the top of a navy-blue or black sock to make the doll's socks.

If you prefer, the sailor suit could be made in white cotton-drill with a blue-cotton collar piped in white.

Fig 43 Sailor

Ballerina
(20in tall)

Difficulty: 3/Colour picture page 51
Body pattern C/Fig 42

½yd felt (36in wide) for body
1oz mohair wool for hair
2 button forms (⅝in) for eyes
1 pair false eyelashes
black, brown and pink thread for features
eyeshadow, blusher, lip pencil

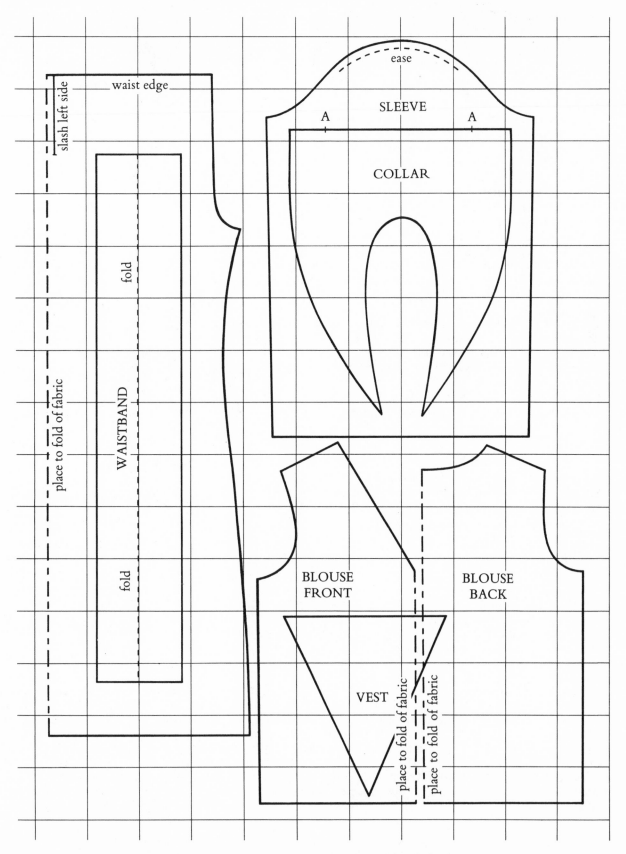

Fig 44 Sailor's clothes patterns

Using body pattern C (Fig 42) cut two bodies, two soles, four arms and four legs. Cut a rectangle 9 x 5in for the head. Stitch the darts on the front and back body pieces — when stuffing the body, mould a small bosom.

Make the head, eyes, eyelids, body and nose exactly as for Thomas and Harriet (see page 66). When positioning the eyes, pin the mohair wool to the head to gauge the effect, but do not stitch the hair until the eyes and nose are in place.

Cut sufficient 16in lengths of wool to cover the head smoothly but not too thickly. Stitch a centre parting through these lengths in matching thread, then stitch them to the doll's head through the parting. Draw the hair to the back of the head and tie it into a pony tail. Turn up the pony tail and secure the loose ends to the back of the head. Plait 12in lengths of wool, coil the plait into a small bun and sew it to the back of the head to cover the ends. Cover the hair with a fine hairnet (a bun net fits well). Once the wool is firmly stitched in place the fronts can be combed smooth and, if necessary, held with a little hair spray.

Trim the false eyelashes and glue them to the lower edge of the eyelids. Embroider the eyebrows in brown thread, and outline the mouth in pink thread. Make-up the doll's face with make-up pencils and powder blusher to give her a slightly theatrical effect.

BALLERINA'S CLOTHES

¼yd white satin (36in wide) for bodice
¼yd white lawn (36in wide) for bodice lining
1yd white net (36in wide) for skirt
¼yd white starched muslin (36in wide) for skirt lining
¼yd pink satin (36in wide) for shoes
1 yd narrow pink-satin ribbon for shoe ribbons
scrap of soft leather or chamois for soles
12 small white fabric flowers
1oz white yarn (2 ply) for shawl
pink tights or stocking
½yd white satin ribbon (½in) for neck

Using the top of the tights or stocking, cut a piece 12in long and wide enough to fit the doll's waist. Sew a 3in centre-back seam from the top, then cut the remainder into two halves for the legs. Stitch across one foot, up the leg, through the crutch then down the other leg and foot. Reinforce the seam, trim and turn through (*see* Fig 18).

Cut one bodice front and two bodice backs in both satin and lawn. The bodice is more realistic with a pointed front waist, but the pattern also

Fig 45 Ballerina

gives a simpler, straight version. Stitch the side seams of both bodice and lining. With right sides together, stitch the lining to the bodice down the backs and around the top edge. Clip the curves, turn through and press.

Fold the net lengthwise to make four layers. Lay the net over the muslin lining and tack through all five layers along one long edge. If using the pointed version of the bodice, cut a shallow corresponding V shape in the centre-front of the skirt. Gather the top edge of the skirt to fit the bodice. Distribute the gathers evenly and stitch the skirt in place to the satin. Turn the lining edge under and hem it over the seam. Trim the bottom edges of the skirt to the required length, and roll a fine hem

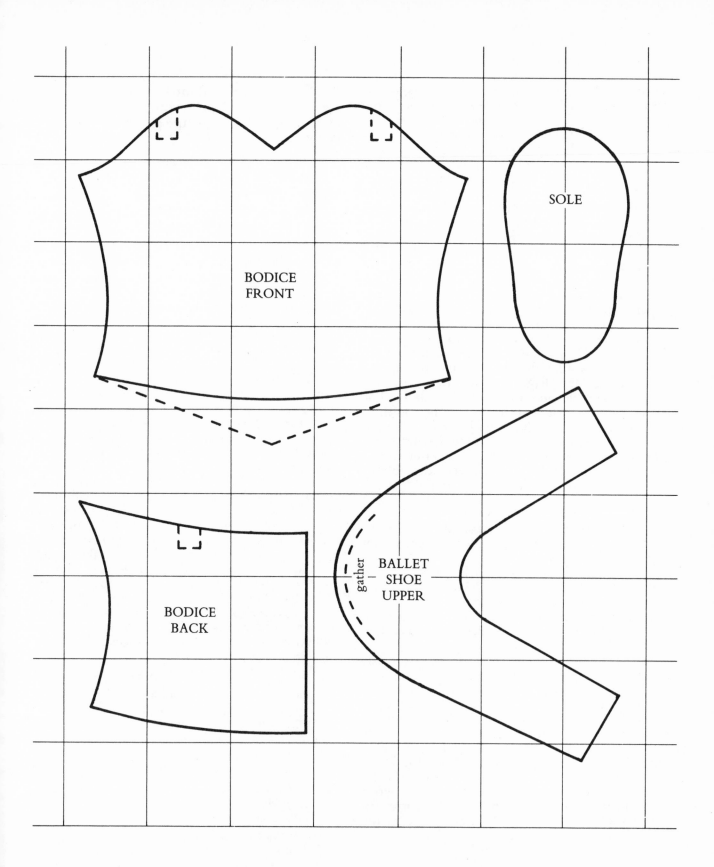

SOLE

BODICE
FRONT

BODICE
BACK

gather

BALLET
SHOE
UPPER

Fig 46 Ballerina's clothes patterns

on the muslin skirt lining. Close the back of the skirt by oversewing each of the five layers separately, making the seams as small as possible. The muslin layer is inclined to fray and will need overcasting. Leave the top 2in of the skirt seams open. Cut the dress straps from scrap satin or use satin ribbon. Stitch them where indicated on the pattern. Fasten the bodice with four small press-studs or hooks and eyes and trim the front with one small flower stitched in place. Twist the stems of the other flowers into a wreath to encircle the doll's head, and pin it to the hair with hair-grips.

Cut two shoe uppers in pink satin, two linings in lawn and two soles in thin leather or chamois. Right sides together, stitch the back seams on the uppers and the linings. Again with right sides together, stitch the linings to the uppers around the top edge; clip the curves, turn through and press. Tack the linings to the uppers around the bottom edge. Gather the curve around the toes and pull up the gathers. Right sides together, stitch the uppers to the soles and turn through. Cut the shoe ribbon into four 9in lengths. Stitch one length to each side of each shoe (level with the ankle bone). Cross the ribbons over the foot and wind twice around the ankle, finishing with a knot (not a bow!) on the inside of the ankle. Trim the ribbons and tuck the loose ends underneath the ankle strap.

The shawl is crocheted in 2-ply yarn. Using a size 13 (2¼mm) crochet hook make 150 ch.

1st row: into the 10th chain from the hook work 1dc, ★ 6ch, miss 3ch, 1dc into next ch, repeat from ★ to end, turn

2nd row: ss across first 3ch, 6ch, 1dc into 3rd ch of next 6ch loop, repeat from ★ to end, working last dc into the first 9ch space, turn

3rd row: ss across first 3ch, continue in pattern to end. Repeat this row to decrease and form a triangle.

Drape the shawl around the doll's shoulders and tie the ends loosely at the front. Tie a white satin ribbon around the neck, with a bow at the back.

If you prefer to make a short tutu, fold the net into eight layers and omit the muslin skirt lining. Eight layers are sufficient to make the short skirts stick out properly, without making the waist seam too bulky. Make up the tutu as described and trim the skirts to the most attractive length. A short white tutu would be suitable for *Swan Lake*, worn with a feathered headdress. A pink tutu worn with a jewelled headdress would be appropriate for the Sugar Plum Fairy.

Fanny
(24in tall)

Difficulty: 3/Colour picture page 51
Body pattern D/Fig 47

½yd felt (36in wide) for body
2 button forms (⅝in) for eyes
1 pair of false eyelashes
blue, black, pink and brown thread for features
eyeshadow, blusher, lip pencil
2 small diamanté stones (optional)

Using body pattern D, cut two bodies, two soles, four arms and four legs. Cut a rectangle 12 x 6in for the head. Stitch the darts in the back and front body pieces — mould a bosom when stuffing. The head and body are made up in exactly the same way as Thomas and Harriet (*see* page 66), except for the hands. Seam the arms together in pairs from the curve AA to the outside of the thumbs and little fingers. Cut carefully on the lines indicated on the pattern to separate the fingers, then oversew by hand around each finger with small tight stitches from the outside of the little finger to the outside of the thumb. Turn the fingers through to the right side (this is a fiddly operation and requires patience — work carefully so that you do not pierce the felt). If you prefer, the fingers can be indicated by stabstitching as for Emily rag doll (*see* page 55) rather than cut separately. Stuff the fingers firmly, then stuff the arms, legs, body and head and make up as for Thomas and Harriet.

Fanny's eyes, nose, mouth and make-up are worked in the same way as the Ballerina's, but she also has a 'twinkle' in each eye made by glueing a small diamanté stone into each pupil. Her 'real-hair' wig is styled with a long curl at either side of her face and the back is swept up into a small bun held with hair grips (wigs from specialist shops).

FANNY'S CLOTHES

¼yd black satin (36in wide) for corset
¼yd black lawn (36in wide) for corset lining
4 collar stiffeners for corset bones
narrow black-lace trimming for corset
2 black petticoat-strap clips for suspenders
¼yd black silk (36in wide) for knickers
½yd black lace (1in wide) for knicker trimming
black stocking
½yd lace for garter
1yd taffeta (36in wide) for dress
1yd satin ribbon for dress trimming
1yd lace for dress trimming
1 zip (6in) for dress

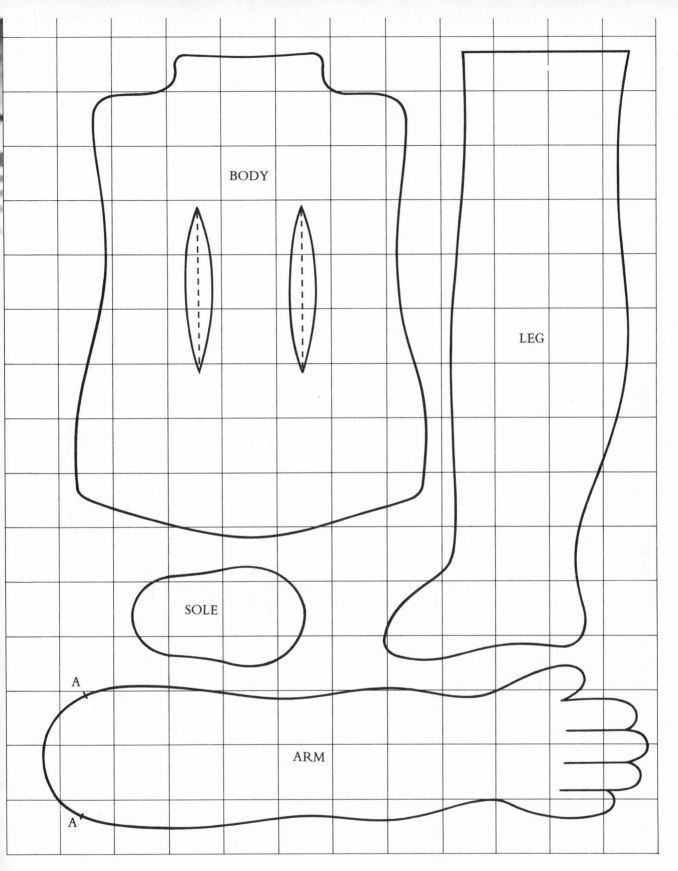

Fig 47 Body pattern D

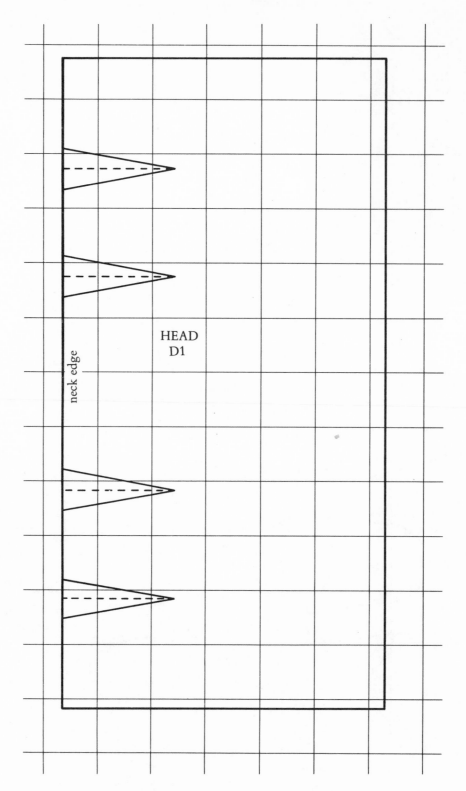

Fig 47a Head pattern D1 (for Emily)

Cut one corset front and two backs in satin, and the same in lawn for the lining. Stitch the side seams and the darts on both satin and lining, and press. With right sides facing, stitch the pieces together down the back edges and around the top, clip the curves, turn through and press. Stitch narrow channels as shown on the pattern through both thicknesses, leaving the bottom edge open. Slip a collar stiffener into each channel. Face the bottom edge of the corset with matching bias binding and trim the top and bottom edges with lace. Fasten the back of the corset with a row of small hooks and eyes placed close together. Attach the petticoat-strap clips (small strips of ribbon with stud fasteners to prevent shoulder straps slipping) to the front lower edges of the corset for suspenders.

Make up the stockings (using the finished top edge of a stocking) and put them onto the doll with the seams at the back of each leg. Clip the suspenders to the top front edge of each stocking.

Cut two knicker pieces in silk, seam each leg, then seam the legs together. Turn hems on each leg and trim them with lace. Turn a casing at the top edge and thread it with elastic to fit the doll's waist. Trim the knickers with tiny ribbon bows on each leg.

To make the garter, cut a 12in length of lace, seam the short ends together and gather it through the centre with doubled shirring elastic to fit the doll's leg just above the knee. Trim it with a tiny ribbon bow.

Cut a bodice front, two bodice backs, two sleeves and two sleeve bands. Cut a piece 8 x 28in for the skirt and 4 x 40in for the skirt frill. Fold the skirt piece in half and cut a shallow V shape at the centre-front to correspond with the bodice. Stitch the bodice pieces together at shoulder and side seams. Stitch a piece of ribbon down the centre-front of the bodice and a piece of lace to either side of the ribbon. Gather the lower edge of the sleeves to fit the sleeve bands and stitch them together. Sew the sleeve seam from the band to the armholes and turn and hem the sleeve bands. Sew lace around the sleeve bands to match the bodice front. Gather the sleeve heads and set the sleeves into the armholes.

Stitch the centre-back seam on the skirt, leaving the top 2½in open. Seam the short edges of the frill together, then fold it in half and press along the length. Gather the top (raw edge) of the frill to fit the lower edge of the skirt and stitch it in place.

Fig 48 Fanny

Stitch ribbon trimming around the skirt above the frill. Gather the top edge of the skirt to fit the bodice and, matching the V at the front, distribute the gathers evenly and stitch it in place. Turn under the back openings in the bodice and the top of the skirt and stitch in the zip. Face the neckline with matching bias binding or a bias-cut strip of dress fabric. Finish the dress with a row of small buttons down the centre of the bodice.

Fanny's bag is made of wide black-satin ribbon. Cut a piece twice as long as the width of the ribbon

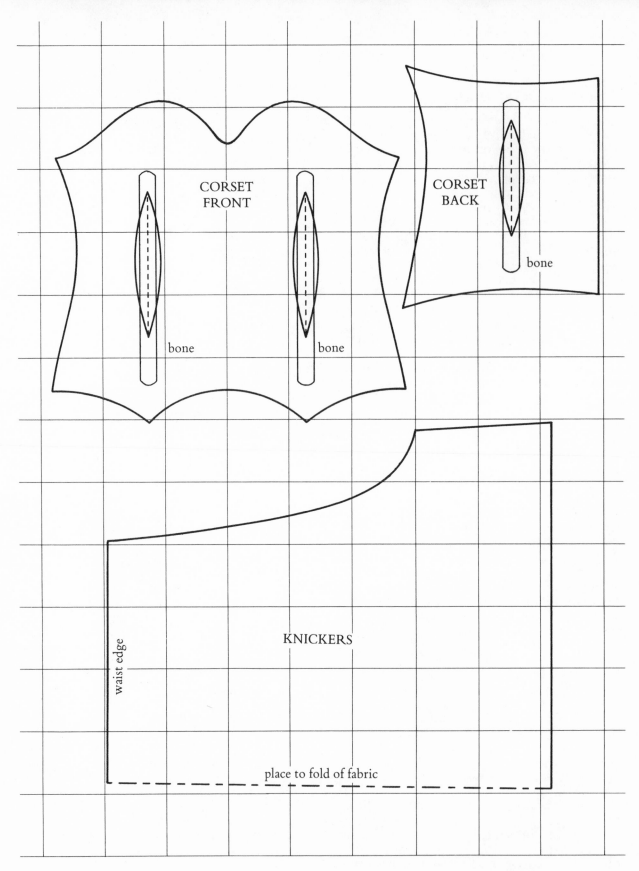

CORSET
FRONT

CORSET
BACK

bone

bone

bone

bone

KNICKERS

waist edge

place to fold of fabric

Fig 49a Fanny's clothes patterns

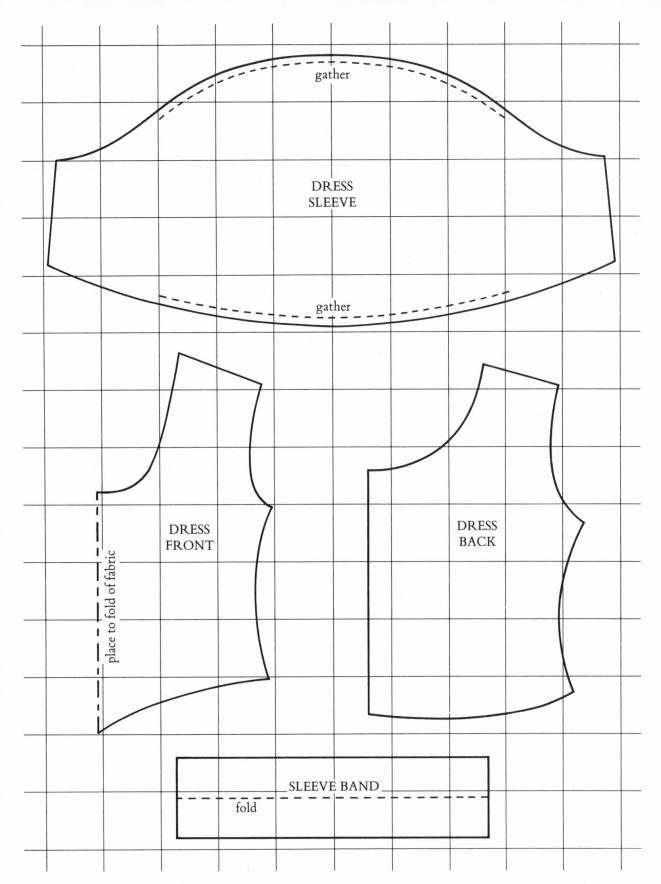

Fig 49b Fanny's clothes patterns

and seam the short ends to make a tube. Oversew the edges together on one side to make a bag and trim with silk-fringed braid (the type sold for trimming lampshades is ideal). Sew a length of cord to either side for a handle. Make a handkerchief in white lawn with a lace edge and, if you have it, add a small perfume bottle.

For the ring, earrings and choker, utilise whatever pieces of costume jewellery are available. Tuck a few artificial flowers or feathers, in a matching colour into the doll's hair.

The mittens which complete Fanny's ensemble are made of wide black lace. Wrap the lace around the doll's arm to gauge the width required, then cut and seam together. Slip the mitten up the doll's arm and catch the lower edges together with a few small stitches between the thumb and fingers.

Fanny wears black-plastic 'Cinderella' shoes, size 4, trimmed with small silver buckles and black-ribbon bows, but if you prefer to make her shoes, use the pattern given for Harriet (Fig 33), which needs to be enlarged slightly using Fanny's sole pattern as a guide. Alternatively, the boots for Emily rag doll (Fig 26) would also be appropriate for Fanny.

8
THE SMALL CHARACTER DOLLS

The three small felt dolls in this chapter are characters, dolls made to represent people. This sort of doll has been made for centuries, perhaps the best known being the crèche figures once found all over Europe. Although they make charming display figures these dolls are equally satisfactory (with minor adaptations for safety's sake) as toys. There is an infinite variety of characters which can be made from the same simple patterns, so a child could have a whole family of these little people to play with.

The first doll, the Pedlar, has a simple skittle-shaped body which can be used to make any doll with long skirts. It is the same size as the costume dolls in the next chapter so is a useful alternative if you do not feel able to model the heads and arms. I used a collection of these skittle dolls to make a nativity display for my son's school; dressing them in long cotton 'nightshirts' for the two shepherds and Joseph, and long silk and velvet robes for the wise men. The baby was a miniature version of the skittle doll and Mary, the only seated figure, was made with legs like the Country Couple.

The pedlar doll seems to be peculiarly British in origin, becoming popular at the end of the eighteenth century. There are fish sellers, stall holders and other artisan dolls from Europe and America — but no pedlars. The dolls are mostly old ladies, but sometimes men or young ladies, equipped with a wealth of miniatures for sale from their trays or baskets. Pedlars were once a common part of rural life, going from house to house with their haberdashery or pots and pans — and sometimes being the complete department store on two feet!

The dolls are always dressed in much the same way: a dark print dress, or blouse and skirt, with a white apron; a black bonnet or hat (the bonnet is more common) and a red cape or shawl. Their goods were usually carried on a large tray suspended from the neck, or sometimes in a basket. Many of these old pedlar dolls have survived in good condition as they were ornaments rather than toys and were often protected by glass domes.

Our Pedlar is a simple felt-stump doll. The stump body enables her to stand firmly upright, balancing the weight of her basket — a doll with legs would need extra support. The doll's body is made of felt, the hair is animal wool (available from chemists' shops) and the eyes are small glass eyes on metal shanks (available from craft shops). If you are unable to obtain eyes small enough, shiny black-headed map pins make a good alternative.

Use only natural fabrics for the Pedlar's clothes, preferably old cotton in a plain subdued colour or a very tiny print. Consider using a faded, coloured-cotton man's handkerchief, which will be the right weight with ready-made hems. Traditionally, the shawl should be red, and the hat black. The basket is made of natural garden raffia, the hat of artificial raffia. Scraps of lace make the collar and cuffs on the dress and a few small artificial flowers trim the hat.

The doll is given legs to make the Country Couple, who could also be an elderly pair with white hair and plumper bodies, or a pair of male and female costume dolls. Stitch the knee joints to make the dolls sit, or insert fine dowelling through the body and down the legs to make them self supporting standing figures. Small stands (from specialist shops) are also available. To make child-sized dolls from these patterns, simply shorten the arms, legs and bodies and slightly reduce the size of the head. It might be amusing to make a wedding party with bride, groom and assorted bridesmaids; a family of parents, grandparents and children, or a schoolroom with teacher and pupils.

The clothes patterns given are basic but used in conjunction with the costume-doll patterns they will make a large variety of styles. It is important to remember the small size of these dolls when choosing fabrics, trimmings and accessories — plain colours with no trimming are preferable to over-large patterns or trimmings.

The success of a character doll depends heavily on using the right style, fabric and colour. However, as the amounts of fabric needed are very small it is easy to experiment, and not costly if the right fabric is expensive. The amounts of fabric needed are small and most should be found amongst your pieces of scrap.

Pedlar
(11in tall)

Difficulty: 2/Colour picture page 52
Body pattern E/Fig 50

12in square of felt for body
scrap of animal wool (approx 8in) for hair
1/4yd fabric (36in wide) for dress
scraps of lace, ribbon etc for trimmings
scrap of white lawn (approx 12 x 7in) for petticoat
scraps of raffia for hat and basket

Using body pattern E cut one front, one back, one base, two arms and one head in felt.

Stitch the bust darts on the body front and, right sides together, stitch the back and front together down the sides from the bottom of the armholes to the base, with a 1/4in seam allowance. Stitch the base circle into the body and turn through to the right side. Cut another base circle in stiff cardboard and push this down into the base of the doll.

Fold the arms along the centre, right sides together, and oversew by hand down the arm and around the hand. Turn through and stuff, pinching the hands to shape as you work. Fill the bottom inch or two of the body with fine sand or rice, packed well down to weight the doll, and then stuff the body up to the underarms. Stuff firmly and mould the waist and bosom as you work. The doll needs a fairly large bosom, not too highly placed (a rather pigeon-chested effect). Oversew one shoulder seam with small tight stitches then attach the arm, oversewing around the armhole. Stuff the chest up to the neck, then oversew the other shoulder seam and sew in the other arm. Ease the shoulders gently downwards so that they slope. Pack stuffing into the neck as firmly as possible.

Seam the two short sides of the head piece and turn through. Gather the bottom edge tightly with strong thread. With your thumbs inside the head, stretch out the gathers then stuff the head very firmly, moulding it to shape as you work. Gather the top edge tightly. (If this thread pulls up easily, there is not enough stuffing in the head — release and add more stuffing.) Fasten off securely. Select the least puckered end of the head to be the chin and, with head seam to centre-back, ladder-stitch the head to the neck.

Cut a length of animal wool about 8in long for the hair, and machine or backstitch a centre parting in matching thread. Pin the hair to the doll's head and backstitch it in place along the parting. Draw the hair to the back of the head, twist it into a coil to make a bun and secure it to the top of the head with a few stitches. Use a spray of hair lacquer if necessary to keep the hair in place.

Gauge the eye positions by pushing black-headed pins into the face. Cut the shanks on the glass eyes (or use map pins) down to one inch and glue the shank and the back of the eye. Press the eyes firmly into the head until the glue is dry, to indent sockets in the face.

Mark the eyebrows and outline the eyes lightly with brown or grey felt pen, and the nose and mouth with pink felt pen. Colour the cheeks with a little powder blusher. This is an old lady so do not use strong colours on the face — try grey or brown (not black) and a soft rose pink. Make-up pencils with sharp points can also be used.

PEDLAR'S CLOTHES

No patterns are given for the Pedlar's clothes, because they are made from rectangles of fabric. The clothes are stitched to the body and are not meant to be removed.

To cover the lower end of the stump body, cut a piece of cotton 7 x 3in and seam the shorter sides together to form a tube. Trim the bottom edge with lace or narrow broderie anglaise and slip it onto the doll. Sew the top to the doll, tucking in the raw edge.

The petticoat is a 12 x 7in piece of cotton lawn or an old white handkerchief. Seam the shorter sides together and turn a small hem along one long edge. Trim the hem with lace or narrow broderie anglaise. Turn in and gather the remaining raw edge. Put the petticoat onto the doll and draw up the gathering to fit just below the waist. Distribute the gathers evenly and slipstitch the top of the petticoat to the body.

The dress sleeves are 4 x 2 1/2in rectangles, seamed along the longer sides to make tubes. Pull these up the doll's arms well onto the shoulder and slipstitch to the body (with the seam to the inside). Turn the raw edges under at the wrists and slipstitch in place. The dress bodice is a piece 7 x 3in. Fold this rectangle in half across the length and width and snip off the corner to make a hole for the neck. Slash open the centre-back. Put the bodice onto the doll, pin it to her front to hold it in place as you slipstitch the back closed, tucking in the raw edges. Pleat the fullness at the shoulders to fit and slipstitch the fold in place. Turn under the raw

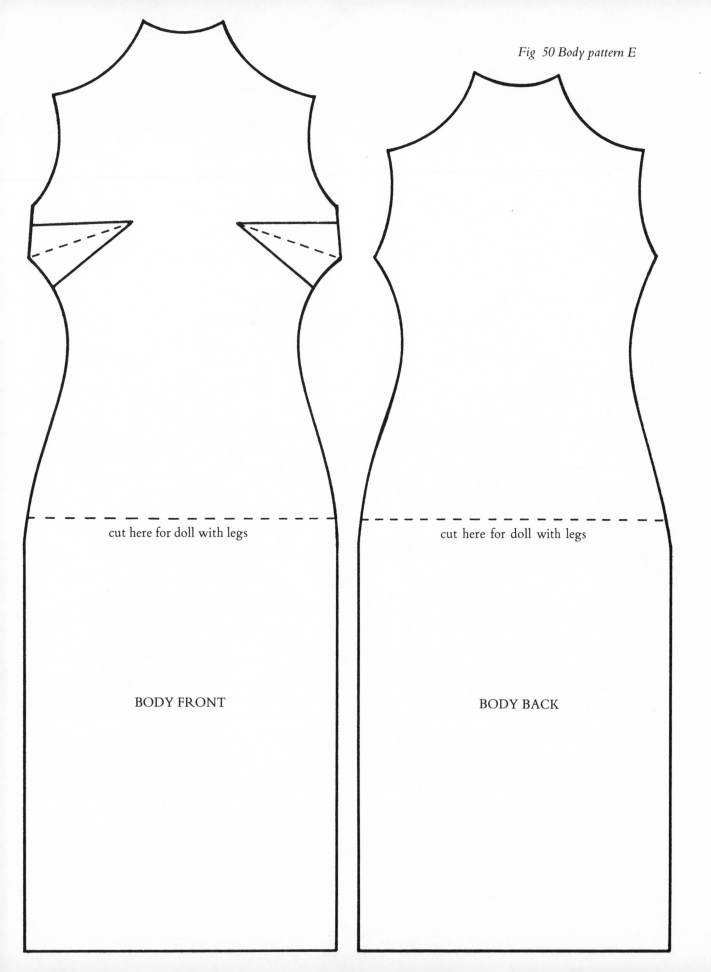

Fig 50 Body pattern E

cut here for doll with legs

cut here for doll with legs

BODY FRONT

BODY BACK

Fig 51 Pedlar

Finish the dress with a little lace trimming at neck and wrists and a narrow-ribbon belt. If you have them, add a tiny belt buckle, a brooch at the throat (a broken earring or bead) and a pair of scissors (a bracelet charm) hung on a fine cord from the waist.

The hat is made from shiny artificial raffia, available in a large range of colours from art and craft shops. Cut and plait together three 6ft strands of raffia. Starting at the centre of the hat crown, coil the plaited raffia and oversew each coil to the next with matching thread and small stitches. Coil until the crown is about 1½in across then work at right-angles for three or four rows to form the side of the hat about ½in deep. Then coil the brim at right-angles to the side. Coil and stitch until the brim is about 3in across, trying the hat on the doll to check that it looks right. When the hat has reached the correct size cut off the extra raffia, tuck the cut end well under the brim and stitch it securely in place. Trim the hat with a piece of narrow ribbon and a few artificial flowers. Use a glass-headed dressmaker's pin as a hatpin to secure the hat to the doll's head.

The Pedlar's basket is made of natural raffia in the same way as the hat. The base of the basket is 2in across and the sides are 1½in deep. The basket handle is a loop of plaited raffia stitched securely inside the basket at either side. The contents of the basket are: lengths of very narrow ribbon and narrow lace wound on cards and tiny buttons tacked to cards; lengths of shirring elastic and fine wool tied in hanks; knitting needles cut from wooden toothpicks; hatpins (glass-headed dressmaker's pins); small brooches (broken earrings) on cards; and cotton reels (½in lengths of fine dowelling) wound with cotton.

I have chosen to fill the basket with haberdashery, because these items are easily found in most homes, but you might prefer to model bread, vegetables or fish in Das clay or bread paste. You could also use many dolls'-house items, such as pots and pans, cups and saucers and books and the really ingenious might try knitting tiny socks and scarves and sewing very small petticoats and drawers.

The shawl is knitted in red 3-ply yarn on size 14 (2mm) needles. Cast on 86 stitches and knit the first row to the end. Continue in garter stitch, decreasing one stitch at the beginning of each row to form a triangle. Alternatively, you could use a triangle of wool fabric.

Drape the shawl around the doll's shoulders, bend the arms into a natural curved position and loop the basket handle over the arm. The Pedlar

edges down both sides and crease sharply with your thumb nail. Slipstitch the sides of the bodice together from underarm to waist and then slipstitch over the shoulders to the tops of the sleeves. For the skirt, cut a piece 13 x 7½in and seam the shorter edges together. Turn a ½in hem along one long edge. Turn under the other raw edge and gather close to the edge. Put the skirt onto the doll and pull up the gathering evenly to fit the waist. Slipstitch the skirt to the bodice.

stands on a small wooden base which is a 3in diameter circle cut from ¼in plywood and stained with dark woodstain. Glue the underside of the doll liberally and press it firmly onto the base. This base is not essential, but it gives a good finish to a doll which is a display doll rather than a toy.

Country Girl
(11in tall)

Difficulty: 3/Colour picture page 52
Body patterns E and E1/Figs 50 and 50a

12in square of felt for body
2 skeins embroidery silk for hair
¼yd cotton (36in wide) for dress
¼yd white lawn (36in wide) for bonnet, apron,
    petticoat and pantalettes
scraps of lace, ribbons and flowers for trimming
scraps of felt, gauze finger bandage, shirring
    elastic etc

Using body pattern E and E1, cut one front and one back body (cutting at the dotted line indicated on the pattern), one head, four legs, two arms and two soles in felt.

Stitch the bust darts on the body front and, right sides together, stitch the back and front together down the sides and along the bottom to form a bag, and turn through. Stitch the legs together in pairs, leaving the top of the leg and the sole of the foot open. Stitch the soles into the feet and turn through. Fold the arms along the centre and oversew by hand along the arm and around the hand and turn through. Stuff the arms, pinching the hands to shape as you stuff. Stuff the legs and, matching the front and back seams, oversew the top edge closed. Stuff the body firmly up to the armholes, working the stuffing well into the hips and moulding a small waist and bosom. Oversew one shoulder seam with small tight stitches, then oversew the top of the arm into the armhole. Push more stuffing in to fill the doll's chest and neck, then seam the other shoulder and attach the other arm in the same way. Make sure that the neck is well-filled and firm. Using strong thread, oversew the legs to the lower edge of the body, working on the back of the doll.

Seam the two short sides of the head piece and turn through. Use strong thread to gather one edge tightly and ease the gathers out evenly. Stuff the head very firmly, moulding it to shape as you stuff, then gather the top edge tightly. Select the least puckered end of the head to be the chin and ladderstitch the head to the neck with the head seam to centre-back.

Fig 52 Country Couple

At the elbow (level with the waist) on each arm, stabstitch right through the arm from side to side to enable the arm to bend. Repeat for the knees.

To make the hair (Fig 53) use two skeins of embroidery silk. Smooth the first skein and backstitch a centre parting in matching thread. Pin this to the doll's head and backstitch it in place along the parting. Cut the second skein at one end to make long strands and put half of these to one side. Cut the remaining strands in half to make bunches. Stitch the bunches to the doll's temples. Twist each bunch into three ringlets, then secure the loose end to the temple. Draw the main part of the hair smoothly over the top of the ringlets to the back of the head and tie it firmly with matching thread into a bunch. Fold this bunch upwards and stitch it to the head. Plait the last length of silk,

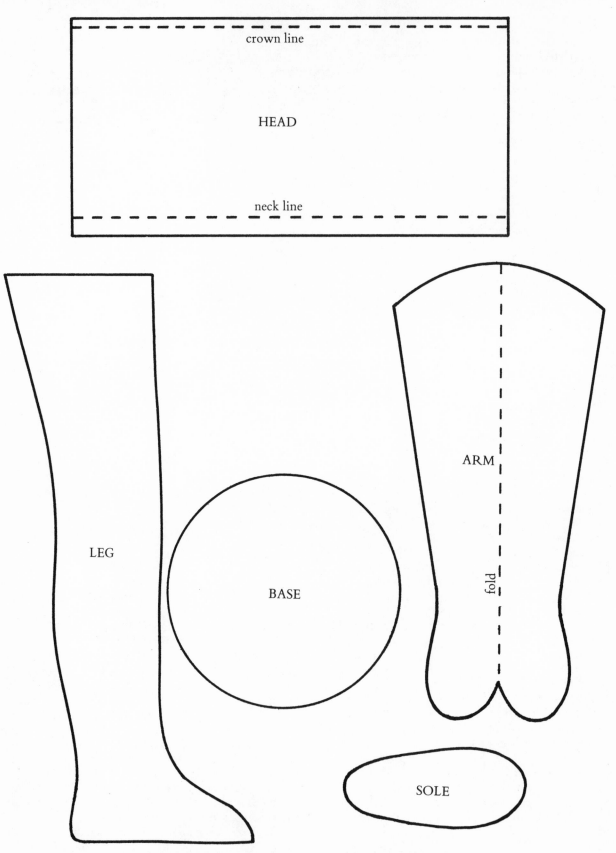

crown line

HEAD

neck line

LEG

BASE

ARM

fold

SOLE

Fig 50a Body pattern E1

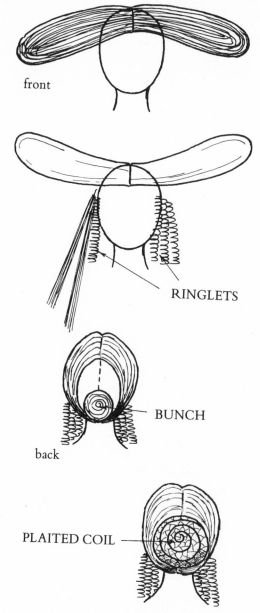

front

RINGLETS

BUNCH

back

PLAITED COIL

Fig 53 Country Girl's hairstyle

then coil and stitch the plait to the back of the head to cover the bald patch.

Gauge the eye positions by pushing black glass-headed dressmaker's pins (or map pins) into the doll's face. Cut the shanks on the glass eyes down to 1in, glue the shank and the back of the eye and push the eyes into the head pressing with your thumbs until the glue is dry to form sockets. If these dolls are made for small children, substitute beads or tiny buttons for the eyes and sew them firmly right through the head before the plaited coil of hair is stitched in place.

Cut a tiny slit under the doll's chin close to the neck seam. Spear a small bead on a darning needle and coat it with glue. Carefully push the bead under the felt into position to make the doll's nose. Pull out the needle and oversew the slit closed. The eyebrows, nostrils, mouth and freckles are drawn in with felt pens or make-up pencils and the cheeks are coloured with a little powder blusher.

COUNTRY GIRL'S CLOTHES

Cut two pantalette pieces in white lawn, seam each leg, and then seam the two legs together. Turn hems on the lower edges and thread shirring elastic above the hems to form a frill. Turn a casing at the waist and thread doubled shirring elastic to fit.

Cut a piece of white lawn 12 x 7in for the petticoat. Seam the short sides together and turn a small hem along one long edge. Trim the hem with lace or narrow broderie anglaise. Turn a small casing at the top edge and thread with doubled shirring elastic to fit the doll's waist.

For the dress, use a small-print or plain-coloured pure cotton (handkerchiefs might be good). Cut one bodice front, two backs, two sleeves and a piece 15 x 7½in for the skirt. Stitch the darts in the bodice front, then stitch the shoulder seams. Gather the heads on the sleeves to fit the armholes. Stitch the sleeves into the armholes. Stitch the sleeve seam from the wrist, through the armhole and down the side seams. Clip the seam if necessary and turn through. Gather the top edge of the skirt evenly to fit the bodice and stitch the waist seam. Stitch the back seam in the skirt to 1in below the waistline. Turn under the open back edges of the bodice and skirt to form facings. Roll a tiny hem around the neckline and trim it with slightly gathered narrow lace. Turn hems at the wrists and gather above them with shirring elastic to form frills. Hem the skirt. Fasten the back of the dress with three very small press-studs.

The sun bonnet is made of lawn with narrow-ribbon ties. Cut two brims and one crown. Stitch the brims together around the curved edge and turn through. Gather the curved edge (AA) of the crown to fit the brim. Distribute the gathers evenly and stitch the brim to the crown. Roll a fine hem on the back edge of the crown, and gather ½in from the hem. Try the bonnet on the doll and pull up the gathers to fit. Stitch ribbon ties at either side of the brim and tie them under the doll's chin.

The apron is a piece of lawn, 5½ x 6in. Hem one short edge and both longer edges. Gather the other short edge. Cut a piece of matching bias binding about 14in long, stitch the gathered edge of the

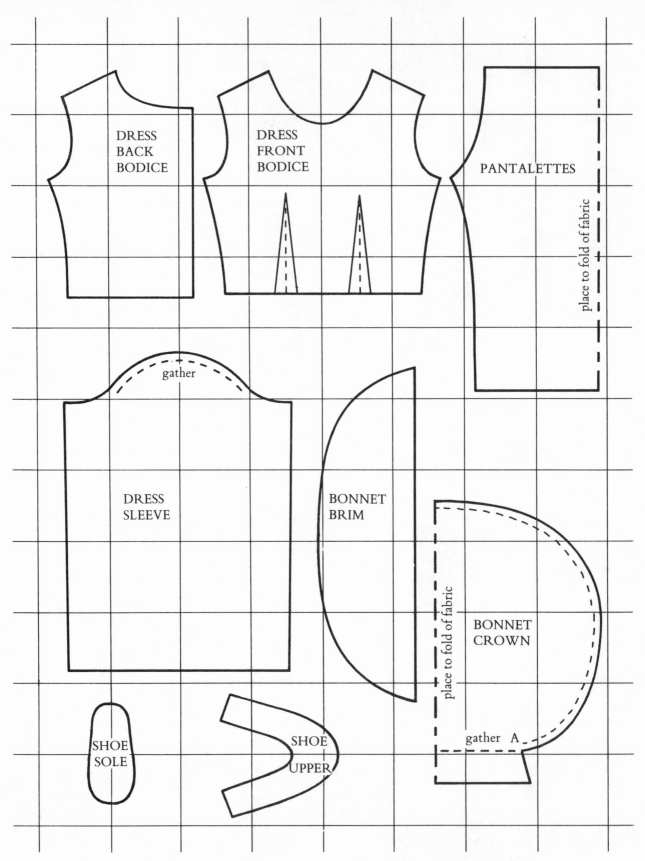

DRESS BACK BODICE

DRESS FRONT BODICE

PANTALETTES

place to fold of fabric

gather

DRESS SLEEVE

BONNET BRIM

place to fold of fabric

BONNET CROWN

gather A

SHOE SOLE

SHOE UPPER

Fig 54 Country Girl's clothes patterns

apron into the centre of the binding, then fold and stitch the binding along its length, enclosing the gathered edge of the apron and forming waistband and ties in one. Neaten the ends of the ties. Cut a 1in square for the pocket. Hem the top edge, fold the three other edges under and stitch the pocket to the apron.

For the stockings, cut two 6in lengths of tubular-gauze finger-bandage. Oversew one cut end on each length and blanketstitch the seam to neaten and strengthen. As this bandage frays easily, it is better to oversew the top of the stocking to the leg, tucking the raw edges inside.

The shoes are made of felt (or soft glove leather). Cut one sole and one upper for each shoe. Oversew the back seam on the upper, right sides together, then blanketstitch the upper to the sole on the outside. Blanketstitch around the top edge of the upper to prevent stretching.

The shawl is crocheted in 3-ply yarn using a size 13 (2¼mm) crochet hook. Make 70 chain.

1st row: into the 10th ch from hook work (1dc, 3ch, 1dc) called 1 picot ⋆ 5ch, miss 3ch, work 1 picot into next ch, repeat from ⋆ to last 4ch, 5ch, miss 3ch, 1dc into last ch, turn

2nd row: ss across first 3ch from hook, ⋆ 5ch, work 1 picot into 3rd ch of first 5ch loop. Repeat from ⋆ to last loop, 5ch, work 1 picot into 3rd ch, 5ch, ss into sixth of the first 9ch, turn. Continue decreasing thus to form a triangle. Knot fringe, using three strands of yarn through each loop.

To complete the Country Girl, catch a small posy of artificial flowers to her hand with a few stitches.

Country Boy ·
(11in tall)

Difficulty: 3/Colour picture page 52
Body pattern E/Figs 50 and 50a

12in square of felt for body
mohair for hair
scrap of lawn or cotton for shirt
scrap of needlecord for trousers
scraps of felt for hat, waistcoat and boots

For the Country Boy cut two backs from pattern E, as you do not need a front body piece with its bust shaping. Otherwise, the method is exactly as for the Country Girl. His beard and hair are made of mohair doll's hair (available from craft shops) glued to the head. Cut a small piece of mohair for the beard, glue the chin (UHU) and press the beard in place. Lay a length of mohair over the head and stitch a side parting to the head with matching

thread. Lift the hair, either side of the parting, glue the head and smooth the hair into place. When the glue is dry trim the hair to shape with small scissors. Apply the beard and hair after the eyes and nose have been inserted. If necessary, spray the hair with lacquer to hold it in place.

COUNTRY BOY'S CLOTHES

For the shirt, use old, fine, faded cotton such as a handkerchief or shirt. Cut two fronts, one back and two sleeves. Stitch the shoulder seams. Gather the sleeve heads slightly, ease into the armholes and stitch in place. Sew the sleeve seams from the wrist, through the armhole and down the side. Cut cuffs to fit around the doll's hand and stitch them to the sleeves, pleating the fullness. Turn back the front edges to make facings and hem the bottom edge. Bind the neck edge with matching fabric or bias binding to form a band collar. Work tiny buttonholes and sew on tiny buttons.

For the trousers use fine needlecord, felt, cotton or wool — again, old fabric is preferable. Cut two trouser pieces, slash an opening on one side and roll a fine hem around the slash. Sew the leg seams, then seam the two pieces together. Cut a waistband to fit the doll's waist with a small overlap and stitch it to the top of the trousers. Turn hems on the trouser legs and fasten the waistband with a small hook and loop. Cut the waistcoat in felt (or glove leather) and oversew the shoulder seams, right sides together. Cut pocket flaps from scrap and stitch them to the waistcoat. Finish the waistcoat by machine-stitching all round the edge and armholes. If you have a tiny buckle, thread it onto a narrow strip of leather to make a belt.

The felt hat is cut in three pieces — brim, crown and side. Cut a circle 3in across for the brim and from its centre cut out a circle 1¾in across. Try this on the doll's head, stretching the hole gently, if necessary, to fit. Cut a strip of felt ½in deep and oversew it to the brim around the edge of the hole, oversewing the short edges together where they meet. Cut a circle 1½in across for the crown and oversew this to the side. Stretch the brim slightly with your fingers to give the hat a battered look.

Make the boots in felt or soft glove leather. Cut one sole and one upper for each boot. Fold the upper, right sides together, and oversew the toecap. Turn through and blanketstitch the upper to the sole on the outside. Use black button thread threaded with a needle for the bootlaces.

To complete the Country Boy, cut a walking stick from a suitable twig and catch it to the hand with a few stitches.

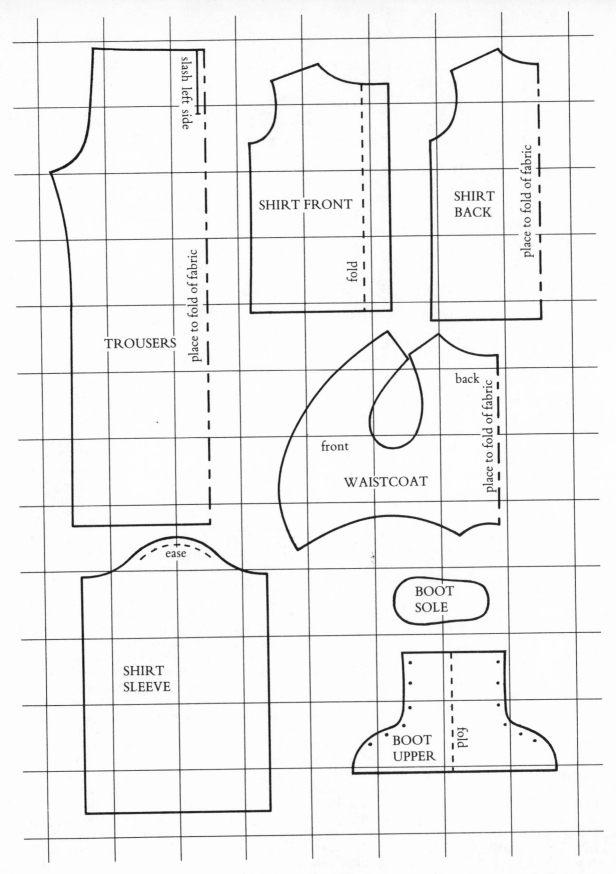

slash left side

place to fold of fabric

TROUSERS

SHIRT FRONT

fold

SHIRT BACK

place to fold of fabric

front

back

place to fold of fabric

WAISTCOAT

ease

SHIRT SLEEVE

BOOT SOLE

BOOT UPPER

fold

Fig 55 Country Boy's clothes patterns

(right, 1–6) The costume dolls: Medieval, Tudor, Georgian, Regency, Victorian and Edwardian, all 11in tall (see Chapter 9)

1

2

3

4

5

6

The Rustic Bench

The bench that the Country Couple are sitting on is made from twigs of approximately ¼in diameter. It is 8in wide and 3in deep. The back is 6in high, the seat 2½in high. Cut a bundle of good straight twigs (hazel is ideal) to allow for waste. Select the thickest twigs for the uprights and assemble the bench following Fig 56 and fixing the joints with UHU glue and panel pins.

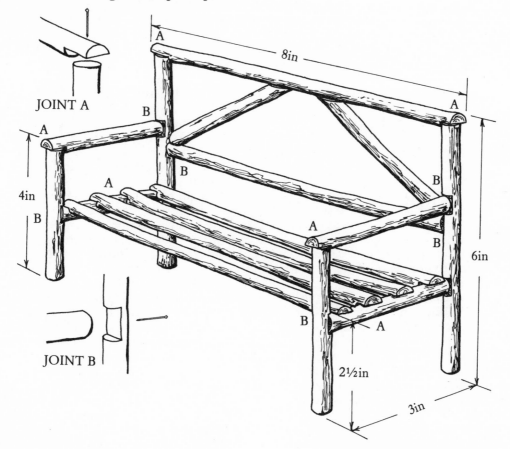

JOINT A

JOINT B

Fig 56 Assembly of rustic bench

(left) *Simple modelled dolls: Sara (seated), 20in tall; Amy, 17in tall; and the Pierrot, 20in tall (see Chapter 10)*

9
THE COSTUME
DOLLS

The dolls in this chapter are designed purely for displaying the six finely-detailed historical costumes. They are simple skittle-shaped stump dolls with heads and lower arms modelled in Das self-hardening clay, dressed in Medieval, Tudor, Georgian, Regency, Victorian and Edwardian costumes. If you feel unable to model the head and arms, use the all-felt stump doll described in Chapter 8 — though self-hardening clay is easy to use and can be effective with even simple modelling.

A costume doll's period should be immediately recognisable. Each period has its fashion clichés; eg a hennin headdress (in fact more fashionable in France than England) is instantly recognisable as medieval, and the Tudor ruff (in fact worn well into the Stuart age) is always associated with Henry VIII and Elizabeth I. I strongly recommend using a good costume reference book as a source of inspiration and a guide to prevailing fashions, and I offer only brief notes here as guidance.

You will see from the pictures that each style has a basic shape which belongs only to that style. The Tudor farthingale and the Victorian crinoline were both hooped petticoats designed to hold skirts out from the body, but the Tudor skirt was cone shaped, the Victorian, bell shaped. The shape of the corset was all-important — witness the long narrow Georgian waist and the bosomy S shape of the Edwardian lady.

The next consideration is the fabric. None of the costumes in this chapter should be made in man-made fabrics but it is sometimes quite impossible to find the 'real thing' which looks right in miniature. I occasionally use nylon lace, for example, because it looks better than the coarser cotton on a particular doll, but as a general rule I recommend cotton lace and silk ribbons rather than nylon or nylon satin.

Colour is also important. For each doll I give notes on the fashionable colours and fabrics — old paintings and costume reference books show how colours were used. In Tudor times for example blue was considered only suitable for servants (it was a cheap dye), velvet was the most popular

fabric and warm-brown and tawny shades or black were the most popular colours. Brown velvet is as 'right' for a Tudor lady's dress as blue cotton would be 'wrong'!

Accessories were an indispensable part of fashion. Fans, muffs, reticules and parasols were a vital part of the lady's toilette. I have noted these where relevant but, as I have tried to avoid repetition, I show only one with each doll, whereas a fashionable lady might carry several. For example, the fan was as popular with Georgian ladies as it was with the Victorians. You must decide these fine points for yourself.

If you plan to display a group of these dolls together it is a good idea to ensure that the colours harmonise. This is not difficult as colours were generally fairly soft until the introduction of aniline dyes in the 1860s when there was a brief fashion for garish colours.

It has been impossible to cut completely authentic patterns to this scale but wherever possible the dolls' clothes are cut like the originals, which means that some require a surprisingly large amount of fabric. The medieval skirt is an almost complete circle cut an inch longer than the doll and the Georgian dress has under-and-over skirts, both of which are very wide. However (not allowing for mistakes), I have found that 1/2yd of fabric (36in wide) has been sufficient for even the most lavish dress.

Although I cannot recommend them, the commercial 11in plastic teenage dolls will fit into clothes made from these patterns. If you do use them, improve their pneumatic modern figures by padding them with strips of terylene wadding to build the correct figure for the period, and paint their features to improve their vacuous expression. Check the skirt length before cutting as these dolls have very long legs.

The final touch to your costume doll is the pose she assumes. These stuffed-felt bodies are very adaptable, and notes are given on the fashionable pose of each period. A few judiciously placed pins will hold any recalcitrant limb in place!

Before you begin, you may find it helpful to read the directions for modelling in Chapter 2. The heads and lower arms may also be wax dipped if you wish — see Chapter 3. Although the patterns for the costumes are fairly simple, because the scale is small they are fiddly to make. Each dollmaker will make the dolls in her own way and there will be slight differences in size due to firmer stuffing, or individual variations in modelling the head and shoulder-plate. Therefore, the patterns should be fitted to the doll. In this small scale ¼in can considerably affect the fit of a garment. I suggest that the pattern pieces are cut in cheap cotton or calico to make a toile, which should be tacked together and fitted to the doll. Minor alterations can then be made and the toile can be unpicked and used as a pattern. This will ensure a good fit, cut down waste and make the sewing less fiddly.

The costumes are sewn onto the dolls and are not meant to be removable — the accessories are glued in place. Dress the doll before applying and styling the hair and paint the features when the doll is completed. Support the doll in a small jar while you are working on it as the base is not fixed until the doll is finished.

Unless you are using a stiff fabric, iron lightweight Vilene to the back of the fabric before cutting the bodice pieces. This reduces fraying, prevents stretching and makes the pieces easier to work with. It also gives the bodice a more rigid, corseted look. Use only the finest needles (I recommend 10 sharps) as tiny stitches are essential. Occasionally, it may be neater to glue a part of the costume rather than sewing it, eg the trimming on the medieval hennin headdress. Apply UHU or a similar all-purpose glue with a toothpick (rather than straight from the tube) for a neat result.

I have chosen to dress this set of lady dolls (except the Victorian doll) in everyday costume of the period, though you may prefer the more elaborate court or evening dress — you could even make a set of splendidly dressed queens 'through the ages'. Use richer fabrics and more lavish trimmings and for crowns, I suggest using the gilt-metal crowns which are sold as stands for decorated eggs.

You could make male consorts for the dolls by adding modelled head and hands to the Country Boy in Chapter 8. Use his clothes as a guide for costumes, with a good reference book as inspiration!

As these dolls are not intended for beginners I have made the instructions brief and to the point. The experienced dollmaker will have her own methods and may prefer to substitute them for some of mine.

Basic Costume Doll
(11in tall)
Difficulty: 5/Colour picture page 101
Body pattern F/Fig 57

To make the basic costume doll you will need a 12in square of felt and a small packet of self-hardening modelling clay (I recommend Das).

Using body pattern F, cut two bodies, two arms and a base in felt. Seam the back and front body pieces together from the underarm to the base with a ¼in seam allowance, leaving the bottom edge open. Stitch the base circle into the body and turn through to the right side. Cut another base circle in stiff cardboard and push this down the body into the base of the doll. Fold the arm pieces down their length, seam them together to form tubes (leaving the top and bottom ends open) and turn through.

Fill the bottom inch or two of the body with fine sand or rice packed well down. Stuff the body up to the underarms, moulding a small bosom.

Oversew one shoulder seam with a few small tight stitches. Oversew the curved top end of the arm into the armhole. Push in more stuffing to fill the top of the chest, then oversew the other shoulder and sew in the other arm. Make sure the body is stuffed firmly to the top then oversew closed with small stitches. Push stuffing up into the arms, ensuring that the top of the arm hangs naturally from the shoulder and the arms move freely.

Take sufficient clay to roll into an egg shape approximately 1½in long for the doll's head. The realistic proportions of this doll require that the head should be about one seventh of the length of the doll. Make a small roll of clay for the neck and join it to the head. Form the nose and depress the eye sockets slightly. Make sure that the head is symmetrical and smooth the surface with water. Roll out a piece of clay about ⅛in thick and cut a rectangle or square for the shoulder-plate. The size of the shoulder-plate will vary slightly with each costume as a low neckline requires a deeper plate, but the width should be the same as the doll's shoulders. From the centre of the shoulder-plate cut out a small circle to fit the lower end of the neck. Lay the shoulder-plate over the doll's shoulders to form the required shape and leave it in place until it begins to dry. When both the head and shoulder-plate are dry enough to handle use a little clay and slip to fix the neck into the hole in the shoulder-plate. Allow to dry thoroughly.

To model the lower arms roll two pieces of clay approximately 2½in long. Form one end of each roll into a shallow spoon shape for the hands and pinch above the hands to narrow the arm into wrists. Leave to dry thoroughly.

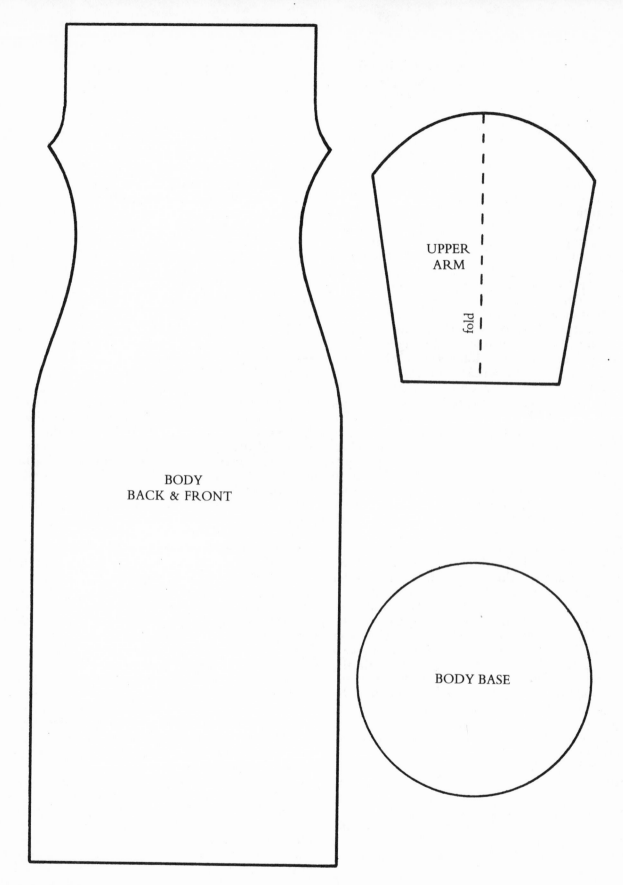

UPPER
ARM

fold

BODY
BACK & FRONT

BODY BASE

Fig 57 Body pattern F

When the clay parts are dry, sand them with medium-grade abrasive paper, smooth them with very fine abrasive paper and paint them flesh colour. Paint the features with a very fine good-quality brush. Glue the underside of the shoulder-plate and press it firmly down onto the body, holding it in place until the glue is dry. Glue the top end of the lower arms and push them into the felt upper arms, holding them in place until the glue is dry and ensuring that the hands are naturally positioned. On this doll, the join is at the elbow. If you are making a doll wearing a short-sleeved costume, cut the felt upper arm shorter and model the clay lower arm longer.

For the base cut a circle of ¼in plywood 3in across, paint or stain and polish it, but do not glue the figure to the base until the costume is completed.

Medieval Doll
(c1460)

This was the era of fabulous headdresses, and the gothic elongated line was the fashion. Gowns were low cut, shoulders sloping and bosoms small and high, with a high waistline and long trailing skirts. Ladies were required to be fragile butterflies, beautiful and delicate, with a high forehead (the eyebrows and hairline were plucked) and a long neck.

Fabrics were soft and rich. Velvet was very popular, also silk, damask, brocade and fine woollens. Colours varied from pastels to rich jewel colours, plain or with all-over patterns, especially large stylised floral motifs. Fur was the main trimming for collars, cuffs and linings.

Fashionable accessories included large, jewelled collars with pendants, rings and brooches, jewelled cauls and stiff wide belts with jewelled clasps. Purses and pomanders hung from the belt and the latter, also carried in the hand, were a practical as well as decorative ornament. The pose was a rather affected backward tilt from the hips, with the hands displayed and holding up the long skirts.

The Medieval doll wears a dark-pink panné velvet gown lined with silk, with a high waistline, long full skirts and very wide sleeves. The low V neckline is trimmed with a collar of gold metallic lace and filled with a plastron of lining silk. The wide belt is of stiffened satin ribbon. The undergown is black silk, with skirts less full than the gown and long tight sleeves. The hennin headdress is pink silk over a cardboard foundation, trimmed with black-and-gold braid and pearls, with a pink-gauze veil. The pendant necklace is an 'opal' on a gilt chain.

Fig 58 Medieval doll

MEDIEVAL COSTUME

½yd velvet (36in wide) for gown
½yd silk (36in wide) for lining
½yd black silk (36in wide) for undergown
scraps of gilt lace, braid, ribbon etc for trimming

Use the pattern (Fig 59b), reducing the fullness, to cut an underskirt in black fabric. Seam the centre-

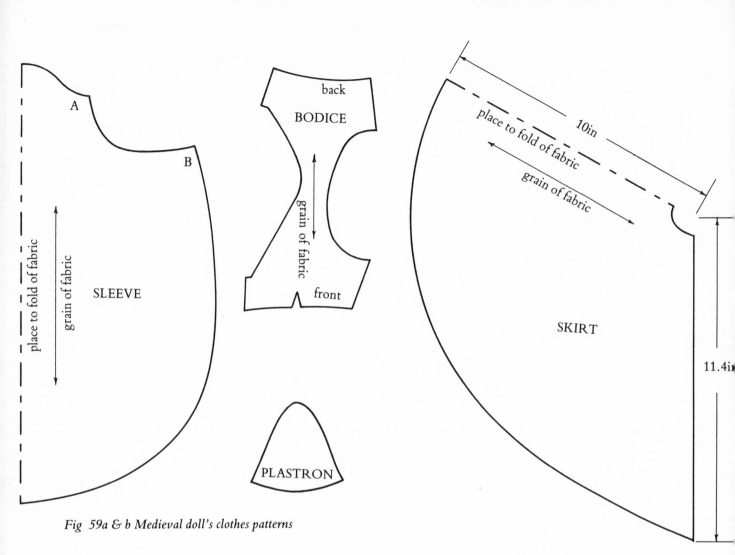

Labels in figure:
A
B
back
BODICE
front
grain of fabric
SLEEVE
place to fold of fabric
grain of fabric
PLASTRON
place to fold of fabric
grain of fabric
10in
SKIRT
11.4in

Fig 59a & b Medieval doll's clothes patterns

back, leaving the top inch or two open, and turn up the hem. Put onto the doll, close the opening and slipstitch to the body above the natural waistline. Cut pieces of the same fabric to make tubes to fit the doll's lower arms. Neaten the lower edges, slip onto the doll's arms and secure the top edges.

Cut the skirt and a skirt lining and stitch centre-back seams leaving the top inch or two open. With right sides together, stitch the lining to the skirt around the hem, turn through and press. Put the skirt onto the doll, slipstitching to the body just below the bosom and close the back opening. Cut two bodice pieces in stiffened fabric, sew the front bust darts and stitch together at centre-front and side seams. Cut the sleeves and sleeve linings and sew the curved underarm seams AB. With right sides together, sew the linings to the sleeves around the lower edge, turn through and press. Set the sleeves into the armholes. Turn up the lower

edge of the bodice, tack and press. Put the bodice onto the doll, turn under the raw edges, slipstitch the back opening closed, and slipstitch the bodice to the skirt.

Make up the plastron in stiffened fabric and tuck it inside the bodice front, securing it at each side. Trim the neckline with metallic gold lace to cover the raw edge. Fur would be equally appropriate, but I have not found a fur or fur substitute which looks realistic in this scale. Cut a piece of stiffened ribbon for the belt and stitch it to the high waistline.

To make the hennin, use a semi-circle of thin cardboard (a postcard is ideal) and roll it in to a cone on the doll's head. When the card shape is correct use it as a pattern to make the fabric covering and as stiffening inside the fabric covering. Trim the front edge of the hennin with braid and glue it to the doll's head (this doll has no visible hair). The veil is a square or rectangle of gauze, cut carefully on the bias of the fabric to minimise fraying, draped over the hennin and secured with a little glue.

To pose the doll, loop the skirts over one arm, secure, if necessary, with pins and arrange the sleeves and skirts in attractive folds. Glue the doll to the base.

Tudor Doll
(c1540)

The Tudor fashion was stiff and formal, with square shoulders, large sleeves and wide cone-shaped skirts. The body shape was distorted by canvas, whalebone and metal corsets which flattened the bosom and shaped a small waist. The skirts were supported by a canvas farthingale with metal hoops (the Spanish farthingale had been introduced into England by Catherine of Aragon). The overall effect was rich and heavy with lavish trimming. The ruff, in fact a slightly later fashion, developed out of the neck frill on the chemise.

Fabrics were heavy velvet, brocade, satin and damask, cut (Genoese) velvet being most popular. Colours were mostly warm reds and browns — tawny/gold and black was very popular. Patterns were large, formal all-over designs, and the richest fabrics were used for petticoats.

The most important and expensive accessory was the girdle. A lavish display of wealth was expected and ladies wore much jewellery; gold chains and pearl ropes, crucifixes and pendants, and jewels on gowns. The fashionable headdress was the French hood (popularised by Anne Boleyn), worn with a black velvet veil.

The pose of the period, to a large extent governed by the merciless corset, was upright, stiff and formal. The ruff forced the chin up, the corset kept the back straight and the large sleeves held the shoulders back and square. The hands were usually loosely clasped at the waist. The Tudor doll wears a brown-velvet gown with a square neckline, large turned-back sleeves and an open skirt. The petticoat and false undersleeves are heavy pink-and-gold brocade. The ruff and wrist frills are white lace. The pearl-trimmed French hood is black and gold, with a black velvet veil. Around the doll's neck are gilt chains, a pearl rope and a ruby pendant. The girdle is a heavy gilt chain with a small crucifix at one end and a pomander at the other.

TUDOR COSTUME

½yd velvet (36in wide) for gown
½yd silk (36in wide) for lining

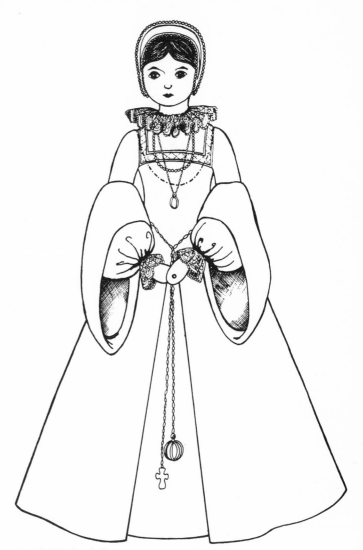

Fig 60 Tudor doll

½yd brocade (36in wide) for petticoat and
*   undersleeves*
scraps of braid, ribbon and jewellery for trimmings
scrap of black velvet for veil
scraps of lace for ruffs

Use the skirt pattern (Fig 61a) as a guide to cut a farthingale in stiff, woven interfacing. Seam the back, turn up the hem, and run a gathering thread around the waist. Put the farthingale onto the doll and pull it up to fit, concentrating the gathers at the back. Slipstitch to the doll's body. Repeat this in petticoat fabric, ensuring that the hemline just touches the floor. The skirt pattern is longer at the centre-back and needs to be trimmed for the farthingale and petticoat.

Cut the skirt and lining from the pattern. With

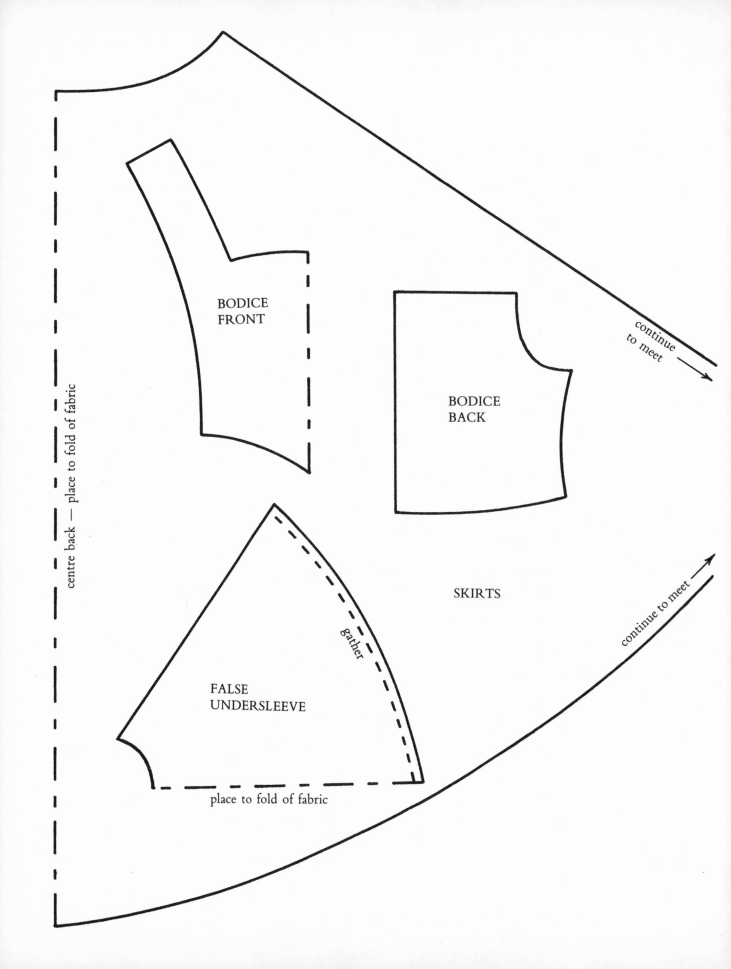

BODICE
FRONT

centre back — place to fold of fabric

BODICE
BACK

continue
to meet

SKIRTS

gather

FALSE
UNDERSLEEVE

continue to meet

place to fold of fabric

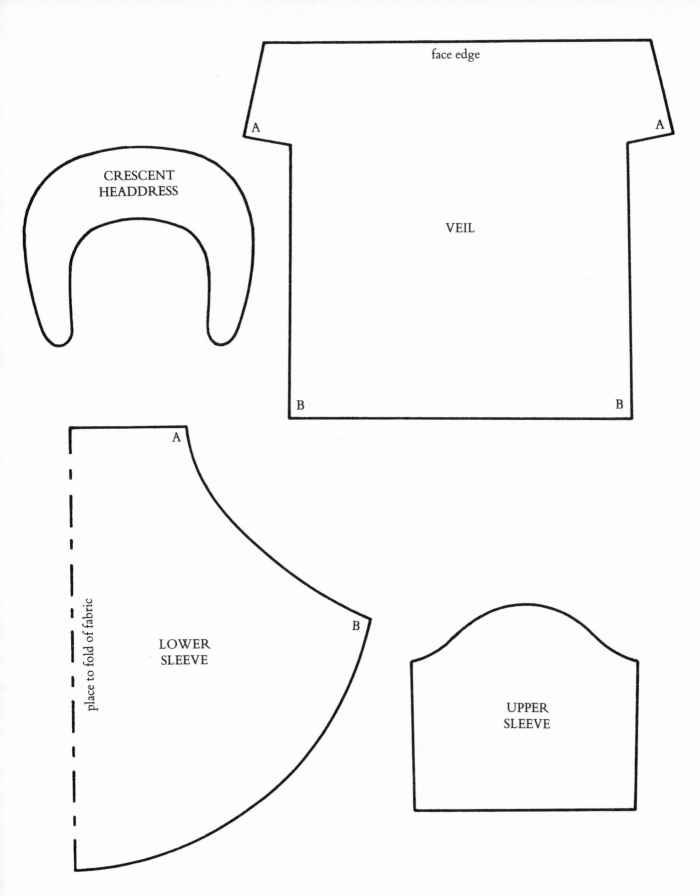

face edge

A A

CRESCENT
HEADDRESS

VEIL

B B

A

place to fold of fabric

LOWER
SLEEVE

B

UPPER
SLEEVE

Fig 61a & b Tudor doll's clothes patterns

right sides facing, sew the lining to the skirt down the centre-fronts and around the bottom edge, turn through and press. Put the skirt onto the doll, tack the centre-front top edges together and gather any fullness in the waist to the back. Slipstitch to the doll's body just above the natural waistline.

Cut the bodice front and backs and the upper sleeves in stiffened fabric. Sew the bodice shoulder and side seams. Stitch the sleeve seams and set the sleeves into the armholes. Turn under the lower edge of the bodice, tack and press. Put the bodice onto the doll, turn under the raw back edges and slipstitch the back opening closed. Slipstitch the waistline to the skirt, ensuring that the V at the front waist is in the centre.

Cut the lower sleeves and linings. Stitch the curved seams AB and, with right sides facing, stitch the lining to the sleeve around the lower edge. Turn through and press. Turn inside-out and pull the lower sleeve, bottom edge first, up the doll's arm and over the upper sleeve. Check that the seams match and stitch both sleeves together about ¼in from the edge. Leave the lower sleeve turned up while you fit the false undersleeves. Stitch the seams in the undersleeves and neaten the wrist edges. Gather the top edge, put onto the doll and pull up the gathers to fit. Tuck the raw edges under the upper sleeves and slipstitch. Pull down the lower sleeves over the false undersleeves.

Stitch braid trimming around the neckline, covering the raw edge and mitring the corners back and front. Further trimming can be applied to the sleeves and the skirt fronts.

To make the ruff, cut a 12in length of 1in wide lace (preferably starched). Neaten the short ends and gather one long edge, to fit tightly round the doll's neck. Make similar frills in narrow lace for the wrists and slipstitch to the undersleeves.

Use black fabric for the veil. Seam together at AB and turn through. Press flat with the seam to the centre. Make a fine hem around the bottom edge (BB), turn under the face edge and tack. To make the crescent headdress use fabric-covered cardboard or braid trimmed with small pearls — the pattern should be used as a guide to the shape, the size will depend on individual modelling. The headdress should frame the face and tilt slightly backwards. The doll's embroidery-silk hair is drawn smoothly back from a centre parting — only the front shows under the headdress. Glue the hair, veil and crescent to the doll's head. For the jewellery use a gilt chain or cord, tiny pearls and stones as available. Pose the doll as shown in the photograph, with the lower sleeves in folds and the hands glued together. Glue the doll to its base.

Georgian Doll
(c1780)

The Georgian fashion was the milkmaid or shepherdess look, inspired by Marie Antoinette playing milkmaid at Le Petit Trianon and popularised by Dresden shepherdesses.

The polonaise gown had a close-fitting bodice with full skirts and elbow-length sleeves. The overskirt was looped up at the back to show the matching petticoat. The general effect was simple, pretty and 'countrified'. Corsets were still worn to give a small waist, but they were not too restrictive. A small pad was tied on at the back to push the skirts out. Dresses of this period were often ankle length (as short as they had ever been).

The most popular fabrics were silks, cottons and chintzes in pastel pinks, blues, yellow and lavender, with delicate, floral sprigs and stripes. Fichus and caps were made of white lawn and muslin and trimmings were lace and ribbons.

Very little jewellery was worn, though lockets, brooches and pearls were popular; fashionable ladies wore artificial flowers, ribbons, bows and a throat ribbon. Accessories such as muffs, gloves, fans and long walking canes, plus cosmetics — especially black face patches — were very popular. The pose was fairly natural, simple and elegant, displaying the costume accessories to advantage.

The Georgian doll's polonaise gown of flower sprigged muslin has a low neckline filled by a lace frill, a deep pointed waist and elbow-length sleeves with frills. The bodice front has an échelle of ribbon bows and the same lilac ribbon trims the looped overskirt and frilled underskirt. Under the gown she wears white-lawn petticoats. Her large mob cap of white lawn, trimmed with lace and lilac ribbons is worn over white 'powdered' hair.

GEORGIAN COSTUME

½yd lightweight fabric (36in wide) for gown and underskirt
2yd narrow ribbon for trimming
scraps of white lawn and lace for petticoat and mob cap
scraps of lace and flowers for trimming

Make a small, stuffed pad (about 1in square) and sew the top edge to the doll at the back just below the waist. Make a full lawn petticoat with lace trimming at the hem, and gather it to fit the doll's waist, concentrating the fullness to the sides and back.

Cut two pieces, approximately 7 x 18in, for the skirts. Seam the centre-back on the underskirt, and stitch a frill approximately 1½in deep to the lower edge. The length of the frill will depend on the thickness of the fabric used, but 1½ times the width of the skirt is usually adequate. Hem the lower edge and gather the top to fit the doll's waist. Slipstitch to the doll, concentrating the fullness to the sides and back.

Hem the overskirt along both short edges and one long edge. Gather the raw top edge. Tack the front top edges together and slipstitch the overskirt to the doll's waist, concentrating the fullness to the sides and back. Make the 'polonaise' on the back of the skirt with rows of gathering at either side, pulled up to give the looped effect.

Cut the bodice front and backs and the sleeves in stiffened fabric. Stitch the shoulder and side seams. Sew the sleeve seams. Roll a fine hem around the outside edge of the sleeve ruffles and sew them to the sleeves, the wider side to the back. Set the sleeves into the armholes. Turn up the lower edge of the bodice, tack and press. Put the bodice onto the doll over the skirt, tuck in the raw edges and slipstitch the back closed. Slipstitch the bodice to the overskirt, leaving the V at the front unstitched.

Trim the neckline with lace to cover the raw edge and gather frills of lace to stitch inside the sleeve ruffles. Stitch ribbon trimming to the bodice, sleeves and skirts and make an échelle (row of bows) down the front of the bodice. Sew bows above the gathering on the back of the skirt, and to the sleeves above the ruffles. Make the ribbon choker trimmed with a tiny flower and tuck a few more flowers into the bosom of the gown.

Use fine lawn or organdie for the cap. Hem and trim the outside edge with lace. Gather along the line indicated on the pattern to fit the doll's head. The animal-wool hair is drawn away from the face and arranged in rolls on the top of the head. Tie ribbon round the gathers on the cap, finishing in a bow at the front.

Thread tiny pearl beads into a bracelet and whittle a walking stick from a length of fine dowelling (or use a paintbrush handle). Glue the doll to its base, and the walking stick to the hand and the base.

Regency Doll
(c1810)

The French Revolution (1789–1794) led to a revolution in costume, bringing simple, pseudo-classical styles. White muslin became universal (cleanliness had become fashionable!). The regency dress had a high waistline, small bodice, puffed sleeves and long slim skirts, and was worn without corsets and with the minimum of petticoats. Extremists dampened the skirts to make them cling to the body. Shawls, small jackets and

Fig 62 Georgian doll

high waisted coats made the fashion possible in the English climate. A youthful figure with a small bosom was the ideal.

Though white muslin with cherry-red trimmings was all the rage, other colours and fabrics were also worn, eg lightweight silks, cottons, poplin and taffeta, with small woven patterns of stripes or spots. Hems were decorated with ruffles and embroidery, the Greek key motif or a flower trail being typical.

Accessories included the reticule (handbag), indispensable because of the lack of pockets; trimmed bonnets, shawls, scarves, long gloves (for short sleeves) and fans. Little jewellery was worn, except cameos, lockets, earrings and throat ribbons. Unrestricted by corsets, the pose was natural.

113

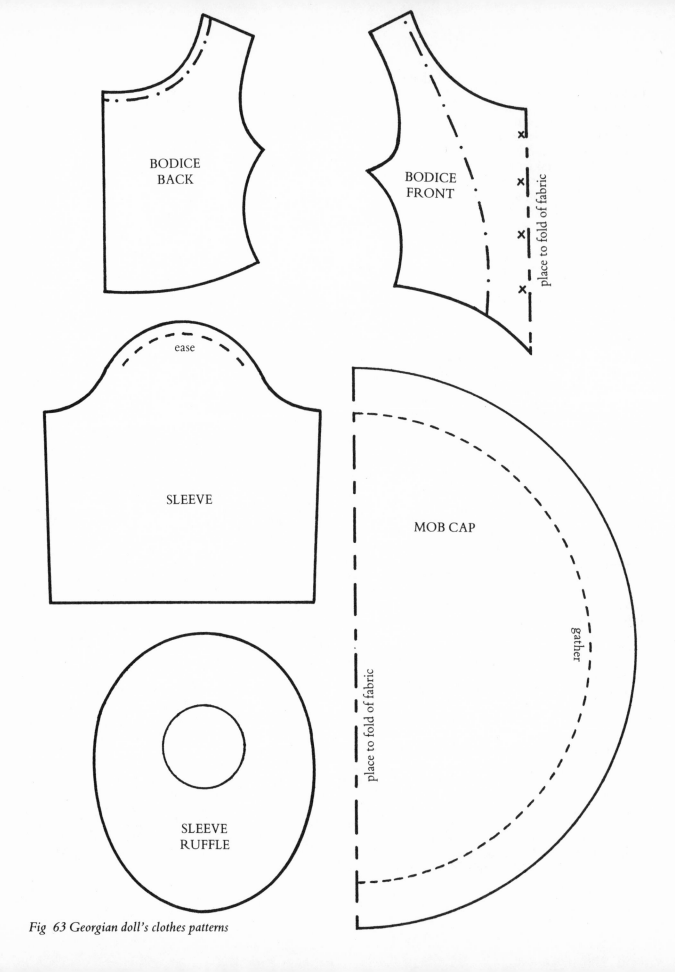

Fig 63 Georgian doll's clothes patterns

Fig 64 Regency doll

back but smooth at the front. The dress is worn over a white-lawn, lace-trimmed petticoat. The straw bonnet is trimmed with pink flowers and ribbons. The costume is completed by a long ribbon sash at the waist and a small white reticule.

REGENCY COSTUME

¼yd lightweight fabric (36in wide) for dress
1yd narrow lace and ribbon for trimming
hat-straw or plaited raffia for bonnet
flowers for trimming
scrap of lace for reticule
scrap of lawn for petticoat

Make a narrow lawn petticoat with lace trimming at the hem. Gather it to fit the doll just above the natural waistline, concentrating the fullness to the back.

Cut the bodice front and backs and the lower sleeves in stiffened fabric, the upper sleeves and skirt in unstiffened fabric. The dress skirt is a rectangle, frilled at the hem (or not as you prefer), approximately 8 x 12in. Sew the centre-back seam in the skirt, adding the frill if required, and hem the lower edge. Gather the top edge and slipstitch to the doll below the bosom, concentrating the fullness to the sides and back.

Sew the darts in the front bodice and sew the shoulder and side seams. Clip the neck edge, turn to the inside and catch down. Alternatively, face the neckline with matching bias binding or fabric. Gather the lower edges of the upper sleeves to fit the lower sleeves. Stitch the sleeve seams, gather the tops of the upper sleeves and set into the armholes. Neaten the wrist edges. Turn up the lower edge of the bodice, tack and press. Put the bodice onto the doll, turn in the raw back edges and slipstitch closed. Slipstitch the bodice to the skirt. Trim the bodice, sleeves and hem with lace and/or ribbon, and use tiny pearl beads as buttons on the bodice front. Tie a narrow ribbon sash around the high waistline.

To make the bonnet use natural hat-straw, plaited raffia or stiffened fabric. Stitch the brim to the back piece and trim with ribbon and flowers. Sew ribbons to either side of the brim and tie them under the doll's chin.

The hair (I have used mohair) has a centre-parting, soft waves at either side of the face and a small bun on the back of the head. The reticule is cotton-lace trimming lined with a scrap of fabric, with a chain-stitched loop for a handle. Insert a small button or bead to give weight and shape to the reticule. Glue the hands together over the handle of the bag, and glue the doll to the base.

The Regency doll wears a pale-pink muslin dress, trimmed with darker-pink silk ribbons and white lace. The small bodice has a scooped neckline and long sleeves with puffed tops. The skirts are long, gathered to the waist at sides and

115

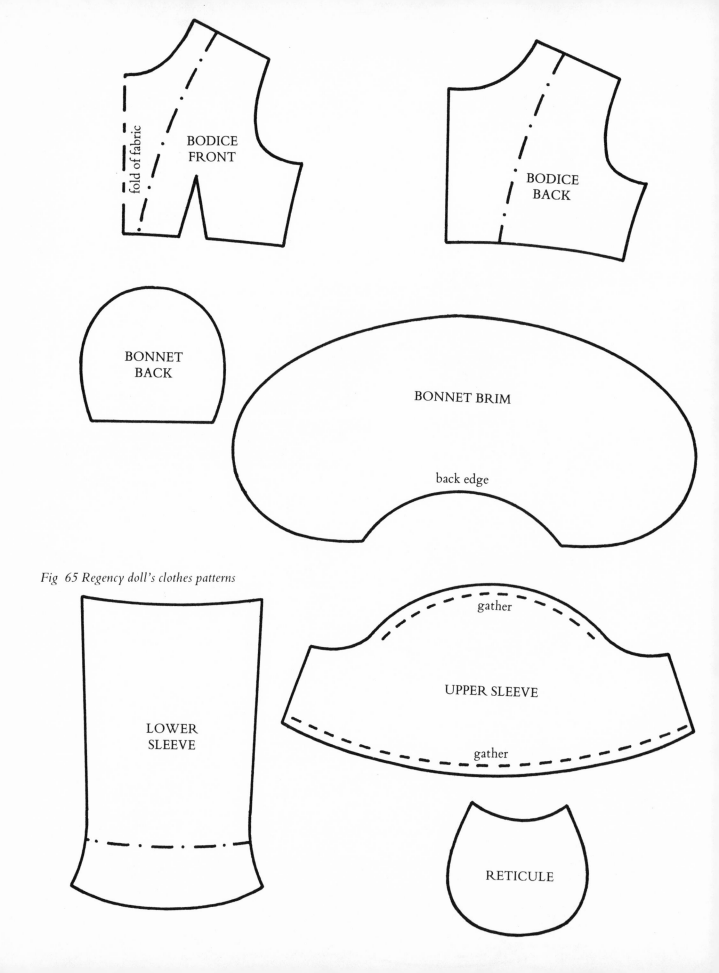

BODICE FRONT

fold of fabric

BODICE BACK

BONNET BACK

BONNET BRIM

back edge

Fig 65 Regency doll's clothes patterns

LOWER SLEEVE

gather

UPPER SLEEVE

gather

RETICULE

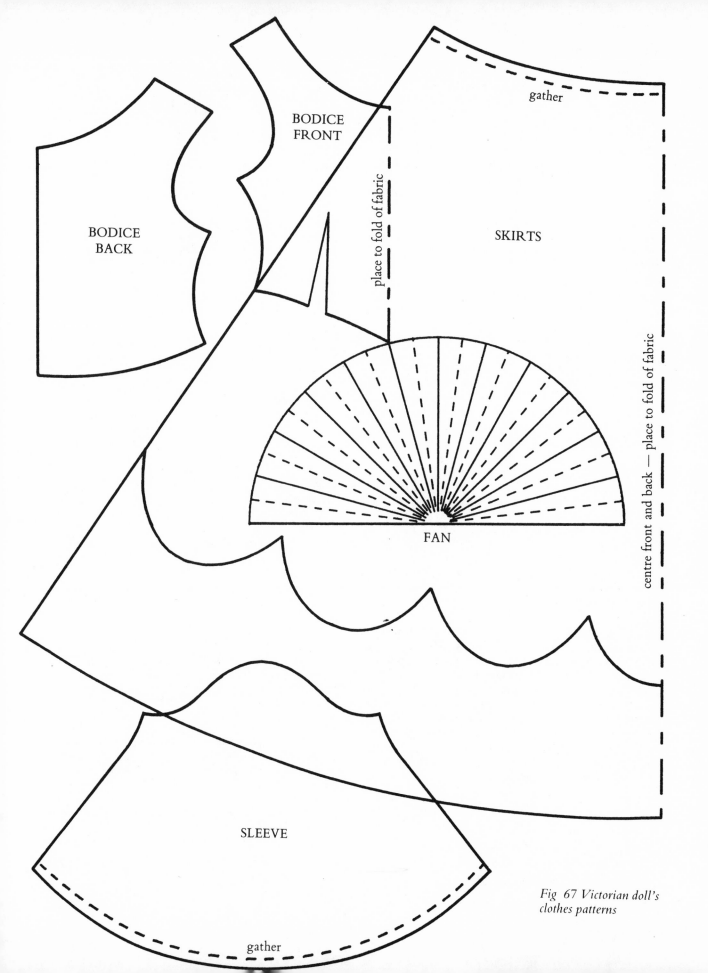

BODICE
FRONT

BODICE
BACK

SKIRTS

gather

place to fold of fabric

centre front and back — place to fold of fabric

FAN

SLEEVE

gather

*Fig 67 Victorian doll's
clothes patterns*

Victorian Doll
(c1840)

The age of the crinoline was beginning, although at this period it had not reached the absurd proportions of the 1860s. Tight corseting was back in fashion, a small waist being the main objective, though in view of the large dinners and families of the time an 18in waist was more often myth than fact, except for young girls. The fashion was demure and elegant. Bell-shaped skirts, sloping shoulders, fairly full sleeves and the small waist created the required womanly shape. Necklines were modestly high for daytime wear and low with a lace berthe collar for evening. Long hair was worn in plaited coils or ringlets with a centre parting. There was an enormous variety of fabrics — wool, cotton, poplin, silk, satin and taffeta — but lighter fabrics were preferred for the very full skirts. Horizontal patterns specially woven for flounces were very fashionable. Pastel colours, especially white were favoured for evening wear.

Large shawls, reticules, parasols, muffs and chatelaines were fashionable accessories, and small bouquets and fans were an indispensable part of evening dress. Caps were worn indoors and under bonnets out-of-doors, but evening headdresses usually consisted of flowers, ribbons, lace or feathers. There was a vogue for roses and rosebuds (real and artificial) and for a time everything was trimmed with them. Jewellery was fairly simple brooches, cameos, lockets and earrings (it was considered bad taste to wear much except for formal occasions).

The pose was fairly natural, though restrained by corset and crinoline. A straight back was the ideal and the hands were held slightly away from the body.

The Victorian doll is wearing an evening dress of white satin and lace, with a scalloped lace ruffle above the hem, a pointed waistline and a scooped neckline with berthe collar. It is decorated with ribbon roses, lace frills and silk-ribbon bows.

Her hair is centre-parted into plaits, coiled around her head and decorated with a white feather plume. She wears a pearl necklace and earrings and a gold bracelet, and carries a white-lace fan. Under the gown she wears a lawn petticoat over a stiff crinoline petticoat.

VICTORIAN COSTUME

¼yd fine fabric (36in wide) for dress
1½yd lace (½in wide) for trimming
1yd narrow ribbon for trimmings
scrap of white lawn for petticoat

Fig 66 Victorian doll

scraps of lace, feather, jewellery etc.
scrap of woven interfacing for crinoline

Use the skirt pattern (slightly less full) to cut a crinoline petticoat in stiff woven interfacing. Seam the two sides, turn up the hem, gather the top edge evenly to fit the doll slightly below the natural waistline, and slipstitch to the doll. Make a lawn petticoat with a lace frill at the hem in the same way. Cut the dress skirt, stitch the side seams and turn up the hem. If using a lace overskirt, tack the two layers together at the waist. Gather the waist

(right) Sophy and Oliver, both 21in tall, with baby Emma, 11in tall (see Chapters 11 and 12)

evenly to fit the doll at the natural waistline and slipstitch to the doll.

Cut the bodice front and backs in stiffened fabric. Stitch the darts and the shoulder and side seams. Sew the sleeve seams, gather the sleeve heads and ease into the armholes. Hem the sleeves and sew on lace trimming. Turn up the lower edge of the bodice, tack and press. Put the bodice onto the doll over the skirts, turn in the raw edges and slipstitch the back opening closed. Slipstitch the bodice to the skirt at the waistline. Gather the sleeves just above the lace frill and pull up to the doll's arms. Sew a gathered-lace frill (or two) to the neckline to cover the raw edge. You might also sew a gathered lace frill to the waistline to form a peplum. Sew gathered lace to the skirt on the line indicated on the pattern to form the scalloped frill. Tie ribbon bows on the sleeves to cover the gathering and a ribbon sash round the waistline.

To make the ribbon roses, use three shades of the same colour on every bunch. Cut 1in lengths of ⅛in wide ribbon, whip the short ends together and gather one edge tightly to form a rosette. Sew three rosettes together over a length of green ribbon folded to form leaves. Stitch one bunch to the bosom and the others around the scalloped frill.

To make the fan, back lace or fabric with stiff iron-on Vilene and trim the top edge with narrow lace. Cut the fan shape from the pattern and machine-stitch along each line marked on the pattern. Fold the fan into pleats on the stitched lines and secure the ends of the pleats with a few stitches at the centre of the fan. Glue the fan to the doll's hand.

The acrylic hair has a centre parting drawn into plaits at each side and wound around the head. A white feather plume is pinned into the hair at one side. Glue pearl beads to either side of the face for earrings, and thread a pearl bead necklace. Use a piece of gilt chain for the bracelet.

Glue the doll to the base.

Edwardian Doll
(c1905)

This was an enormously elegant fashion, characterised by large, lavishly trimmed hats, high stiff collars and the S-bend figure. The corset made a small waist and pushed the hips backwards, and the fashionable full bosom was emphasised by a

(left) *The Fashion doll, 20in tall, a waxed and clay-modelled lady doll dressed in a walking costume of the 1870s, with her own trunk of accessories (see Chapter 13)*

Fig 68 Edwardian doll

pouched front blouse and the fullness at the back of the skirt. The matronly figure was the ideal and mature women rather than girls were the reigning beauties for once!

Lightweight fabrics were fashionable; silk, lawn and faille for summer and evening wear, fine woollens and velvet for cooler weather. Lace was enormously popular especially for blouses, and taffeta was all the rage for petticoats. Colours were mainly pastels, with black, brown and navy for skirts and there was a vogue for coffee-coloured lace.

Accessories included parasols, feather boas, fur stoles, gloves, handbags and some jewellery, such as brooches, cameos, earrings, long necklaces, bar pins and long jewelled (and necessary) hatpins. Hair was generally swept up over a pad of false hair in the popular cottage-loaf style which helped to support the large hats. The pose was dictated by the corset, which thrust the hips backwards and made the figure appear to lean forward from the waist. The head was held very erect to support the hat and the hands were displayed elegantly.

The Edwardian doll is wearing a white-lawn blouse with a high band collar. The pouched front is gathered into a square yoke trimmed with a lace frill. The sleeves are long, the fullness gathered into a standing head at the top and cuffs at the wrist. The black moiré-taffeta skirt is cut in gores with the fullness concentrated at the back and a belt at the waist. The lace-trimmed petticoats are white lawn. The large straw hat is trimmed with flowers, feathers and ribbons. The doll wears a feather boa and carries a bronze-silk parasol trimmed with black lace.

EDWARDIAN COSTUME

1/4yd fabric (36in wide) for blouse and skirt
1/2yd lace (1/2in wide) for trimming
scrap of white lawn for petticoat
hat-straw or plaited raffia and trimming for hat
scrap of fabric for parasol
9in marabou for boa

This costume may be made as a blouse and skirt, using different fabrics, or as a dress, using the same fabric for both.

Make a lawn or taffeta petticoat, with a lace or self-fabric frill at the hem, and gather it to fit the doll's waist, concentrating the fullness to the back.

Cut the blouse pieces in soft unstiffened fabric. Gather the blouse front to the yoke front, and the blouse backs to the yoke backs. Seam together at shoulders and sides. Sew the sleeve seams, gather the sleeve heads and set the sleeves into the armholes. Put the blouse onto the doll turn in the raw back edges and slipstitch closed. Fold the collar along the lines indicated, press and slipstitch it to the neckline. Gather the sleeves to fit the doll's wrists. Fold and press the cuffs along the line indicated, press and slipstitch over the gathered wrist edges. Stitch gathered lace trimming around the blouse yoke.

Seam the skirt pieces together at sides and centre-back. Turn up the skirt hem and gather the top edge of the back skirt to fit the waist. Slipstitch the skirt to the doll at the natural waistline, pulling the blouse out a little as you work to form a pouched front. Use narrow ribbon or a piece of folded fabric for a belt and slipstitch over the raw skirt edge. Trim with a tiny buckle if you have one.

Use natural hat-straw, plaited raffia or a stiffened straw-effect fabric for the hat and make up with a wide brim as shown on the pattern (for full straw-hat instructions see the Pedlar, Chapter 8). Trim the hat lavishly with ribbons, feathers and flowers and secure it to the doll's hair with a glass-headed pin as a hatpin. Style the doll's hair (I have used mohair) into a cottage loaf to support the hat, and glue tiny pearl beads to either side of the face for earrings. Use a small piece of jewellery or a pretty bead as a brooch at the throat.

The feather boa is a 9in length of marabou trimming. To make the parasol, cut a length of fine dowelling (or use a paintbrush handle) and whittle a handle at one end (or use a bead). Cut a cover, seam, then hem and trim the top edge. Push the stick down through the point of the cover and stick with a little glue. Twist and fold the cover around the handle and secure it with narrow ribbon. Glue the parasol to the doll's hand and glue the doll to the base.

Fig 69a Edwardian doll's clothes patterns

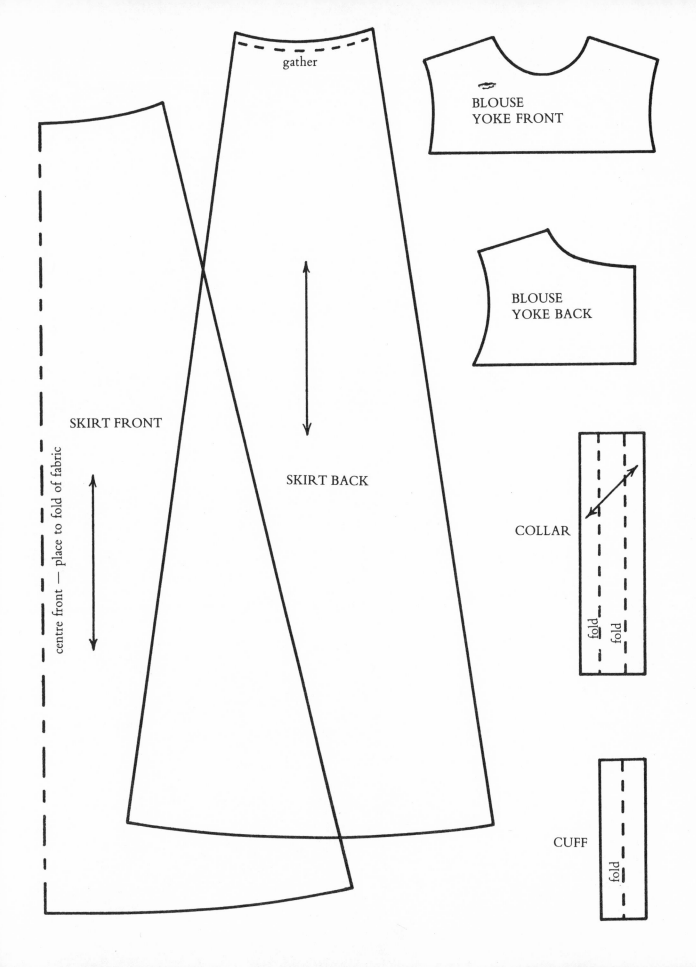

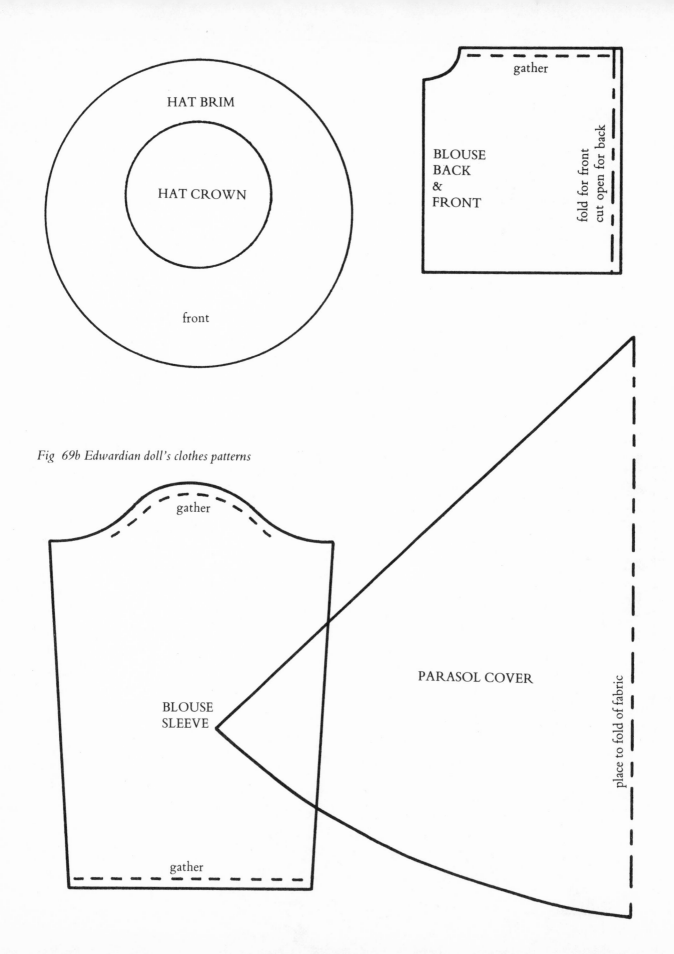

HAT BRIM

HAT CROWN

front

gather

BLOUSE
BACK
&
FRONT

fold for front
cut open for back

Fig 69b Edwardian doll's clothes patterns

gather

BLOUSE
SLEEVE

gather

PARASOL COVER

place to fold of fabric

10
THE SIMPLE MODELLED DOLLS

The three dolls in this chapter, Amy, Sara and the Pierrot, have felt bodies and clay heads and lower arms. The modelling on the heads is simply a shaped nose and depressed eye sockets, and the features are painted. If you have never modelled before these are the dolls to try. Consult Chapter 2 for the basic techniques and use one of the self-hardening clays, such as Das. Patience rather than skill is necessary to ensure that the head is a natural and symmetrical shape and that the simple hands are the right size. Careful smoothing and sanding gives a good finish, and the eyes, mouth and eyebrows can be painted in as much detail as you want.

Amy is a little-girl doll. Her head is rounded, with chubby cheeks and a small nose, her hands are small. Sara and the Pierrot, both adult dolls, have egg-shaped heads and larger noses and hands. Each head is attached to a shoulder-plate which is moulded on the doll's body for a good fit. Amy is dressed in 'Kate Greenaway' style, complete with bonnet and bag. Sara is a modern lady and the Pierrot wears the traditional costume. These dolls are the same sizes as the felt dolls, so costume patterns can be swapped around as you please.

Obviously, as the clay heads are fairly fragile, these dolls are not suitable for young children. They would, however, please a careful older child, and, when well made, they certainly qualify as collector's dolls.

The scope for characters is enormous; because of the simple modelling virtually any face can be painted — young, old, male, female, happy, or sad. The adult and child dolls have different-shaped heads, but male and female dolls are distinguished by their painted features (though a male doll might have a larger nose). Men generally have stronger eyebrows and darker complexions, women's mouths are smaller and more delicately shaped, and their eyes are more clearly defined.

You could try modelling more than just nose and eye sockets. Try building up the brow, cheeks and chin, or modelling eyes and ears. You may well be surprised by your own talent, but if not, smooth away the mistakes and settle for a simply modelled head with painted features! Full modelling instructions can be found in Chapter 2 so they are repeated only briefly for each doll. These dolls may also be wax dipped if you wish, see Chapter 3.

Amy
(17in tall)
Difficulty: 4/Colour picture page 102
Body pattern G/Fig 70

½yd felt (36in wide) for body
1 packet Das clay for head and lower arms
1 ball (2½in diameter) for head
paints
doll's wig
terylene stuffing

Using body pattern G, cut two bodies, two arms, two soles and four legs in felt. Seam the body pieces together, leaving the top edge AA open to form a bag. Turn through, stuff the body firmly and slipstitch closed.

Seam the legs together in pairs, stitch in the soles, turn through, stuff firmly, turn in the top edge and slipstitch closed. Oversew the legs to the lower back edge of the body.

Fold the upper arms in half, matching BB, and seam from that point to the elbow, leaving the curved top open.

Roll out the clay to approximately ⅜in thick. Shape the head and neck round the ball, building up the nose and depressing shallow eye sockets. Check that the head is symmetrical and smooth thoroughly with a paintbrush and water. For the shoulder-plate, cut a rectangle the width of the shoulders and approximately 3½in deep. Cut out a circle from the centre of the shoulder-plate to accommodate the lower end of the neck. Mould the shoulder-plate over the doll's shoulders and leave to dry.

For the lower arms use rolls of clay thick enough to fit into the felt upper arm at the elbow. Flatten out the hand to a spoon shape and cut the fingers

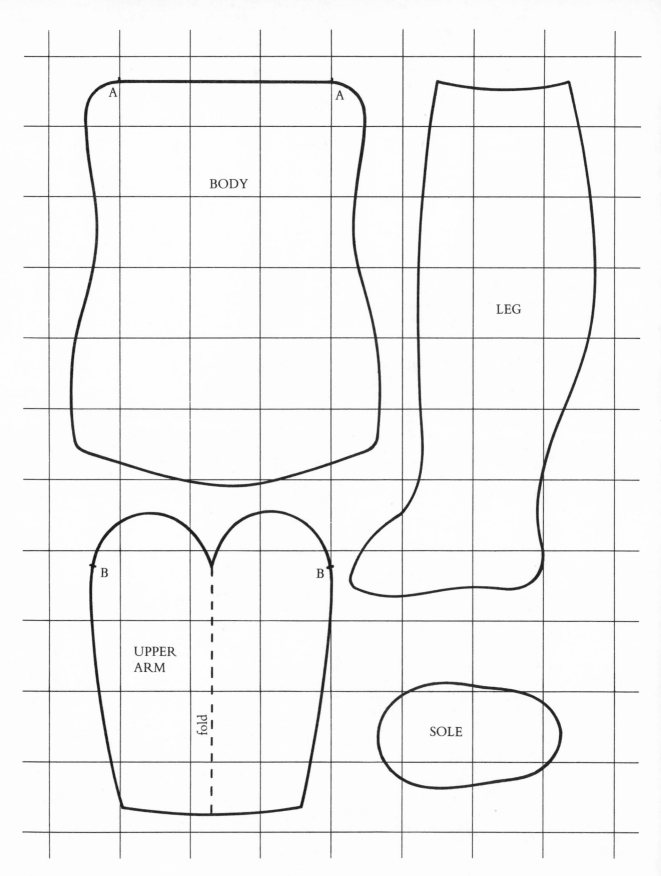

BODY

LEG

A   A

B   B

UPPER
ARM

fold

SOLE

Fig 70 Body pattern G

Fig 71 Amy

necessary with a craft knife. Paint the head, shoulder-plate and lower arms with flesh-coloured paint.

Tie the lower and upper arms together, aligning the seam with the thumb (*see* Fig 12). Stuff the upper arm and slipstitch the curved top edge closed. Oversew the arms to the shoulders, checking that both thumbs face forwards.

Glue the underside of the shoulder-plate liberally and seat it firmly onto the body, holding it in place until the glue dries.

Try the doll's wig, and mark the position of the eyes and mouth. Remove the wig and paint the eyes, mouth and eyebrows with a fine paintbrush. Colour the cheeks slightly pink. When the paint is thoroughly dry, polish the head and arms with a soft cloth. Glue the wig in place and touch in the fingernails with natural-coloured nail varnish or paint.

AMY'S CLOTHES

½yd white lawn (36in wide) for combinations
1yd white lace for trimming
4 small buttons
1 yd ribbon (⅛in)
½yd fabric (36in wide) for dress, bonnet and bag
1yd lace for trimming
½yd velvet ribbon for sash
½yd silk/satin ribbon for bonnet
scrap of stiffening for bonnet brim

For the combinations, cut two pieces in white lawn. Stitch the centre-back seam from neck to crutch. Stitch the centre-fronts together for 1in from the crutch, then turn back the remainder of the centre-front to form facings and hem. Stitch the inside-leg seams, up one leg, through the crutch and down the other leg. Turn a hem on each leg, and make a small casing. Roll a narrow hem around the neck to form a casing and the armholes (or face with bias strip). Stitch lace trimming to the armholes and legs. Work buttonholes on the right front and sew buttons on to the left. Thread ⅛in ribbon through the neck and the leg casings, draw up to fit the doll and tie in bows.

To make the dress, cut one bodice front, two backs, two upper sleeves, two lower sleeves and a rectangle 12 x 26in for the skirt. Seam bodice shoulder and side seams. Gather the upper sleeves to fit the lower sleeves and stitch. Sew the sleeve seams. Gather the upper sleeves to fit the armholes and stitch. Gather the skirt evenly to fit the bodice, leaving the centre-front of the skirt ungathered and stitch the waist seam. Stitch the skirt back seam up to 2in below the waist. Turn

and thumb. Roll and curve them to shape, depress the palm and pinch the wrist. Score grooves ½in below the elbow for tying on. When the arms are satisfactory, smooth with a paintbrush and water and leave to dry.

When the head and shoulder-plate are dry enough to handle, fix the neck into the shoulder-plate with clay and slip, checking that the head sits on the shoulders at a natural angle, and leave to dry thoroughly. When the clay parts are completely dry, remove the core-ball from the head and sand the pieces thoroughly, correcting the shaping if

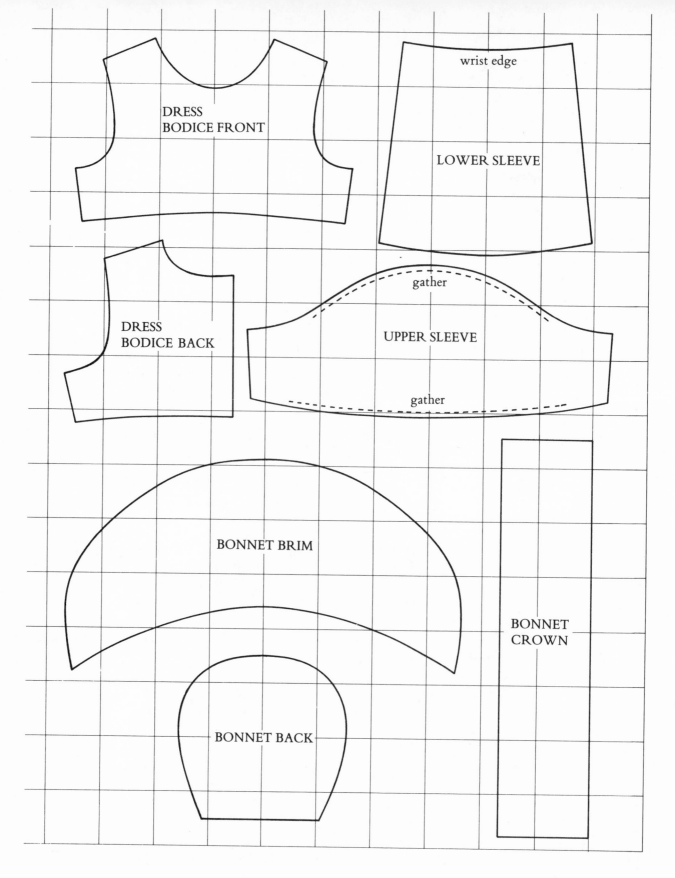

Fig 72a Amy's clothes patterns

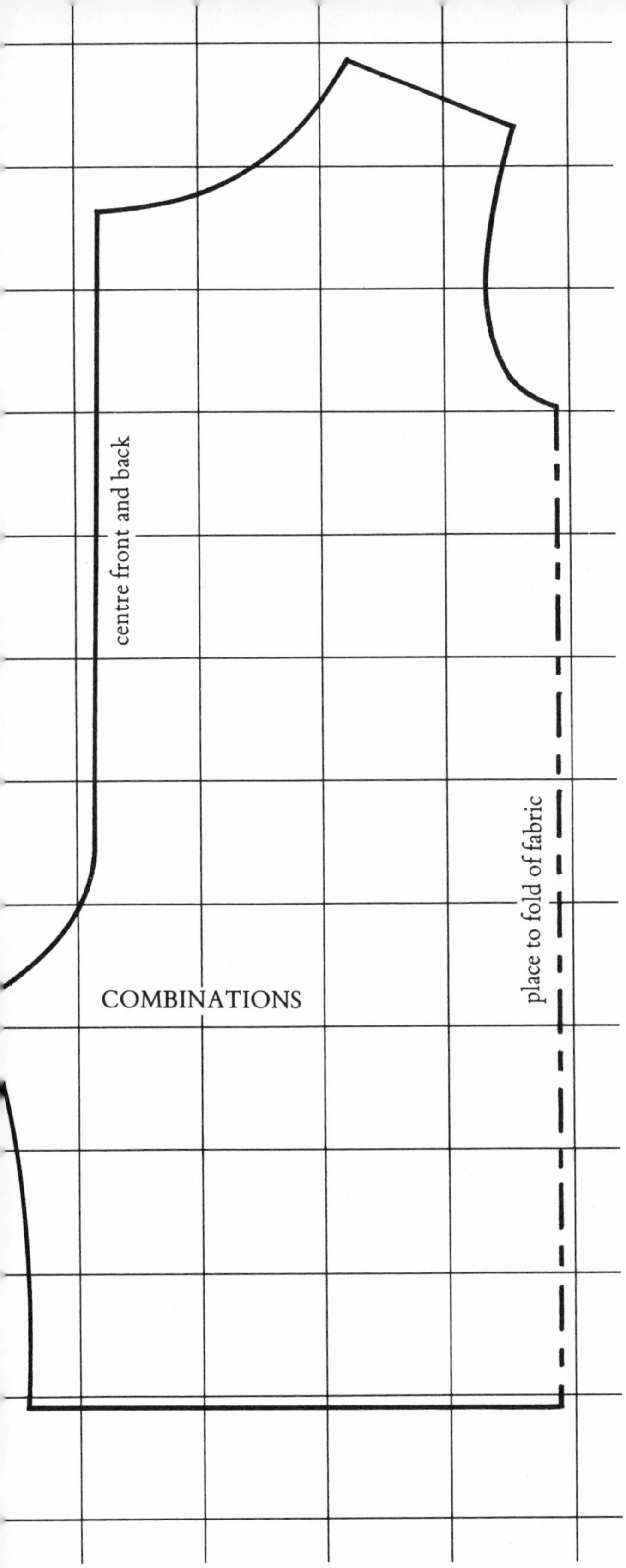

The pattern diagram contains the following labels:

centre front and back

COMBINATIONS

place to fold of fabric

Fig 72b Amy's clothes patterns

under the open back edges of the bodice and skirt to form facings and hem. Face the neckline with bias strip and hem the sleeves. Sew lace trimming to the neckline and the sleeves. Turn up and hem the skirt, and fasten the bodice with three small press-studs. Tie the velvet ribbon around the high waistline.

To make the bonnet, cut two brims, one back and one crown and stiffen each piece with iron-on Vilene. Cut a second crown and back to use as lining. Stitch the two brims together, right sides facing, around the outside curved edge, then clip, turn through and press. Stitch one long side of the crown to the back, and the other long side to the brim. Stitch the lining crown to the lining back. With right sides facing, slip the lining over the bonnet and stitch across the lower edges of the crown and back. Turn through and slipstitch the long edge of the lining over the crown brim seam. Trim the bonnet brim with lace edging to match the dress and sew ribbon ties to either side of the crown.

For the bag, cut a base circle 2in across and stiffen with iron-on Vilene. Cut a piece 3½ x 8in and seam the two short sides together. Gather the lower edge to fit the base and stitch. Turn in the top edge, hem and trim with lace edging. Gather the bag 1in from the top with doubled shirring elastic and make a cord or ribbon handle. Amy's bag contains a lace-edged handkerchief and tiny purse.

The stockings are cut from a white sock and she wears pink-plastic 'Cinderella' shoes size 2. If you prefer to make her shoes use Fig 33.

Amy's clothes look best in a lightweight cotton or lawn fabric in soft colours or pretty prints. The bonnet could be trimmed with artificial flowers (a plain colour is effective) and she might have a shawl (*see* page 94).

Amy will also fit any of the children's clothes in Chapter 6, and vice versa. The combinations also fit the Fashion doll in Chapter 13 — this thoroughly impractical garment should of course be made in white although coloured ribbons are quite acceptable!

Sara
(20in tall)
Difficulty: 4/Colour picture page 101
Body pattern H/Fig 73

The materials for Sara are the same as for Amy, page 125. Using body pattern H, cut two bodies, two arms, two soles and four legs. Stitch the darts marked on the pattern in the front piece and mould

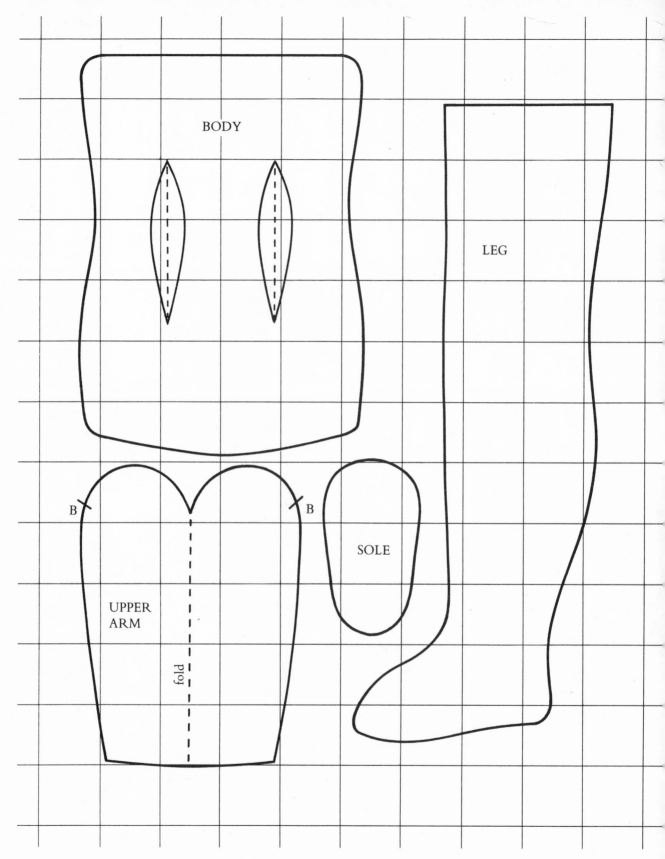

BODY

LEG

B

B

UPPER
ARM

fold

SOLE

Fig 73 Body pattern H

Fig 74 Sara

a small bosom when stuffing. Sara's body, head, shoulder-plate and lower arms are made in exactly the same way as Amy's (page 125), except that, as this is an adult doll, the head is rather more egg-shaped than round (*see* Fig 6). Build-up the top of the head and, if necessary, the chin, so that the doll's cheeks are less pronounced. Sara is a modern doll so, when painting the face, give her a made-up look by using a lipstick colour on the mouth (harmonising with the clothes). Choose a wig which can be styled in a modern way and colour the fingernails with nail varnish to match the lips.

(Obviously, if you dress this doll in period clothes these things will not apply.)

SARA'S CLOTHES

scrap of stretch nylon for panties
nylon for tights
¼yd fabric (36in wide) for petticoat
½yd lace for petticoat trimming
narrow elastic
½yd fabric (36in wide) for dress
1½yd ribbon for trimming
½yd lace for trimming
scrap of velvet ribbon and pendant for choker
leather (or similar) for shoes
small buckles and ribbon scraps for shoe trims

Cut the simple panties (*see* Chapter 4) in stretch nylon, stitch the side seams, roll narrow hems around the legs and turn a casing at the top. Thread narrow elastic to fit the doll.

Cut the tights from a nylon stocking or pair of tights, using the top edge. Cut a piece 12in long and wide enough to fit the doll's waist. Sew the back edges together for 3in from the top, then cut the remainder into two halves for the legs. Seam from one foot, up the leg, through the crutch then down the other leg and foot. Reinforce the seam, trim and turn through.

For the petticoat, cut a piece 9 x 18in and seam the short sides together. Turn a hem along one long edge and sew on the lace trimming. Turn a casing on the other long edge and thread elastic to fit the doll's waist.

Cut a bodice front and two backs in dress fabric and in lining; two sleeves and a piece 11 x 22in for the skirt. Sew the bust darts in bodice front and lining. Sew the shoulder and side seams on bodice and lining. With right sides facing, sew lining to bodice down the back edges and around the neckline. Clip the curves and corners, turn through and press. Sew the sleeve seams, gather the sleeve heads and sew into the armholes. Turn up the sleeve hems and make a casing above the hem. Turn under the back edges of the skirt, gather the top evenly to fit the bodice and stitch the waist seam. Stitch the centre-back skirt seam up to 2in below the waist. Turn up the skirt hem and trim with a ribbon band on the stitching line. Trim the sleeves with lace and thread narrow elastic through the casings. Tie ribbons over the casings, catching the ribbon to the sleeve at the inside-arm seam.

Measure from the front waist seam over the shoulder to the back waist and cut ribbons to fit,

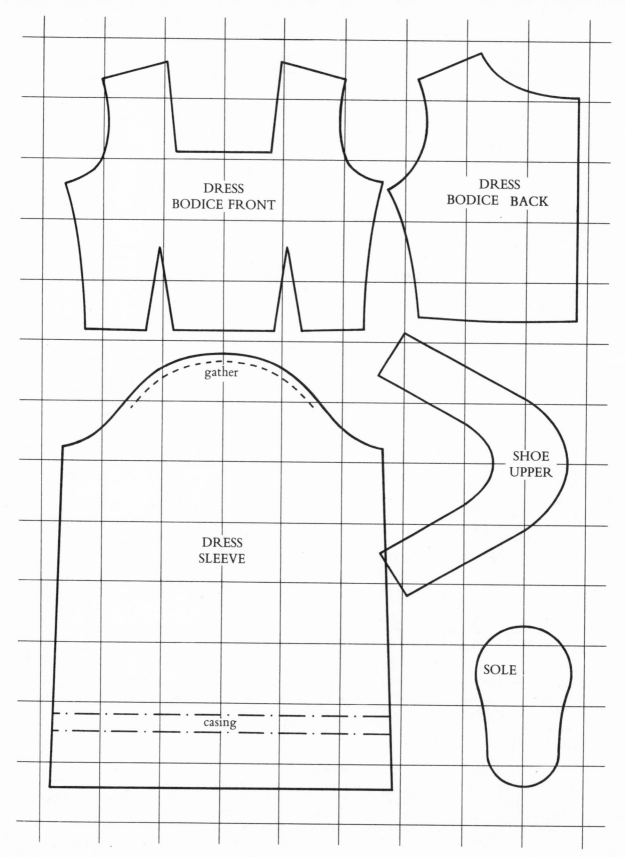

Fig 75 Sara's clothes patterns

allowing ½in at each end to turn under. Cut narrow frills from scrap and gather them to fit the ribbons. Stitch the ribbons to the frills then stitch to the bodice, tucking in the raw ends. Fasten the bodice with three small press-studs (or a zip).

Cut one upper and one sole for each shoe, in soft leather, plastic or suede. Right sides together, stitch the back seam in the upper, then stitch the upper to the sole and turn through. Trim with tiny silver buckles and ribbon bows. Cut a length of narrow velvet ribbon for the choker and hem the ends. Stitch on a small press-stud and attach a pendant.

Sara is a modern-lady doll — a type much neglected by most collectors but obviously of interest to the next generation. Her dress is rather 'Laura Ashley' in style, and the hairstyle, make-up and coloured tights are thoroughly modern. Any fabric which is a tiny version of modern fashions is appropriate, but the man-mades will not gather and hang as well as natural fabrics, so cotton is still best.

The children's clothes patterns in Chapter 6 and Amy's patterns (suitably lengthened and allowance made for a bosom) can be used to dress Sara in a variety of modern clothes; perhaps a shirt and dungarees, a smock, or a blouse and pinafore dress. (The Sailor's and the Pierrot's patterns will also fit Sara — to make jeans or lounging pyjamas.)

With a suitable wig and a more subtly painted face, Sara could make a charming period doll if dressed in pantalettes, petticoats (see Polly, page 61) and a longer version of this dress in an old-fashioned print or soft colour. She could be a Twenties flapper wearing silk lounging pyjamas with marabou trimming, a bobbed wig, jewellery, silk slippers and carrying a long cigarette holder. Other possibilities include a gypsy girl with a dirndl skirt, laced bodice and blouse, long hair tied in coloured ribbons and perhaps a miniature tambourine or bunch of flowers.

If you wish to make the Fashion doll in Chapter 13 but do not feel able to make the elaborately modelled and waxed head, this simpler head is a good alternative. Both dolls are the same size so the head will be correctly proportioned, but you would need to use the Fashion doll's body patterns (Fig 88) as her clothes do not fit Sara's body.

Pierrot
(20in tall)

Difficulty: 4/Colour picture page 102
Body pattern H/Fig 73

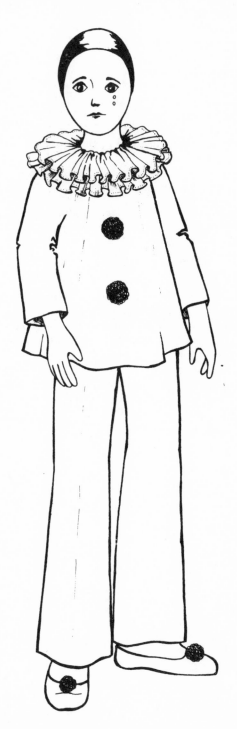

Fig 76 Pierrot

Materials are the same as for Amy (page 125), omitting the wig. From body pattern H, cut two bodies, two arms, two soles and four legs. Do not sew the body darts (these are for Sara). The Pierrot is made up in exactly the same way as Sara (with an egg-shaped head), except that the head and arms are painted white instead of flesh colour. It is best to paint the doll's features after the cap is made up as this doll has no wig. The Pierrot should have a sad expression — the tear drops are small diamanté stones glued to the cheek.

The doll can be polished with a good-quality furniture polish and buffed with a soft cloth to imitate porcelain. This finish looks rather unnatural on flesh-coloured dolls but is attractive on the white Pierrot.

PIERROT'S CLOTHES

1/2yd white silk (36in wide) for suit
1/4yd black silk (36in wide) for ruffles
4 pompoms (2 large and 2 small)
black felt for the cap and slippers
1/2yd fine black cord

Cut two trouser pieces and one smock in white silk. Stitch the trousers together (back and front) from waist to crutch. Stitch the inside-leg seams, up one leg, through the crutch and down the other leg. Turn up the legs. Turn a casing and thread elastic to fit the doll's waist. Stitch the smock side seams from wrist, under the arm and down the sides. Turn up the sleeves and bottom edge and hem. Face the neckline with bias binding or bias-cut fabric and thread elastic to fit loosely around the doll's neck. Sew large pompoms to the front of the smock.

To make the ruffles, fold the strip of fabric in half along its length and stitch together along one short edge and the long edge to form a tube. Turn through, press flat and slipstitch the other short end closed. Fold in half along the length and stitch a casing 1/2in from the fold. Thread fine cord through the casing and pull it up to form a double ruffle. Tie it round the doll's neck.

Cut four cap pieces in felt and seam them together. Steam the cap over a kettle and stretch it over the doll's head to fit smoothly. If necessary, sew on white hat elastic to fit under the chin.

Cut two uppers and two soles in felt for the slippers. Right sides together, stitch the back seams in the uppers, stitch the uppers to the soles and turn through. If necessary, cut cardboard soles to go inside the slippers. Blanketstitch around the tops to prevent stretching and sew the small pompoms to the fronts. The Pierrot wears white socks cut from a child's sock.

This traditional Pierrot is dressed in black and white silk (imitation silk or satin also look well, but the fabric should be soft and fine), but he would look equally attractive in pink satin with white ruffles. Alternatively, he could be dressed as a clown (sad or happy) using clown's make-up and bright colours for the clothes.

134

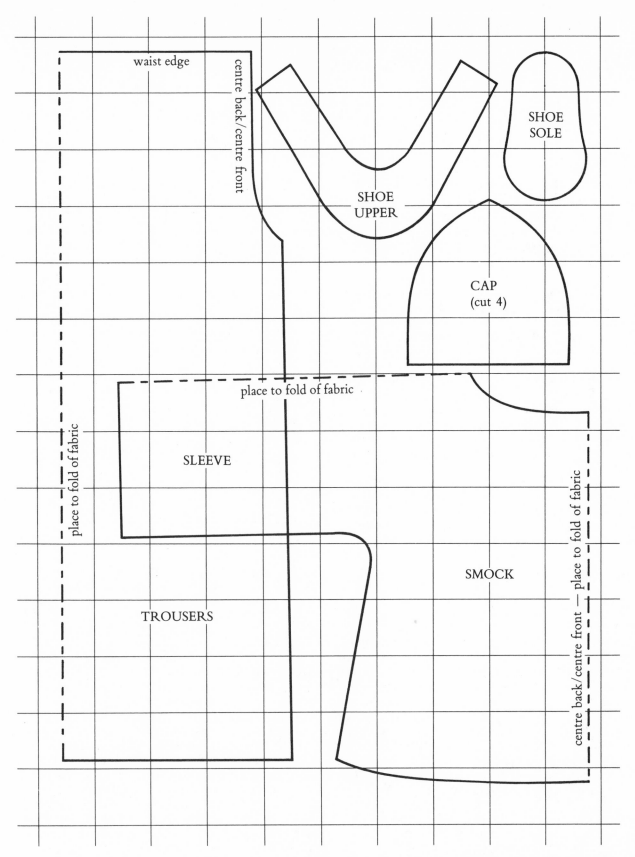

Fig 77 Pierrot's clothes patterns

11
THE FULLY MODELLED DOLLS

Sophy and Oliver are modern dolls with a rather wistful old-fashioned air due to their Edwardian clothes. They are brother and sister teenagers, slightly idealised, but with definite character. Their heads and lower arms are modelled in detail in self-hardening clay and they have inset acrylic eyes and real-hair wigs. The bodies are felt.

Sophy's loose, smock-shaped dress is a version of the new turn-of-the-century style championed by female educators and more enlightened doctors as a revolt against corsets and constricting clothes for girls. The mid-calf-length skirt and loose hair were also an indication of age — when she reached eighteen, she would put up her hair and lengthen her skirts to the ankle.

Oliver's brown velvet 'Lord Fauntleroy' suit is worn over a cream-silk shirt with a lace-trimmed collar. This fashion derived from the book *Little Lord Fauntleroy,* and was worn by boys of all ages. Made in dark-coloured velvet, it had long trousers for older boys and knee-length trousers or knickerbockers for younger ones. Lace collars, long curls and sometimes a sash were *de rigueur*. It was the sort of fashion which their mamas loved, but the boys themselves hated!

Both costumes are simple to make. They are made here in silk or velvet for 'best' but could be made in wool or cotton for everyday clothes.

When modelling clay heads, the finished results will depend on your own skill and taste, no two dollmakers will produce the same thing. You may want to make doll-like dolls like those of the last century, rather than characters. No great degree of skill is necessary to work in self-hardening clay as it stays malleable for hours, so even a beginner, given patience, should produce a satisfying head. You could use a live model, a book on modelling or pictures of dolls as guides.

Again, I recommend natural fabrics for the clothes. You could also adapt patterns from elsewhere in this book, or use your own patterns.

When the heads are painted and wigged they usually suggest a type or period of their own, so it is better not to have strong preconceived ideas on

costume — wait and see how the doll turns out before you decide how to dress it.

Acrylic eyes and wigs are available from specialist doll shops. Before beginning you might find it helpful to read Chapter 2 and refer to it as necessary. These dolls may also be wax dipped if you wish — see Chapter 3.

Sophy and Oliver
(21in tall)

Difficulty: 5/Colour picture page 119
Body pattern I/Fig 78

1yd felt (36in wide) for bodies
2 packets self-hardening clay
2 pairs 16mm oval acrylic eyes
2 wigs
paints
stuffing
2 balls (2³⁄4in diameter) for heads

Sophy and Oliver are made in exactly the same way. Using body pattern I, cut two bodies, two arms, two soles and four legs for each doll in felt. Seam the body pieces together to form a bag, leaving the top edge AA open. Turn through, stuff firmly and slipstitch closed.

Seam the legs together in pairs and stitch in the soles. Turn through, stuff firmly (stabstitching knee joints if you wish), turn in the top edges and slipstitch closed. Oversew the legs to the back of the doll. Fold the arms in half and seam from BB to the elbow, leaving the curved top open.

Roll the clay out to approximately ³⁄8in thick. Shape the head and neck round the ball. Build up the brow, cheeks and chin, shape the nose and ears, press in the eyes. Check that the head is symmetrical and the eyes and ears are level. Model the nostrils and eyelids and shape the mouth. Check the doll from all angles each side, above and below. Try the wig on the head to check that it fits well with the features and adjust the head (or try a different wig) if the result is not satisfactory. When the modelling is complete, smooth the head

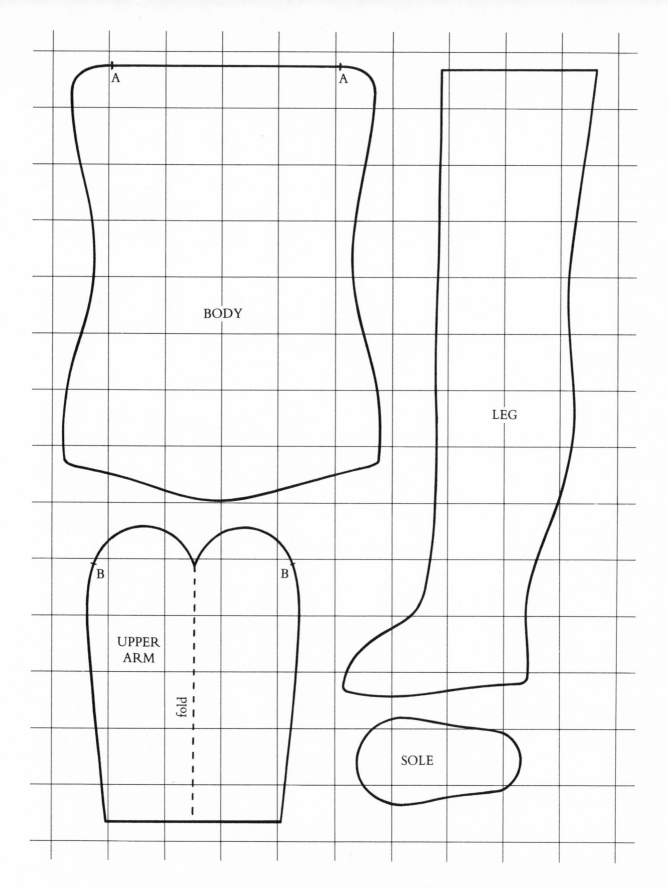

Fig 78 Body pattern I

Fig 79 Sophy and Oliver

Smooth with paintbrush and water and leave to dry.

When the head and shoulder-plate are dry enough to handle fix them together with clay and slip, checking that the head sits on the shoulders at a natural angle. Leave to dry thoroughly. When the clay parts are completely dry, remove the core-ball from the head and sand the pieces thoroughly, correcting the shaping if necessary with a craft knife. Paint the head, shoulder-plate and arms with flesh-coloured paint. Allow the paint to dry thoroughly.

Tie lower and upper arms together, aligning the seam above the thumb. Stuff the upper arm loosely at the elbow for a flexible joint, and firmly above the elbow. Slipstitch the curved top closed. Oversew the arms to the shoulders, with the thumbs facing forwards. Glue the underside of the shoulder-plate liberally (UHU is ideal) and seat it firmly onto the body. Hold it in place until the glue is dry.

You can glue the wig to the doll's head before painting the features — this is sometimes a little inconvenient but it gives a clearer impression of how the face will look as you work.

With a fine paintbrush and subtle colours paint in the eyebrows, lashes, mouth and cheek colouring. Soft browns and greys usually look better than black around the eyes and a mixture of red, brown and white makes a more natural lip colour than pink. Paint in freckles or beauty spots with brown paint. During painting, the acrylic eyes will probably become paint smeared — clean them gently with cotton buds and, if necessary, a wooden toothpick, but take care not to scratch them. Colour the fingernails with natural-coloured nail polish or paint. When the paint is thoroughly dry polish the head and arms with a soft cloth, and if you have not already done so glue the wig in place.

Style the wig to suit the doll's face; real-hair wigs can be treated like your own hair, but acrylic wigs are usually permanently styled and can only be brushed to shape. All wigs can be sprayed with hair lacquer.

If at this stage you find that you dislike your creation, do not panic! Try changing the wig (it is amazing the amount of difference this can make) or repainting the face. A different colour for the mouth, or a change of emphasis around the eyes will also make a considerable difference. If however the problem is one of shape, eg the cheeks are too fat, remove the wig, wrap the doll in a tea towel to prevent it getting messy and pare down with a craft knife until the offending part looks

thoroughly with paintbrush and water. For the shoulder-plate cut a rectangle the width of the shoulders and the depth required (about 4in). Cut out a circle to accommodate the neck. Mould the shoulder-plate over the doll, smooth and leave to dry.

For the lower arms use rolls of clay thick enough to fit into the felt upper arm. Flatten out the hand to a spoon shape, cut the fingers and thumb, then roll and curve them to a natural shape and position. Pinch the wrist and depress the centre of the palm. Check the hands from all angles and refine them until satisfactory using your own hands as models. Score a groove ½in below the elbow for tying on.

138

right. Then sand thoroughly and repaint.

You can use a needle to bore fine holes through the earlobes for earrings (many old dolls wore them) and between the fingers for rings. Should you snap off a finger or drop and break the doll, repairs can be made with a glue such as UHU. When the glue is dry, sand the part carefully and repaint. Because of this clay's fibrous nature, such repairs are usually almost invisible.

SOPHY'S CLOTHES

1yd white cotton lawn (36in wide) for underwear
1yd fabric (36in wide) for dress
1½yd lace for trimming
1 yd soft satin ribbon (2in wide) for sash
5 tiny buttons for dress
stockings and shoes

Cut two pantalette pieces in white cotton and slash one side. Seam each leg, then seam together. Roll a fine hem around the slashed opening. Gather the top edge. Cut a waistband to fit the doll's waist, allowing for a button-and-buttonhole fastening. Stitch the waistband to the gathered top edge of the pantalettes, work a buttonhole and sew on a button. Turn hems on the legs and trim with lace. Make casings above the hems and thread elastic or narrow ribbon. If using ribbon, tie the loose ends in bows.

For the petticoat, cut one bodice front, two backs and a rectangle 10 x 26in for the skirt. Sew the bodice shoulder and side seams. Roll fine hems round the armholes and neckline (or face with bias strip). Gather the skirt evenly to fit the bodice, and stitch. Sew the centre-back skirt seam up to 2in below the bodice. Turn back the open back edges of bodice and skirt to make facings and hem. Work three ¼in wide pintucks parallel with the bottom of the skirt and turn up the hem behind the lowest pintuck. Sew lace to the hem to match the pantalettes. Fasten the bodice with three small press-studs.

To make the dress, cut one front yoke and two back yokes in fabric and in lining, plus two sleeves, two cuffs and one skirt in fabric. (Please note that the skirt pattern needs to be extended 4½in to the back edges.) Seam the yoke and the yoke lining together at the shoulders, then, with right sides facing, sew the lining to the yoke down the back and around the neckline. Clip, turn through and press. Gather the skirt evenly to fit the yoke, and stitch, tucking the centre-back edges of the skirt under. Roll a fine hem around the slashed opening on the sleeves and sew the seams. Gather the

sleeves to fit the cuffs, allowing for a button-and-buttonhole fastening, and stitch. Gather the sleeve heads and set the sleeves into the armholes. Seam the skirt back seam up to 2in below the yoke and hem the remaining turned-under edges. Work buttonholes on each cuff and three down the back of the yoke, and sew on the buttons. Stitch the skirt hem. Embroider the yoke front or sew on embroidered appliqués. Pleat the satin-ribbon sash and tie it in a large bow over the hips.

Sophy wears bought white-cotton stockings and leather shoes, but stockings can be made from a white sock, and shoes can be made from the pattern given for Sara (Fig 75), slightly enlarged.

Sophy wears a pink satin-ribbon bow in her hair, a small pearl necklace and a gilt-chain bracelet. She has a lace-edged handkerchief tucked into her cuff.

Sophy's dress is pure silk, but as this is expensive and easily spoiled you need to be an experienced needlewoman to use it. Fine lawn or wool or Viyella are easier and equally suitable alternatives. As the smock shape is simple, velveteen could also be used, with a reduced width of sleeve and skirt for this thicker fabric. The underclothes should be white for an Edwardian doll, though coloured-ribbon trimmings might be used. See Stockists for suppliers of dolls' cotton stockings and leather shoes.

OLIVER'S CLOTHES

1yd fabric (36in wide) for suit
1yd silk braid (½in wide) for trimming
¼yd lining (36in wide) for jacket
½yd fabric (36in wide) for shirt
1yd lace for shirt frills
6 small buttons for shirt
½yd satin ribbon (1in wide) for neck bow
socks and shoes or boots

Cut two shirt fronts, one back, two collars, two sleeves and two cuffs. With right sides facing, stitch the collars together around the outside edge, clip, turn through and press. Stitch shoulder and side seams. Fold back front facings and hem. Roll a fine hem around the slashed openings in the sleeves, and stitch the sleeve seams. Stitch the sleeves to the cuffs, pleating in the fullness. Gather the sleeve heads, ease and stitch into the armholes. Stitch the collar to the neckline, enclosing the raw edges. Turn up the lower edge and hem. Work button-holes on each cuff and four on the left shirt front and sew on buttons. Gather the lace and whip it to the collar and cuffs, turning under and hemming the raw ends.

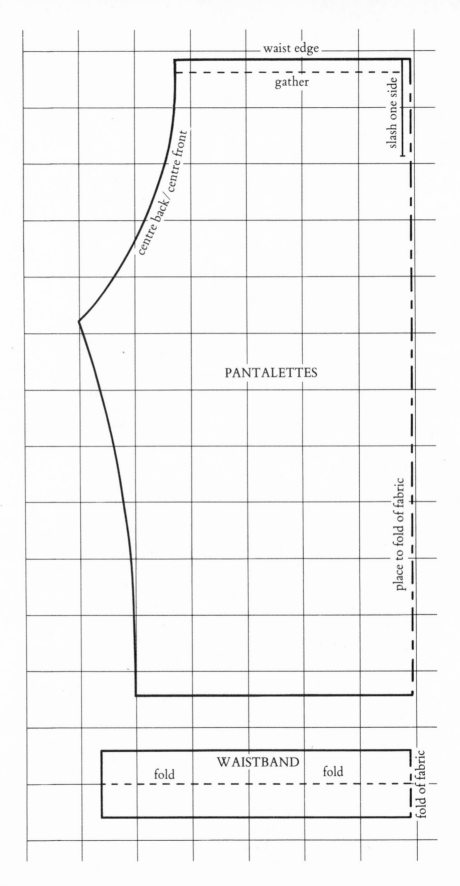

waist edge

gather

slash one side

centre back / centre front

PANTALETTES

place to fold of fabric

WAISTBAND

fold   fold

fold of fabric

Fig 80a Sophy's clothes patterns

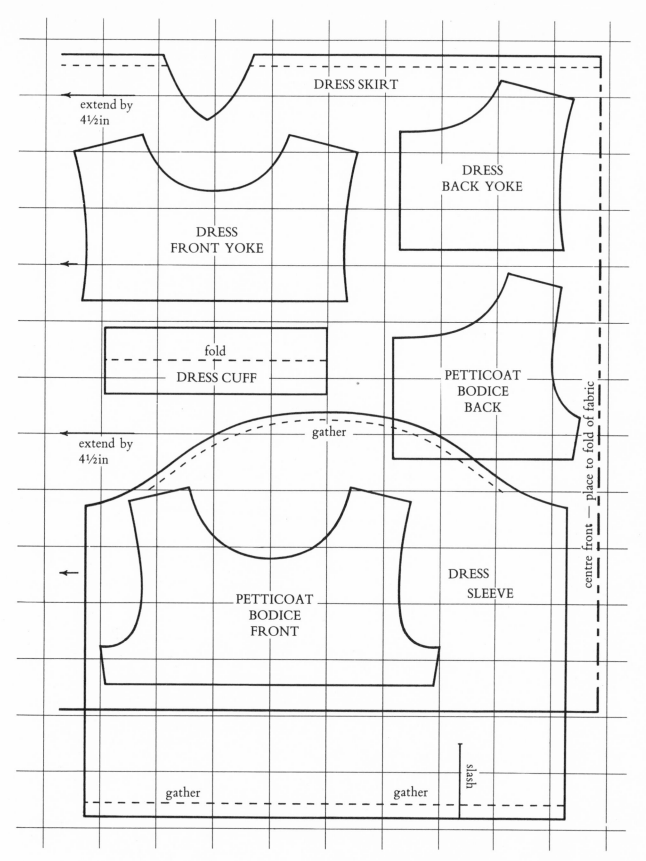

Fig 80b Sophy's clothes patterns

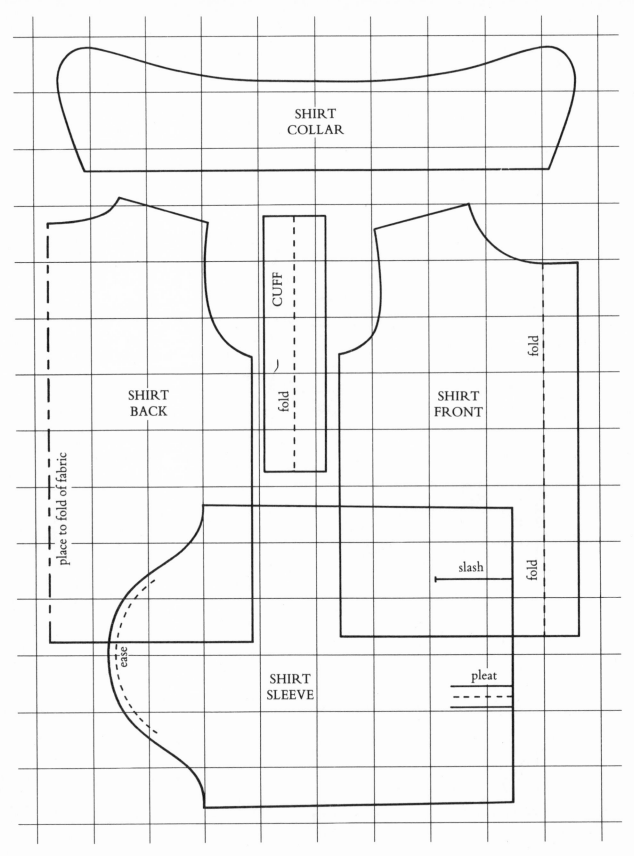

SHIRT
COLLAR

CUFF

fold

SHIRT
BACK

SHIRT
FRONT

fold

place to fold of fabric

slash

fold

ease

SHIRT
SLEEVE

pleat

Fig 81a Oliver's clothes patterns

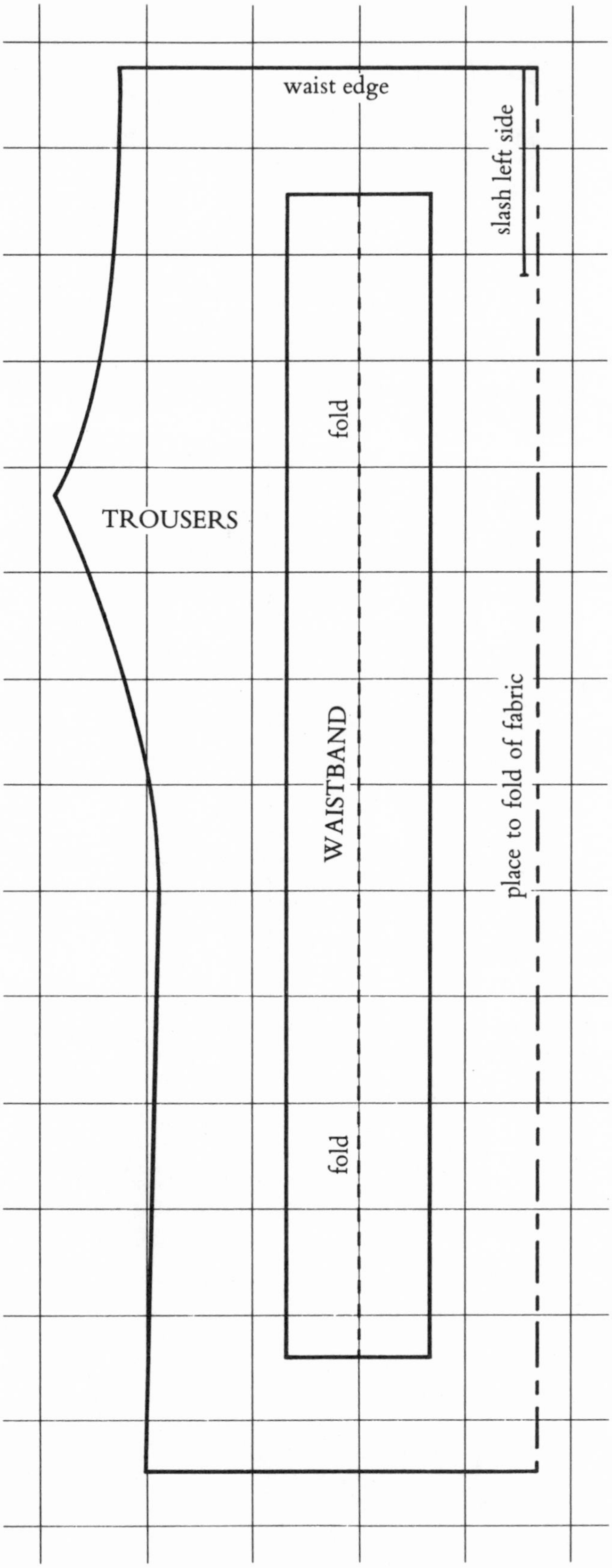

waist edge

slash left side

fold

TROUSERS

WAISTBAND

place to fold of fabric

fold

Fig 81b Oliver's clothes patterns

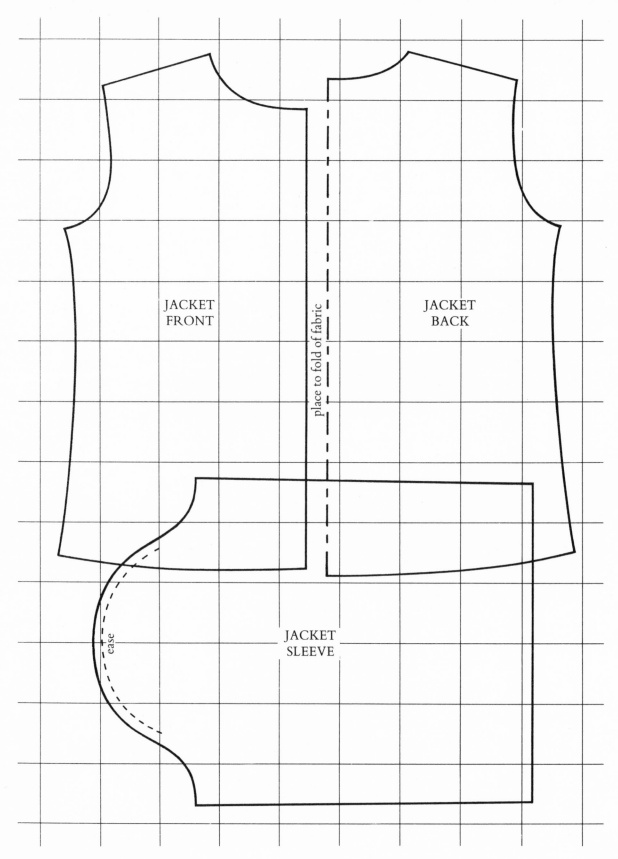

JACKET
FRONT

place to fold of fabric

JACKET
BACK

ease

JACKET
SLEEVE

Fig 81c Oliver's clothes patterns

To make the trousers, cut two pieces and the waistband (when working with velvet, ensure that all pattern pieces are cut with the pile in the same direction). Slash the left-side opening, and face with matching bias binding. Seam the legs, then seam together. Check that the waistband fits the doll, with an overlap for fastening. Stitch the waistband to the trousers and fasten with a button and buttonhole or hooks and eyes. Turn up the legs and hem. On bulky fabrics, face the trouser hems with matching bias binding.

For the jacket, cut one back, two fronts, and two sleeves in both fabric and lining. Stitch the jacket shoulder and side seams. Stitch the jacket sleeve seams, gather the sleeve heads, ease and stitch into the armholes. Repeat for the lining. Press the seams open flat. With right sides facing, stitch the lining to the jacket all the way round the outside edge, leaving a gap in the lower edge at the back to turn through. Clip the curves and corners and turn through. Slipstitch the opening closed and press. Pull the sleeve lining through the sleeves and tack together around the wrist edges. Turn the sleeves inside out and turn up the cuff hems, catching to the lining. Turn through.

Stitch silky braid all round the outside edge and around the cuffs. Tie the satin ribbon under the shirt collar into a bow at the neck.

Oliver wears bought black cotton socks and leather boots, but socks can be cut from a child's sock and boots to fit Oliver can be made from the pattern given for Emily (Fig 26).

Oliver's shirt is pure silk but fine cotton or Viyella would be equally suitable. The suit is extremely simple so even fairly thick velvet poses no problems, but wool, tweed or needlecord could also be used. The braid is one sold for trimming lampshades.

Sophy and Oliver were dressed as an Edwardian pair because that's the way their faces turned out! Consider making Victorian children in sailor suits and pinafores, or Regency children in 'skeleton' suits and long high-waisted dresses — perhaps a Tudor or Stuart pair in the elaborate costumes of those times.

I do advise that you wait and see how the dolls look when finished before you decide how to dress them. Dolls with modelled faces and realistic eyes have very definite characters, and look their best when dressed to suit their personalities. Sometimes they turn out stubbornly modern and look ill at ease in period clothes but stunning in modern dress. It is for you to decide.

145

12

THE CLAY AND WAXED BABIES

The history of the baby doll is surprisingly short, reaching back only to the middle of the last century. With the exception of wax portraits and a few doll's-house babies, the first baby dolls were made as toys for rich Victorian children. These early babies had poured-wax heads on cloth bodies and represented the Victorian concept of the idealised child — beautiful but unrealistic. Later, it became fashionable to make baby dolls which looked like real babies. The later dolls were usually made in bisque and were often modelled on real children, sometimes with very lifelike results. The two dolls in this chapter, William and Emma, represent both views. They are made in basically the same way, with modelled-clay heads and lower arms on felt bodies. They have inset acrylic eyes and 'real-hair' wigs and wear long baby gowns.

William has been modelled to represent the idealised baby — with a pretty face; his head and lower arms are dipped in wax, which gives him a smooth finish and makes him look very like the Victorian wax babies. Emma's face is modelled with rather more realism; she is not as pretty as William, and bears a strong family resemblance to her big sister and brother Sophy and Oliver.

William's dress and bonnet are made in cream broderie anglaise (white would look equally pretty), from a very simple pattern. Emma's white-lawn dress and bonnet, lavishly trimmed with lace and pintucks, are rather more complicated and are recommended for the more experienced needleperson. Instructions are also given for the nappies, petticoats and bootees which both dolls wear under their gowns, and for Emma's satin-covered carrying pillow and William's cradle.

Emma
(11in tall)
Difficulty: 5/Colour picture page 119
Body pattern J/Fig 82

ball (1¾in diameter) for head
self-hardening clay for head and arms

2 squares of felt (12 x 12in) for body
1 pair oval acrylic eyes (12mm)
wig
stuffing
paints

Full instructions for modelling are given in Chapter 2 and are repeated only briefly here.

Using body pattern J, cut two bodies, two arms, two soles and four legs in felt. Seam the body pieces together, leaving the neck edge and the lower curved edge AA open, and turn through. Seam the legs together in pairs, leaving the sole of the foot and the top curved edge AA open. Stitch the soles into the feet, turn through, stuff and close the curved opening. Seam the arms, matching AA and leaving open the lower edge and the top curved edge.

Roll the clay out to approximately ⅜in thick and model the doll's head and neck round the core-ball. Babies' heads are rather round, with full cheeks and small noses (it is helpful to use pictures, a doll or a live baby as models). Press in the eyes fairly deeply and make sure that the eyelids cover the whites above the iris, otherwise the baby will look like a startled horse! If you model ears, keep them very small and set close to the head. Dimples can be made in the cheek or chin with a cocktail stick and the mouth should be small and well shaped. As a general rule, babies' features are smaller, softer and less well defined than adults'. This doll has no shoulder-plate — the neck should not be modelled too long as it is attached directly to the body. Roll the clay arms to fit into the felt arms at the elbow. Make the arms rounded, the hands small and the fingers curled into a natural position. (Lower legs may also be modelled in clay if you wish.) Check the head and arms carefully from all angles, smooth with paintbrush and water and leave to dry. When the parts are thoroughly dry, remove the core-ball from the head, sand with medium-grade then fine abrasive paper, taking care to avoid scratching the eyes, and paint flesh colour.

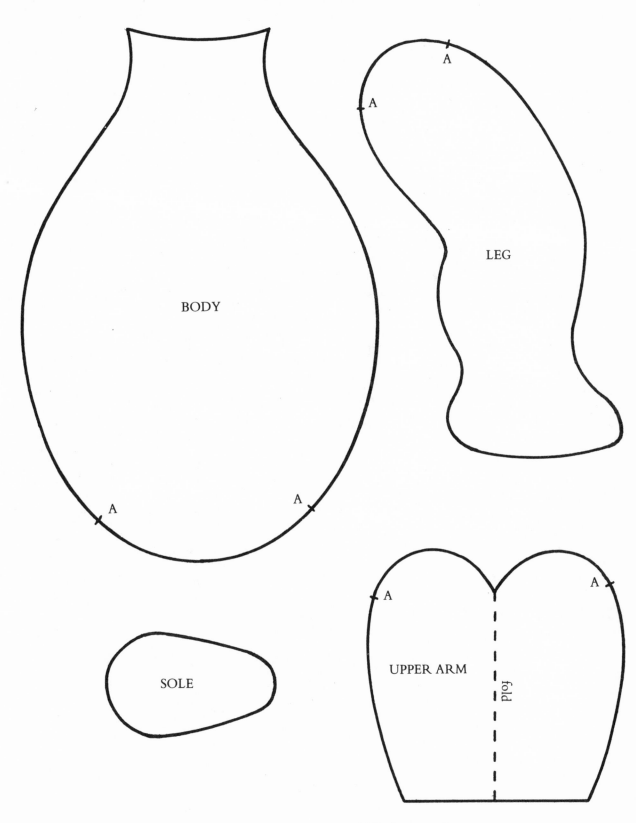

Fig 82 Body pattern J

When the paint is dry, tie on the lower arms with the seam above the thumb, stuff the upper arm and close the top curved opening (*see* Fig 12).

To attach the head to the body, glue the inside of the clay neck liberally then put your hand inside the body with your fingers inside the neck (as if holding a glove puppet) and lower the head over the felt neck. Press the felt firmly to the inside of the clay neck, and hold it until the glue is dry.

Stuff from the lower end, pushing stuffing up into the neck then the body and moulding a rounded tummy as you work. Slipstitch the curved opening closed. Ladderstitch the arms to the body on the side seams, ½in below the neck, with the thumbs to the inside. Ladderstitch the legs to the body on the side seams — at right angles to the body for a sitting baby, in line with the body for a lying baby (Fig 83).

Paint the eyes, eyebrows, mouth and cheeks very delicately, using soft colours and a very fine brush. For the hair, use a bought wig, or tufts of fur fabric or human hair. Emma's wig was made from strips of hair cut from a life-sized wig and glued to the head. It is not essential to make a wig for baby dolls; the head can be left bald or painted to suggest hair, or a few wisps of fur fabric can be glued to the front of the head, the rest being covered by the bonnet.

The clay parts of the doll can be lightly polished with a good-quality wax furniture polish and a soft cloth.

EMMA'S CLOTHES

1yd white lawn for dress, bonnet and petticoat
3yd lace trimming (½in wide)
1yd narrow ribbon
2 tiny buttons
white face flannel for nappy
½oz yarn (2-ply) for bootees

Cut the face flannel in half diagonally and hem the raw edge to make a nappy, fasten with a small safety pin. Knit the bootees on size 14 (2mm) needles. To make each bootee:

Cast on 43 stitches. Work 10 rows of st st.
With right side facing, k 19, sl 1, k1, psso, k1, k2 tog, knit to end.
Next row, p. Next row, k18, sl 1, k1, psso, k1, k2 tog, knit to end. Repeat the last two rows once more so that you have decreased six stitches altogether. Continue in st st for 1 cm. Work 1cm in garter stitch, cast off. Press, fold in half and sew back and underfoot seams. Tie narrow ribbons in bows around the ankles.

Make the petticoat from the bodice given for William (Fig 87) plus a piece of white lawn 10 x 16in for the skirt. Use the instructions given for William on page 152. Whip lace trimming to the neckline, armholes and hem and sew a small ribbon bow to one side of the hem.

To make the dress, cut two dress and sleeve pieces, one front panel and two yokes (one yoke is used as lining) in white lawn.

Work the pintucks and lace bands on the front panel as shown on the pattern. Work the pintucks and lace bands on the sleeves as shown on the pattern. With right sides facing, sew the yokes together down the centre-backs and round the neck. Clip the curves, turn through and press. Stitch the front panel to the sides and cover the seams with lace edging. Gather the skirt and sleeves and stitch them to the yoke, turning under the back seam of the skirt. Turn under the lining yoke and oversew over the seam to neaten. Stitch the back skirt seam, leaving the top 2in open. Hem the open edges to neaten. Stitch the sleeve and side seams from the wrists, through the underarms and down the skirt.

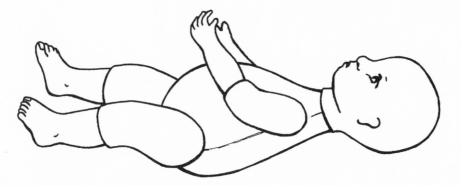

Fig 83 Assembly for baby with modelled head, lower arms and legs

Fig 84 Emma, the clay baby

through the sleeve casings, pull up and tie in bows at the wrists. Fasten the back yoke with two tiny buttons and worked buttonholes.

To make the bonnet, cut two crowns, two backs and one frill in white lawn. With right sides facing, stitch the crowns together along both short edges and the front edge, turn through, press and gather the back edge. Stitch the backs together along the straight edge, then stitch the crown to the back round the curved edge. Turn under the back lining and oversew it over the seam to neaten.

Make a fine hem all round the frill and trim both long edges with lace. Make two rows of gathering along the frill as shown on the pattern and pull them up to fit the crown. Stitch the frill to the crown through the gathering. Stitch ribbon over the gathered centre of the frill, the ends of the ribbon forming the bonnet ties. Underneath the bonnet oversew the front edge of the crown to the frill.

THE CARRYING PILLOW

stiff cardboard
½yd satin (36in wide)
½yd cotton fabric (36in wide)
1yd wide lace trimming
1yd satin ribbon (½in wide)
terylene wadding

Make a stiff cardboard base, 13 x 6in, fold terylene wadding around it and oversew the edges. Use the padded cardboard as a pattern to cut a cotton undercover (2 pieces) and a satin cover (2 pieces). Seam three sides of the cotton cover, ease it over the padded card and slipstitch closed. Seam three sides of the satin cover, hem the open edge and stitch on small press-studs so that the cover can be removed for washing. Ease the satin cover over the cotton undercover. Make a stuffed cotton pillow, 5½ x 3in, and a satin pillow case trimmed with wide-frilled lace and fastened with press-studs. Tack the small pillow lightly in place. Stitch lengths of ribbon to either side of the carrying pillow to tie over the baby.

William
(11in tall)
Difficulty: 5/Colour picture page 152
Body pattern J/Fig 82

Materials are the same as for Emma (page 146), plus approximately 1lb of wax for dipping. Full instructions for wax-dipping are given in Chapter 3 and are repeated only briefly here.

Hem the sleeves to form casings and trim with lace. Gather and hem a strip of fabric to make a 2in frill at the skirt hem and trim it with lace. Gather a strip of lace trimming and stitch it around the yoke. Stitch ungathered lace to the neckline to form a standing collar. Thread narrow ribbon

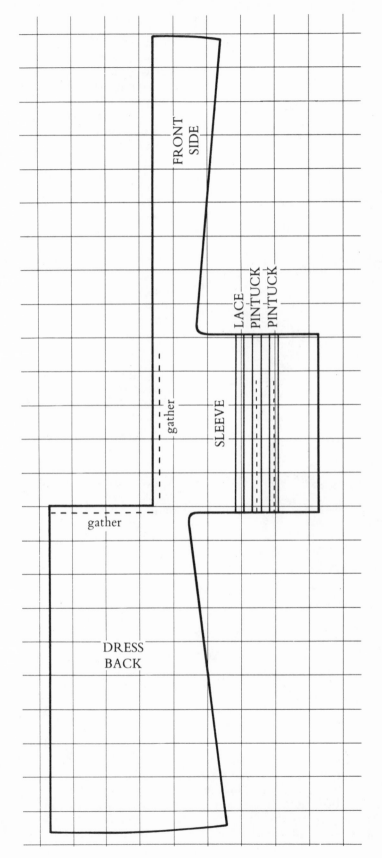

Fig 85a Emma's clothes patterns

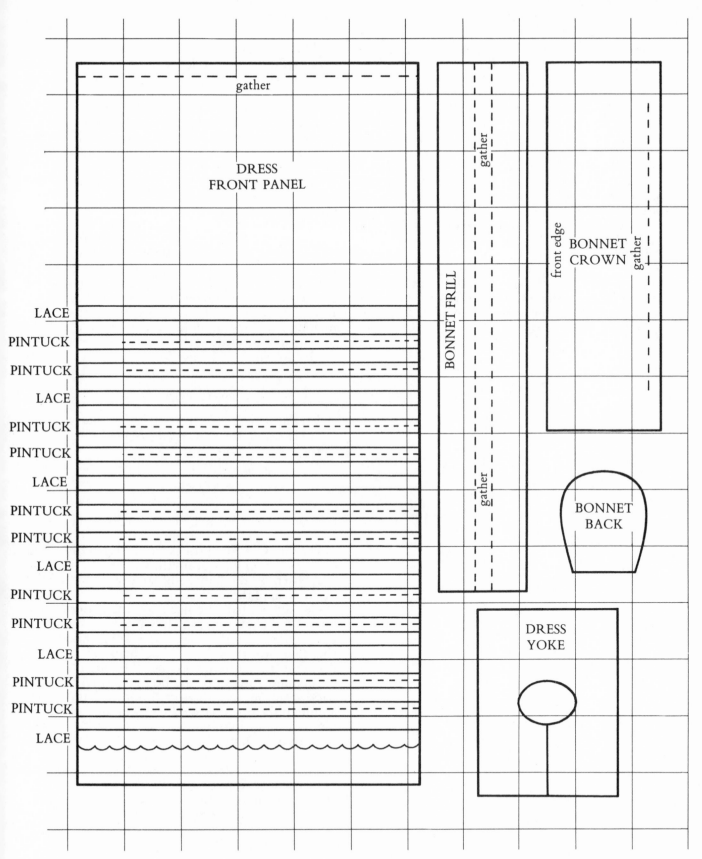

Fig 85b Emma's clothes patterns

Make up the felt body (Fig 82), clay head and lower arms exactly as for Emma, but model the face to represent a 'pretty' baby.

Tie on the arms, seat the head onto the body and stuff as for Emma, but do not sew the legs and arms to the body at this stage. Paint the head and lower arms before dipping. Do so rather more strongly than for an unwaxed doll as some definition will be lost under the wax.

In a double-boiler, or a pyrex jug inside a saucepan of water, melt sufficient wax to cover the head. Melt it slowly and carefully, taking the safety precautions recommended on page 35. Turn off the heat before dipping.

Hold the body and dip the head upside-down into the wax — carefully, so that the wax reaches only the edge of the clay neck and does not seep onto the body. When a satisfactory coat of wax is achieved leave the head aside to cool and harden.

Fig 86 William, the waxed baby

Hold the upper arms and dip the lower arms (and legs — if these are modelled) in the same way.

When the waxed parts are cool and hard cut away the wax from the eyes with a sharp craft knife. This requires care and patience to ensure that the eyes and the wax are not scratched. Remove tiny pieces left behind and smooth a clean edge around the eyes with turpentine and a cotton bud.

Small imperfections in the wax coating can be smoothed by rubbing gently with a piece of soft cloth and a little turpentine. If the features have not been painted strongly enough they can be retouched with paints, using a fine paintbrush; or if only a little more colouring is needed use waxy make-up pencils.

Ladderstitch the arms and legs to the body (*see* Fig 83) and fit the wig in the same way as for Emma, or you could try the Victorian method of making hair for wax dolls, which involves inserting the hair into the scalp — if the wax coating is thick enough (*see* Chapter 3).

WILLIAM'S CLOTHES

½yd broderie anglaise (36in) for dress and bonnet
2yd matching broderie-anglaise trimming
1yd narrow ribbon
½yd white lawn (36in wide) for petticoat
white face flannel for nappy
scraps of stretch towelling for bootees

Cut the face flannel in half diagonally and hem the raw edge to make a nappy; fasten with a small safety pin. Cut small socks from stretch towelling to make the bootees; seam them, hem the top edge and fasten on the doll with narrow ribbon tied in bows around the ankles.

Cut the petticoat bodice from the pattern and a piece 10 x 16in for the skirt in white lawn (use these instructions for Emma, page 148). Stitch the shoulder seams and roll fine hems around the neckline and armholes. Gather the top of the skirt evenly and stitch it to the bodice. Stitch the skirt back seam, leaving the top 2in open. Turn under and hem the open back edges of bodice and skirt. Hem the bottom of the skirt and fasten the bodice with two small press-studs. Trim with lace if you wish.

To make the dress, cut two yoke fronts, four yoke backs (one yoke is used as lining), two sleeves and a skirt in broderie anglaise. Sew the shoulder seams on both yokes, then stitch the yokes together with right sides facing down the backs and round the neck. Clip the curves, turn through and

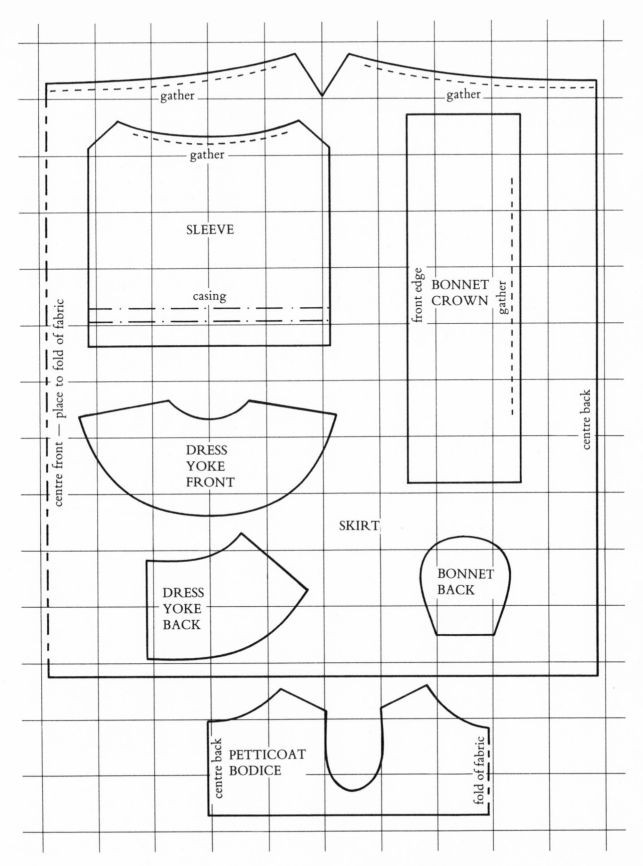

Fig 87 William's clothes patterns

press. Stitch the sleeve seams, then stitch the sleeves into the armholes. Place a length of trimming on the top edge of the skirt and sleeves and gather the two layers evenly. Stitch to the yoke. Oversew the yoke lining over the seam to neaten. Sew trimming to the sleeve ends and make casings. Stitch the centre-back skirt seam to the lower edge of the yoke. Stitch a frill of gathered trimming to the skirt hem and a standing collar of un-gathered trimming to the neckline. Fasten the back yoke with two small press-studs, thread narrow ribbons through the sleeve casings and tie them in bows round the wrists.

To make the bonnet, cut two crowns and two backs and a length of trimming for the frill. Put the two crowns together, right sides facing, sandwich the gathered-trimming frill between the two front edges, and stitch along both short sides and the front edge. Turn through and press. Gather the back edge of the crown. Stitch the two back pieces together, right sides facing, along the straight edge. Stitch the gathered edge of the crown to the wrong side of one back piece, then turn under the other back and oversew it over the seam to neaten. Sew ribbon ties to either side of the crown.

THE CRADLE

oval breadbasket approximately 13 x 7in
1yd of lightweight printed cotton fabric (36in wide)
terylene wadding

Measure the top circumference and the depth of the basket and add 1in to both measurements. Cut a rectangle of wadding to this size and seam the shorter sides together. Cut a piece of fabric the same length and twice the width of the wadding, seam the shorter sides together and fold in half lengthways. Put the wadding inside the fabric, pushing it well into the fold, and run a gathering thread round the bottom edge. Fit the covered wadding into the basket with the gathered edge to the bottom and the top edge rolled over the rim of the basket to the outside. Pull up the gathers and tack the lower edge to the bottom of the basket. Tack the top edge to the outside of the basket.

Cut a piece of stiff cardboard to fit into the bottom of the basket, pad with wadding and cover with fabric glued to the underside. Glue the base into the basket.

For the frill, cut a rectangle of fabric one-and-a-half times the circumference of the basket and slightly more than twice the depth required. Seam the shorter sides together then, with right sides facing, fold the fabric in half and seam along the length, leaving a gap to turn through. Turn through, slipstitch closed and press. Make a casing 1in from the edge along one side. Thread elastic through the casing and pull it up to fit around the basket.

Make a small pillow with a matching fabric cover to fit into the cradle.

13
AN ELEGANT
WAXED DOLL

Fashion dolls with their trunks of exquisite minia-ture clothes and accessories were a rich child's toy around 1860–80. These Parisiennes (the majority were made in France) were very expensive and a whole industry was devoted to making, dressing and equipping them. They came complete with corsets, gloves, hats, shoes, parasols and toilet articles, all beautifully made in the finest detail. The dolls themselves had bisque or wax heads with glass eyes, wooden or stuffed-kid bodies and real-hair wigs.

The Fashion doll described here offers a real challenge to the dollmaker, from the modelling of her face and delicate hands to the fine needlework involved in her clothes. The head is dipped in wax to give the doll a fine complexion and she has large acrylic eyes and a luxuriant real-hair wig, which all combine to give this modern doll a very Victorian look. A slim body and long legs accommodate the many layers of clothing and display the costume to advantage.

Over the frilled and lacy underclothes, she wears a walking costume of the early 1870s in smoky-blue silk crêpe — a skirt and polonaise tunic lavishly trimmed with brown-velvet ribbon, coffee lace and blue embroidered flowers. She carries a matching parasol and a small, fringed silk-braid handbag. She also wears a bonnet, though bonnets were out of fashion at this time, because it suits the shape of her face. You might prefer to make a small, lavishly-trimmed hat, which would be more typical of the period. The brown 'leather' trunk, complete with initials, contains the ward-robe of clothes and accessories indispensable to a lady of fashion.

Research into period costume is vital to select the appropriate colours, styles and trimmings and to make the costumes reasonably authentic. For example, the polonaise overskirt on this doll's costume is properly looped with tapes on the in-side rather than faked with gathering. I am not however concerned with making reproduction 'antiques', but aim rather to make an elegant and pretty doll, sacrificing total accuracy to taste, as

with the bonnet. This is a matter for the individual dollmaker to decide.

Again, use natural fabrics as the synthetics will not gather and drape in the same way. This par-ticular costume can be expensive to make, but, if you are prepared to spend the time and effort re-quired to make this doll, the expense on materials is fully justified by the results!

As alternatives to this costume (also as addi-tional clothes to fill her trunk) you can design your own clothes by adapting other patterns given in this book. Sara, Amy, the Ballerina and the felt children all have similar proportions and their pat-terns can be adapted to fit the Fashion doll. Scaled up to this size, the costume-doll patterns (Chapter 9) can be used to dress the Fashion doll in a variety of period costumes. She would also look quite stunning dressed as a bride!

Fashion Doll
(20in tall)
Difficulty: 5/Colour picture page 120
Body pattern K/Fig 88

ball for head (2¼in diameter)
self-hardening clay for head and arms
1 pair oval acrylic eyes (16mm)
1lb wax for dipping
½yd felt (36in wide) for body
wig
stuffing
paints

As full instructions for modelling and wax dipping are given in Chapters 2 and 3 the instructions given here are repeated only briefly.

Using body pattern K, cut two bodies, two arms, four legs and two soles in felt. Stitch the body darts on both back and front pieces. Seam the body pieces together to form a bag, leaving open the edge AA. Turn through and stuff very firmly, moulding a bosom as you work. Close AA.

Seam the legs together in pairs, leaving the sole of the foot and the edge AA open. Stitch the soles

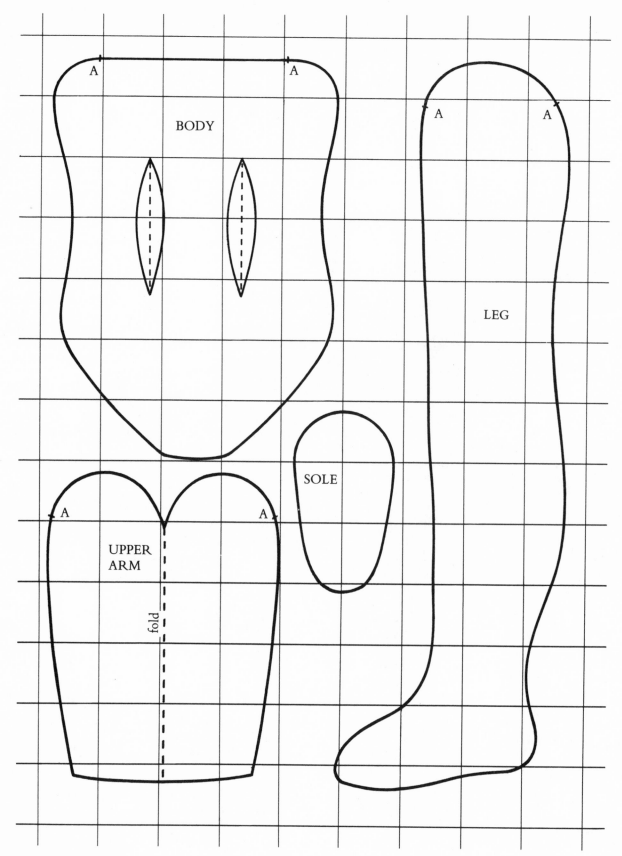

Fig 88 Body pattern K

into the feet and turn through. Stuff the legs very firmly. Dowelling rods can be inserted in the legs during stuffing for extra support. Slipstitch the curved top opening closed. Depress sockets at the hips on the body and ladderstitch the legs to the body so that the tops of the legs form the doll's hips (see Fig 89). The doll's body and legs should be quite rigid — *very* firmly stuffed, with no movement at the hips. Stitch the arm seams matching AA and leaving the lower edge and the top curved edge open. Do not stuff.

Roll the clay to approximately ³⁄₈in thick and model the doll's head and neck round the core-ball, making a pretty adult face with delicate features fairly sharply defined. Cut a shoulder-plate the width of the doll's shoulders and deep enough to accommodate the proposed costume, and mould this over the body. Do not forget to cut out a circle from the centre.

Roll the clay to fit into the felt arms at the elbow and shape the wrists and hands. The Fashion doll has small hands, the fingers bent to a natural curved position to hold accessories. If the proposed costume has tight sleeves, the hands will need to be small enough to go through them.

All the modelled pieces should be checked carefully from all angles, smoothed with water and a paintbrush and left to dry. When the head and shoulder-plate are dry enough to handle, fix the neck into the shoulder-plate with clay and slip. Pose the head carefully — usually a slight tilt to left or right, up or down, looks more effective than a straight head-on position. It helps to try the wig in position while gauging the most attractive angle for the head.

Leave the modelled pieces to dry thoroughly, then remove the core-ball from the head. Sand thoroughly with medium-grade then fine abrasive paper, taking particular care with the fingers and avoiding scratching the eyes. Paint the pieces flesh colour. Then paint the eyes, eyebrows, mouth and cheeks, rather more strongly than you would if the doll were not to be waxed, as some definition is lost under the wax. Define the fingernails with paint or nail varnish.

Tie the lower to the upper arms, with the seam above the thumb. Stuff the upper arms fairly loosely at the elbow to allow some flexibility, more firmly in the upper arms, and close the curved top openings (see Fig 12).

Much of the fine modelling of the fingers is lost when wax coated, so the arms are not dipped. Sew the arms to the shoulders into slightly depressed sockets. (If you prefer to dip the arms, hold the upper arms to dip, and stitch the arms to the body

after waxing.) In a double boiler or a pyrex jug inside a saucepan of water melt sufficient wax to cover the head and shoulder-plate. Melt the wax, slowly and carefully, taking the safety precautions recommended on page 35. Turn off the heat before dipping.

Fix a support into the head, blocking the neck and leaving a handle well clear of the wax (see Fig 15). Hold this handle and dip the head, upside down, into the wax, right up to the edges of the shoulder-plate. (Do not worry about seepage onto the inside of the shoulder-plate, this can be removed later.) When a satisfactory wax coat is achieved, leave the head to cool and harden. Hold the upper arms and dip the lower arms in the same way if required. Remove head support.

When the head is cool and hard cut away the wax from the eyes with a sharp craft knife, with care and patience. Then use a cotton bud and turpentine to clean away any tiny pieces left behind and smooth a clean edge around the eyes. Use the craft knife to scrape off any wax which has seeped onto the inside of the shoulder-plate.

Glue the underside of the shoulder-plate and seat it firmly onto the body, holding it in place until the glue is dry. If the arms have also been waxed, sew them to the shoulders before attaching the shoulder-plate.

Small imperfections in the wax coating can be smoothed by rubbing gently with a soft cloth and a little turpentine. The features can be retouched with paints, using a fine brush; or, if only a little more colouring is needed, use make-up pencils.

Glue the wig to the doll's head and style it, or consider implanting hair if the wax coating is thick enough.

FASHION DOLL'S CLOTHES

For the underwear
    1½yd white lawn (36in wide)
    2yd lace or broderie anglaise
    narrow silk ribbon for ties and bows
    8 small buttons
    white cotton sock

For the costume
    1½yd silk or other lightweight fabric (36in wide)
    2yd velvet ribbon (¼in wide)
    4yd of lace (½in wide)
    20 embroidered flower motifs
    hat-straw (or plaited raffia)
    1½yd satin ribbon (½in wide)
    artificial flowers
    pearl beads

Fig 89 Assembly for the Fashion doll

stiffeners. If the corset is worn under the combinations, the suspenders can be used to hold up the stockings. Cut the stockings from a white cotton sock or use bought cotton doll's stockings (I have tried using a silk stocking, but find that it ladders too badly to be usable — you might however like to knit stockings in silk thread!).

For the waist petticoat cut a piece of lawn 14 x 26in and a waistband to fit the doll's waist, with an overlap for a button-and-buttonhole fastening.

Use the pattern (Fig 72) and instructions (page 127) given for Amy to make a pair of combinations; the pattern needs no alteration. Make the combinations in white lawn trimmed with lace and silk ribbons and fasten them with four small buttons and buttonholes down the front.

If you wish to make a corset, use the pattern (Fig 49) and instructions (page 84) given for Fanny, reducing the pattern to fit the Fashion doll. Make the corset in pale-pink, blue or white satin, lined with lawn, trimmed with lace and boned with collar-

Fig 90 Fashion doll

158

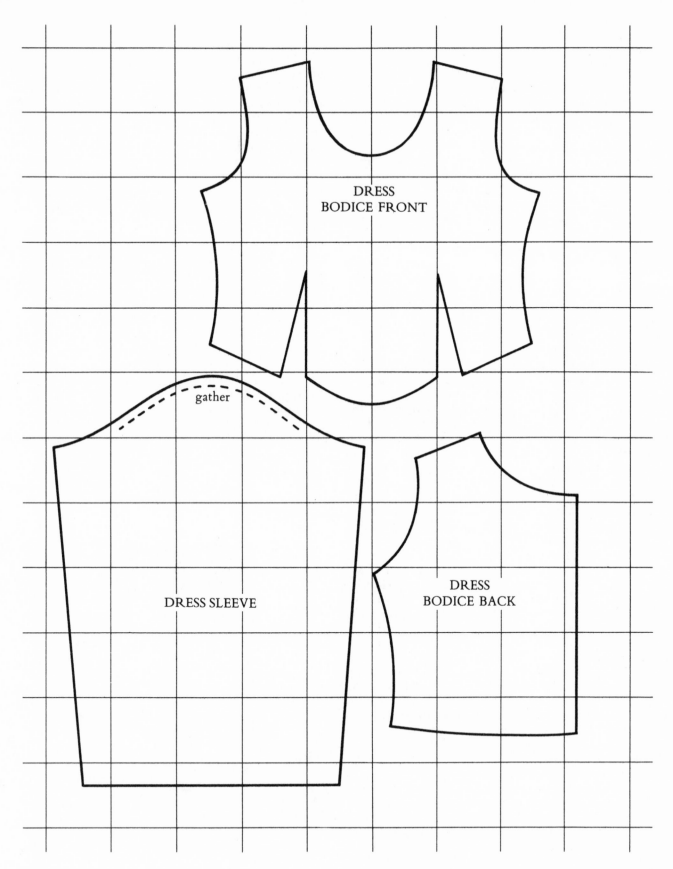

DRESS
BODICE FRONT

gather

DRESS SLEEVE

DRESS
BODICE BACK

Fig 91 Fashion doll's clothes patterns

Stitch the centre-back seam, leaving the top 2in open, and turn under and hem the opening. Turn up a hem on the lower edge and work several rows of pintucks above the hem. Gather the top edge and stitch to the waistband, concentrating the fullness to the back. Fasten the waistband with a worked buttonhole and button at the back.

For the full-length petticoat, cut a bodice from the dress-bodice pattern and a piece 12 x 27in for the skirt. Sew the darts in the front bodice and stitch the shoulder and side seams. Roll fine hems round the neck and armholes (or face with bias binding).

Gather the top of the skirt and stitch it to the bodice, concentrating the fullness to the sides and back. Stitch the skirt back seam, leaving the top 2in open, and turn under and hem the open back seam in bodice and skirt to form facings. Turn up the skirt hem and trim it with lace or broderie anglaise and ribbon bows. Fasten the bodice with three buttons and worked buttonholes.

Before cutting the dress bodice, make a toile in cheap cotton or calico and fit this to the doll over the underclothes. Make any necessary alterations, then unpick the toile and use it as a pattern for the dress. This will ensure a perfect fit (individual dolls will vary in size according to the firmness of stuffing, size of bosom and amount of underclothes) and will prevent expensive mistakes.

Using the toile as a pattern, cut the dress bodice, front, backs and sleeves in stiffened fabric, ie with lightweight Vilene ironed on to the back of the piece. Cut a piece of fabric 14 x 30in for the underskirt, and a waistband to fit the doll's waist with a hook and eye closure. Cut a piece 50 x 11in for the overskirt and a frill 1½in deep. The length of the frill will vary according to the weight of the fabric, but 1¾ times the width of the skirt is usually right.

To make the underskirt, seam the centre-back, leaving the top 2in open and turn under and hem the opening. Gather the top edge to the waistband, concentrating the fullness to the back. Put the skirt onto the doll, over the underclothes, and turn up the hem; it should just touch the ground. Stitch the hem and trim the skirt with a band of lace, a band of velvet ribbon and seven evenly spaced embroidered flower motifs. Fasten the waistband with hooks and eyes.

Stitch the darts in the front bodice and stitch the shoulder and side seams. Face the neck edge with bias-cut fabric. Sew the sleeve seams, gather the heads and stitch them into the armholes. Turn small hems on the sleeves. Stitch two gathered lace ruffles to each sleeve and trim with bands of velvet ribbon and flower motifs.

Whip two 3in lengths of velvet ribbon together and stitch them down the front of the bodice, tucking in the raw ends. Gather a length of lace trimming and stitch it to the neckline of the dress, from the centre-back to the front, and down and around the velvet ribbon. Stitch small pearl beads down the centre of the velvet ribbon.

To make the overskirt, stitch the centre-back seam, leaving the top 2in open, turn under and hem the opening. Hem and gather the frill to the lower edge. Trim with a band of lace, a band of velvet ribbon and eleven evenly spaced flower motifs. Gather the skirt and stitch it to the bodice, concentrating the fullness to the sides and back and turning under the back edges of the bodice to form facings enclosing the back edges of the skirt. The bodice is designed to meet edge-to-edge with a hook-and-loop fastening. With the dress inside-out, sew tapes to the back waistline at either side, and to one side of the opening. Sew loops to the skirt, half-way down its length, to line up with the tapes. Sew tapes to either side of the skirt, 2in above the frill (Fig 92). Thread the waist tapes through the loops, pull up evenly and tie. Tie the side tapes together, drawing in the fullness of the skirt (you could do this when the dress is on the doll). Sew small hooks and loops close together

Fig 92 Placement for tapes to loop polonaise skirt

down the back of the bodice and open part of the skirt and sew half of a press-stud to the outside of the dress at the centre-back waist. Cut and hem a strip of dress fabric, tie it into a large bow, sew the other half of the press-stud to the centre of the bow and fasten it to the waist.

To make the bonnet use hat-straw or plaited raffia. Alternatively, use the pattern for Amy's bonnet (Fig 72) and stiffened fabric. Shape the back of the bonnet, with a small rounded crown, then work outwards to make a large curved brim. Line the bonnet with a strip of dress fabric, gathered along both sides to flute it, and a lace frill. Trim the bonnet with ribbon and artificial flowers in colours to complement the dress. Stitch satin ribbons to either side of the brim and tie them in a bow to one side under the doll's chin. If you prefer to make a

hat, see the instructions given for the Pedlar doll (page 94).

Make leather shoes from the pattern given for Sara (Fig 75) and trim them with tiny buckles and ribbon bows. You could use bought leather doll's shoes (from specialist shops).

Whittle a length of dowelling for the parasol, shaping the handle and tapering the stick — or use a long paintbrush handle. Cut the cover from dress fabric, using a dinner plate as a guide to cut a circle. Fold the circle in half, right sides together, and sew round the curved edge, leaving a small opening to turn through. Turn through, slipstitch the opening closed and press. Fold in half again and seam down the straight edges. Turn through. Sew lace trimming to the top edge and push the stick down through the point, holding it in place with a little

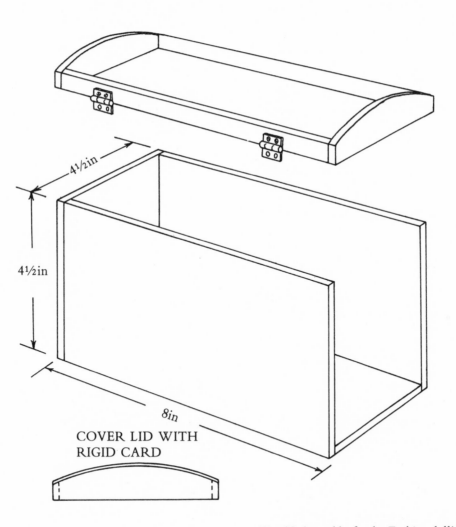

4½in

4½in

8in

COVER LID WITH
RIGID CARD

Fig 93 Assembly for the Fashion doll's trunk

glue. Fold and wrap the cover around the stick and secure it with ribbon tied in a bow.

For the bag, use silky fringed braid or pretty ribbon. Work buttonholestitch loops around the top edge and thread a gilt chain for a handle. The bag contains a lace-edged handkerchief, a tiny perfume bottle, a purse and a small notebook and pencil. The bracelet is made from a small piece of broken necklace — any similar pieces of jewellery would be suitable and you could add a necklace, earrings or brooch.

The doll is permanently supported by a doll stand which fits under her clothes and is completely concealed by the full skirts. The rigidity of the body allows the stand to keep the doll completely stable (from specialist shops).

The trunk is made of Daler board, but thin wood such as obeche would be equally suitable. The curved lid is made of firm cardboard. Following Fig 93, glue and pin the pieces with small panel pins. Cover the outside of the trunk with leather-effect Fablon (or thin leather) and line it with printed paper. Attach two ½in brass hinges and a fancy gilt clasp. The finishing touch is the gilt initials on the front. Fill the trunk with a selection of clothes and accessories suitable for a lady of fashion!

STOCKISTS

Sunday Dolls, 7 Park Drive, London SW14 8RB
Specialise in fine lace, silk ribbons and other small scale
trimmings, fabrics, flowers, feathers, buckles, buttons etc.
Also wigs, hat-straw and accessories. They also have a range
of fine porcelain doll kits.

**Hello Dolly, Gwavas Lane, Newlyn, Penzance,
Cornwall**
A good selection of wigs, doll stands, stuffing, shoes,
stockings, lace, ribbons and trimmings. Also doll paint,
clothes patterns, eyes, books and reasonably priced quality
porcelain doll kits.

**Ridings Crafts, 4–6 Brandycarr, Wakefield,
W Yorkshire WF2 0RG**
A wide range of fabrics, trimmings, flowers, feathers,
buttons, buckles etc, also eyes, joints, wigs, doll stands and
stuffing. They also have a selection of patterns and dolls'
clothes including straw hats — and pottery and porcelain doll
kits.

**Recollect, 82c Trafalgar Street, Brighton,
Sussex BN1 4EB**
Good quality wigs and eyes, shoes and clothes. They are
specialists in porcelain dollmaking equipment and books,
and carry a range of reproduction-bisque doll kits.

Contact the above addresses for details of their catalogues
and mail-order service, enclosing sae.

BIBLIOGRAPHY

Coleman, Dorothy S. etc *The Collectors' Book of Doll's Clothes* Robert Hale (1976)

Coleman, Dorothy S. etc *The Collectors' Encyclopedia of Dolls* Robert Hale (1970)

Johnson, Audrey *Dressing Dolls* Bell and Hyman (1969)

Johnson, Audrey *How to Repair and Dress Old Dolls* G. Bell (1967)

King, Constance Eileen *Dolls and Dolls' Houses* Hamlyn (1977)

INDEX